MEMOIR

OF

GENERAL GRAHAM

WITH

NOTICES OF THE CAMPAIGNS IN WHICH HE
WAS ENGAGED FROM 1779 TO 1801

EDITED BY HIS SON

COLONEL JAMES J. GRAHAM,

AUTHOR OF THE 'ART OF WAR'

> " Generous as brave—
> Affection, kindness, the sweet offices
> Of love and duty, were to him as needful
> As his daily bread."
>
> ROGERS

EDINBURGH ·

PRIVATELY PRINTED BY R. & R. CLARK

1862

PREFACE.

THE circumstances under which this volume has been brought into existence are briefly these. The manuscript which forms the nucleus appears to have been designed by the late General Graham with the twofold purpose of serving as a tribute to the memory of a very dear friend of his early life, Lieutenant-Colonel Gordon, and of vindicating his friend's memory in connection with an expenditure of the public money, which Colonel Gordon, acting in his official capacity, had very properly sanctioned, in order to obtain the release of Captain Asgill, but which the auditors of the public accounts, on some frivolous pretext, long hesitated to ratify.

Whatever may have been the real object of General Graham in drawing up a narrative of

PREFACE.

transactions during the last four years of the American war, the result is a sketch expressed in plain and homely language, but with all the truth and power of an original drawing. To read it is, to a certain extent, to realize the dire suspense of the young officers at Lancaster on the night previous to their being assembled to cast lots for life or death.

In deciding to put the General's manuscript in type, the editor felt the satisfaction of a person about to give effect to one of the last wishes of a revered parent. In the execution of this resolution he felt an irresistible desire to add to the narrative in his possession some account of his father's career subsequent to his captivity in America, that the monument about to be raised to the memory of Colonel Gordon might become a memorial also of the attached friend by whom it was first designed.

The materials available for such a memoir being scanty, he has been obliged to confine himself to an outline of the services upon which the General was engaged, interspersed with a few personal recollections and letters calculated

PREFACE. vii

to illustrate the General's history and private life.

To the judgment which may be passed upon his undertaking the editor cannot feel indifferent; but he is more disposed to rely on the indulgence of his readers than to add anything further with a view to modifying or influencing their judgment.

Having, in the course of his researches, felt the want of a more satisfactory account of the Duke of York's campaigns than any he has been able to meet with, he takes this opportunity of noticing that circumstance, as the campaigns of the British army from 1793 to 1795, although attended with less favourable results than other wars in which we have been since engaged, present many questions of considerable professional interest, which merit more attention than they seem to have hitherto received.

The editor's task being now completed, he presents the book to those for whom it is specially intended—the friends and relatives of the late General Graham—in the hope that the old friends of the General may find in its pages some traces

viii   PREFACE.

of the amiable cheerful companion of former days; and that the descendants of the General may find in them an incitement to emulate his honourable career.

LONDON, 18*th April* 1862

CONTENTS.

CHAPTER I·

PAGE

Birth-place... Parents.. Account of Paisley.. Education... Entrance into the army   .   .   .   1

CHAPTER II.

Account of the raising of the 76th Highlanders and 80th or Edinburgh regiment.. Strictness of the Highlanders on duty...Dislike of the Highlanders to stoppages from their pay for messing...Court-martial...Embarkation for Jersey...Attachment of the Highlanders to national costume...Return to Spithead...Sail for America   .   .   8

CHAPTER III·

First acquaintance with Major Gordon·· His family.. Colonel Maitland, 71st regiment...Earl of Stirling crosses to Staten Island. General Knyphausen crosses into the Jersies and tries to draw Washington from his position...Conspiracy at Charleston...

x   CONTENTS

PAGE

Gates moves into North Carolina...Battle of Camden...Daring conduct of Partizans...General Wayne attacks them...Soldiers make great progress in learning their duty.. General Arnold and Major André...General Leslie's expedition...Activity of Major Ferguson as a partizan...Takes post on King's mountain, is defeated, and killed...Lord Cornwallis retires to Winnsborough...American partizans—General Phillips sails for the Chesapeake—Expedition under General Arnold. Sudden attack on picquet...Sudden break up of a wedding party—Desultory warfare near Petersburg   .   .   .   17

CHAPTER IV

Lord Cornwallis prepares to move from Winnsborough... The Cowpens—Morgan pursued—Green's movements...Battle of Guilford...March to Cross Creek ..Second battle of Camden..Siege of Ninety-six raised by Lord Rawdon—Lord Cornwallis unites his forces with those lately commanded by General Phillips   38

CHAPTER V.

Major Gordon noticed by Lord Cornwallis. Picturesque bivouac . Action at James' city.. York and Gloucester occupied by Lord Cornwallis' army...Vigorous efforts to fortify the former—Americans reinforced by the arrival of French troops...Rapid progress made by the besiegers.. Gallant sortie of the garrison under Colonel Abercromby...Surrender of York town...Arrangements with regard to prisoners—Politeness of the French officers   .   .   51

CONTENTS.

XI

CHAPTER VI.

PAGE

Prisoners march into Virginia...Anecdote on march .
Arrive at Winchester...Complaint of insufficient
accommodation. Letter in reply from General
Morgan, and anecdote of that officer ...Irregular
supply of rations.. Remove to Little York...Death
of Lieutenant Cunningham   .   66

CHAPTER VII

Warfare between the American royalists and the republicans .Correspondence between General Washington and Sir Henry Clinton and Sir Guy
Carleton relative to the execution of Captain Huddy
. All the British captains, prisoners of war, ordered
to assemble at Lancaster .American General Hazan
reads his order to select one of them as a victim
for retaliation ...Lots drawn for the unfortunate..
Judicious and energetic measures taken by Major
Gordon   75

CHAPTER VIII

Captain Asgill leaves Lancaster Arrives at Philadelphia .Exertions of Major Gordon...His interview with the French ambassador and the members
of Congress .Asgill at Philadelphia . Letter to
Colonel Dayton. General Washington's orders...
Further correspondence Escape of Asgill planned
...Letters from Washington to Asgill...Asgill's
release...Letter from Count de Vergennes.. Lady
Asgill's letter to Count de Vergennes.. Asgill's
return to England   90

xii CONTENTS.

CHAPTER IX.

PAGE

Major Gordon's return to Lancaster...His promotion... Description of Morris' house and surrounding scenery...Death of Colonel Gordon...Copy of Lady Asgill's letter to Colonel Gordon delivered to General Graham on his death bed . . . 104

CHAPTER X.

Anecdotes...Old Highland customs...War with France ...Error committed in undertaking the siege of Dunkirk...Relief of Nieuport 110

CHAPTER XI

Campaign in Holland...Alison's inaccuracy with regard to the movements of Lord Moira's corps...Lord Moira's stratagem...The hardships suffered by his troops...General orders, etc....Plundering...Rules to be observed on a halt...Communications to be made on front and flanks...Marauding...Order of march...Cutting down forage...Roll calls and patrols to prevent plundering...Bad bread to be exchanged...Returns for bread and forage...Removal of nuisances about camp...Quarter-master's returns...Bât horses...Returns for wood, straw, bât and forage, money and ammunition...Drivers for the ordnance...Keeping up communications between corps...Posts at Duffel...Allotment of waggons, and weight to be carried, etc...Deputy-provost-marshal...Lord Moira's farewell order... Order of march 21st July...Directions for move-

CONTENTS. XIII

PAGE

ment of outposts .No huts or straw to be set on fire.. Order of march 22d July...Order of march 23d July.. Sentries over wells, and safeguards to protect private property.. Plundering and marauding...Outlying and inlying picquets ..Assignment of quarters...Order of march 24th July. .Difference in currency...Watering cavalry horses and sinking wells ... Formation of troops, three deep and two deep ... Army to be under arms for inspection in order of battle.. Orders for conducting bread and forage waggons ..Order of march 28th July...Troops to provide themselves with green forage...Men not to be sent on duty without subsistence.. Order of march 29th July...Evening states . Conveyance of sick . Distribution of Cattle ..Regiments to furnish men for additional gunners 120

CHAPTER XII.

Narrative of a spy.. His escape from Paris...Joins the Duke of York at Famars...Is recommended to Colonel Calvert, the officer in charge of the secret intelligence department.. Result of his first mission ...Critical position.. Taken prisoner by the French ...Their inhuman treatment...Narrow escape from being hanged...Is taken to Paillencour.. His acquaintance with Adjutant-General Cherin ..Is offered a command in the Republican army...Hospitality of General Cherin and his officers...Interview with Custine.. Tempting offer made by Custine ..Set at liberty and is escorted to the English camp by a party of dragoons...Interview with Major O'Brady...His conduct is highly commended by the Duke of York. . . 174

b

xiv CONTENTS.

CHAPTER XIII.

PAGE

General Clairfayt is defeated...The Duke passes the Waal...Evacuation of Nimeguen...800 Dutch taken prisoners...The time to make a move according to the Dutchman's maxim...Sickness amongst the troops...The Duke of York returns to England... Count Walmoden succeeds His Royal Highness... The enemy pass the Waal on the ice and surprise the Dutch...Are driven back again by Major-General Dundas...The severe frost and hardships of the troops...The enemy dislodged at Surgen by Lord Cathcart...Affair at Eldermalsen...Dreadful sufferings on the march...Popular excitement...Embarkation of the troops at Lake Bremen . . 192

CHAPTER XIV.

Scenery at St. Vincent.. Description of the Caribs... Revolt of the Caribs...French revolutionary agents ...2d West India Regiment raised . . . 208

CHAPTER XV.

Arrival at St. Vincent...Major-General Irving in command...Attempt on the Vigie...The citadel evacuated...Colonel Graham ordered to take Blackett's Bluff...Orders countermanded...Surprise of camp and retreat to Bellevue Ridge... Colonel Graham covers the retreat...Major-General Hunter takes command...Arrival of General Abercrombie with reinforcements...Assault of Vigie...Distress of the Caribs...Negotiations for peace...Fresh hostilities ...Colonel Graham severely wounded... Wounds dressed by a soldier's wife...Is sent to England... Wonderful recovery 215

CONTENTS.   XV

CHAPTER XVI.

PAGE

Takes the command of the 27th . Is ordered to
Holland...Action at the Helder...Is severely
wounded in the eye...Rejoicings in England on
the troops landing at the Helder...A public letter
of thanks. Rejoins 27th regiment at Swinly camp
...Ferrol expedition   229

CHAPTER XVII.

27th regiment joins the expedition under Abercromby
at Gibralter...Sickness amongst the troops...De-
tention at Malta...Arrival in Egypt...Cut made
across the Isthmus separating the Lake of Aboukir
from the dry bed of Lake Mariotis...Inundation
completely successful...Surrender of the Castle
St. Julien...Surrender of General Belliard...
Operations undertaken to the westward of Alexandria...Lieutenant-Colonel Graham leads the advance of General Cootes' division . French corps
under General Efflar driven from their position
between Marabout and Alexandria .Investment
of Alexandria completed.. Surrender of General
Menon   237

CHAPTER XVIII.

Returns with his regiment to Malta...Is sent home...
General Ferrier's place at Dumbarton Castle filled
up before his death.. Appointment of General
Graham to Stirling Castle and employment on the
staff . Marriage. .Verses by Robert Burns on Mrs.
Graham...Letter from Lady Charlotte Campbell..

xvi CONTENTS.

PAGE

Letter from Sheridan ... Staff employment in Ireland ... Discipline without the lash ... Lord Hill wishes him to go to Portugal . Letter from Sir W. H. Clinton ... Letter from Sir John Floyd ... Letter from Sir Frederick Adam . Seeks to be employed in Holland ... Letter from Sir Thomas Graham . 247

CHAPTER XIX.

Conclusion of peace ... Is struck off the staff ... Retires to his government at Stirling Castle .. List of the sieges of the Castle ... Its defence by General Blakeney ... Dress of the old garrison corps ... Gardening under difficulties ... The Stirling heads published by Mrs Graham ... Encouragement given to the arts by the royal house of Stuart ... Skilful carving in Scotland . The general enthusiasm about Scotland only of recent date ... Effect produced by Scott's novels ... Striking view from the top of the castle ... Letters from Sir Walter Scott 265

CHAPTER XX.

Great prosperity of England during the French war succeeded by distress and suffering on the return of peace ... Demand for reform in Parliament ... Meetings in various parts of England.. Act for their suppression ... Union societies in Scotland ... Addresses posted in manufacturing towns declaring for equality of rights, etc ... Strike of 60,000 artizans and mechanics ... Proclamations of the magistrates, cautioning the people from taking part in the tumult ... Glasgow sharpshooters ... Skirmish at

CONTENTS.   xvii

PAGE

Bonnymuir...Arrival of prisoners at Stirling Castle
...Report of Lieutenant Hodgson to General
Graham...Trial of the prisoners...The formation of
veteran battalions 278

CHAPTER XXI.

Stirling a favorite resort of artists...Visit of Wilkie...
Letter from him...Letter from Dr. Gregory of
Edinburgh...Letter from Mr. Williams...Letter
from Herman Ryland, Esq ...Death of General
Graham 286

ERRATA.

Page 13, line 19, comma after, instead of before, *only*.
   ,, 67, ,,   6, for *Wallace's*, read *Wallis's*
   ,, 179, ,,   4, for *drum*, read *drive*.
   ,, 183, for Appendix *D*, read *C*.
   ,, 191,   ,,   *E*, read *D*.
   ,, 233, lines 15-16, for *recruited*, read *recovered*.

ADDENDA.

Page 30, at foot of page, add—" See Appendix A.
   ,, 37, line 8, after the word *watched*, add—" Some of these
                officers were surprised and made prisoners on
                our entering the town."
   ,, 37, at foot of page, add—" See Appendix B.
   ,, 68,   ,,   ,,   ,,   AA.
   ,, 82,   ,,   ,,   ,,   BB.
   ,, 86,   ,,   ,,   ,,   AB
   ,, 121,   ,,   ,,   ,,   BA.

MEMOIR OF GENERAL GRAHAM.

CHAPTER THE FIRST.

Early life, and entrance into the Army.

SAMUEL GRAHAM,* Lieutenant-General, and Lieutenant-Governor of Stirling Castle—the son of Mr. John Graham and Euphanel Stenson, his wife—was born at Paisley n the 20th May 1756.

The period at which his father's family were first attracted to the shrine of St. Mirren† is involved in an uncertainty, the solution of which it is not intended at present to attempt, but for several years previous to his

---

* Buchanan of Auchmar classes the surname Graham amongst he surnames of families now reputed Scotch, whose descent is from England. He says—" According to Buchanan and some others of ur historians and antiquaries, the Grahams are descended from ne Fulgentius, a nobleman lineally descended from the ancient kings of the Britons, who, in the beginning of the third century of he Christian era, with an army of his countrymen attempting to free themselves and country from the Roman servitude, their just

† Patron saint of the Abbey of Paisley.

MEMOIR OF GENERAL GRAHAM.

birth, Paisley seems to have been their residence. By his maternal grandmother, whose maiden name was Cecilia Millar, he was descended from a common ancestor with the family of Millar of Earnock, in Lanarkshire.

endeavours were nevertheless frustrated by the superior power of their adversaries, in which exigency Fulgentius and divers of his associates were obliged to flee for refuge to Donald, first of that name, king of the Scots, then at war with the Romans, who not only gave a very kind reception to these strangers, but bestowed estates upon Fulgentius and some other principal men of them, whose posterity remained always thereafter in Scotland The principal person of Fulgentius' progeny having, after the battle of Dun, in which Eugenius, king of the Scots, with the greatest part of his nobility and others of any account of the Scottish nation, were killed by Maximus, the Roman Legate, in conjunction with the perfidious Picts gone with divers other Scots into Denmark, he continued there till the restoration of King Fergus II., *anno* 404, or, as Boece, 423

" That person of Fulgentius' race who went to Denmark, whose proper name was Græme married in Denmark, and his daughter was married to Fergus II., though others relate that Græme's daughter was mother to King Fergus, being married to Erthus, his father, which carries little probability, in regard Græme was not only a principal assistant to King Fergus in his own lifetime, but was after his death elected governor or regent of the kingdom during the minority of his son Eugenius, and having in that time broke over the wall of Abercorn, greatly harassed the dominions of the Britons, so that, from that adventure, that wall is said to have obtained the denomination retained as yet, of Graham's dyke, which denomination others assert to be taken from the Emperor Severus, who repaired that wall which was first begun by Julius Agricola, in the reign of the Emperor Domitian. The reason given for the last is, that Severus being born in Africa was of very black and swarthy complexion and that thence the dyke

BIRTHPLACE 3

The rise of Paisley to its present standing of importance as a commercial town, has taken place since the time now referred to, in the middle of the last century, the population of the town did not exceed 5000 souls,

was termed Grim's dyke; grim in Irish, signifying black or swarthy, whence the Scottish word grim is derived However this be, the first seems the most probable. And that which very much evinces Græme's origin, as above asserted, is that his grandchild Eugenius, upon assumption of the government (as our historians relate) gave for pretence of the war commenced by him against the Britons, the restitution of his grandfather Graham's lands

"Our history gives no account of the posterity of this Græme for some ages The first to be met with of them is that Graham who, with Dunbar and the forces of Lothian, appeared in the rear of the Danes when in battle with King Indulph and his army, which was the occasion of the defeat of the first

"The next was Constantine, married to Avila, daughter to Kenneth, one of the ancestors of the Stewarts, in the year 1030, and in the year 1125 William de Graham is witness to the foundation-charter of Holyrood House, in the reign of King David I. The said William's son, Sir David, got charters of Charletoun and other lands in Forfarshire in the reign of King William of Scotland; as did his son, another Sir David, from Malduin, Earl of Lennox, of the land of Strablane, and from Patrick Dunbar, Earl of Dunbar or March, of the lands of Dundaff and Strathcarron, in the reign of King Alexander II, as did his successor, also David, the lands of Kincardine from Malise Forteth, Earl of Strathern, in the reign of King Alexander III Before all which lands mentioned in the above charters, that surname seems to have been in possession of Abercorn, Ehestoun, and other lands in Lothian And although one Muir is reported to have had Abercorn in the reign of King Alexander III, yet in all probability he has had but some part thereof, acquired from the Grahams, which, after having continued some little time with

4   MEMOIR OF GENERAL GRAHAM.

but it was then, as it must always continue to be, a place of great historical interest

The earliest notice of Paisley on record is the description of the station established there during the occupation of the country by the Romans. The "Prætorium" is stated to have embraced within its boundary the compass of a mile, and to have been fortified by three fosses and dykes of earth, including great part of the ground on which the old town now stands ; but when Paisley was selected as the site of a great ecclesiastical edifice in

Muir, returned to the Grahams again, and went from them with Margaret, heiress thereof, to James, brother to the Earl of Douglas, in the reign of King James I.

" There were two principal families of this name in the reign of King Alexander III , the one being of Abercorn. Both these are mentioned among the *magnates Scotiæ*, in cognition of the debate betwixt Bruce and Baliol anent the Scottish kingdom, as also inserted in that famous letter written by King Robert I to the pope in the year 1320 These two thereafter were united when Patrick Graham of Eliestoun and Kilbride, second son to Sir Patrick Graham of Kincardine, in the reign of King Robert III., married his only daughter and heiress of David, Earl of Strathern, and by her obtained that Earldom whose son Malise was deprived of the same by King James I in regard that estate was entailed to heirs-male , but he gave Malise, in lieu of Strathern, the earldom of Monteith, *anno* 1428, whose posterity continued for nine generations earls thereof William, the ninth Earl, having no issue, disponed his estate to the Marquis of Montrose, and died *anno* 1694.

" The first cadet of this family was Sir John Graham of Kilbride, Gartmore's ancestor. And the last cadet of any repute was Walter, ancestor to Graham of Gartur "

ABBEY OF PAISLEY.

1163, no town or even hamlet appears to have been then in existence

The abbey was founded by Walter, the steward of David I., King of Scotland, and several of the descendants of the founder added to the original endowment by gifts both of money and lands.

By the peculiar sanctity of character attributed to the patron saint of the abbey St Mirren, this religious establishment soon acquired great celebrity, and pilgrims from all parts of the kingdom were attracted in numbers to its shrine, many of whom eventually made it their permanent residence In point of wealth and magnificence, this monastery, although the foundation of a private family, rivalled the religious houses founded by royalty at Dunfermline and St Andrews Its deer-park was of more than a mile in extent Its orchards and gardens equalled those of any similar establishment, and the ecclesiastics attached to the monastery were accommodated in a style of splendour in keeping with the general magnificence of the endowment.

This ancient pile was the burying-place of the Stewarts previous to their accession to the throne of Scotland and subsequent to their accession. Elizabeth Mure and Euphemia Ross, consorts of Robert II., were interred there, as well as Robert III.

The abbots of Paisley having always shewn themselves hostile to Edward I., the abbey was burned by

6 MEMOIR OF GENERAL GRAHAM.

the English army in 1307, but it was subsequently restored in a style surpassing even its original magnificence, and continued to flourish until the Reformation, when its walls were again laid in ruins, and its revenues secularized in favour of the ancestors of the Abercorn family

Surrounded by such venerable relics as these at a period of life when the mind is most susceptible of impressions, it is not surprising that the subject of this memoir should have imbibed a love for the legends of bygone days. This was a taste which grew with his years, and in after life few people excelled him in a knowledge of the history of his native country and its antiquities.

He received the rudiments of his education at the grammar school of Paisley. At a subsequent period he was removed to the High School of Edinburgh; and having completed his education at the College of Edinburgh, he was sent to France, where he acquired a proficiency in the French language, which often proved useful to him in after life

When it became necessary for him to choose a profession, he gave the preference to a military life, and having obtained an ensigncy, by purchase, in the 31st Regiment, on the recommendation of Sir Adolphus Oughton, he joined the additional companies of the regiment in Edinburgh Castle in the year 1777.

FIRST PROMOTION.

In the same year, the war with America caused an augmentation of the army, and several regiments were evied in Scotland. By raising a quota of men he was promoted to a lieutenancy in the 76th Highlanders, and, in April 1779, succeeded to the captain-lieutenancy of the regiment.

The following account of the various events at this period of his life has been left in his own handwriting.

CHAPTER THE SECOND.

Raising of 76th and 80th Regiments—Arrival in America.

THE late 76th and 80th Regiments were raised in North Britain in the beginning of the year 1778. The first consisted of 1000 Scotch Highlanders, and the other of the same number of Scotch Lowlanders, divided into ten companies, with the usual number of officers and non-commissioned officers. Lord Macdonald having patronized the Highland regiment, recommended most of the officers, who were nominally to raise a quota of men for their commissions. Such of them as were doing duty with regiments from which they were promoted, began to enlist men, and marched with their parties to Inverness, in the north of Scotland, the place appointed for the assembling of the regiment; there were also some officers appointed from half-pay, who enlisted men in the Highlands, but the most of the subalterns were connections of his Lordship's family. A Highland chieftain in those days was still invested with considerable power and influence, and this influence his Lordship made use of, by directing a body of men of a certain age and description to be sent from his extensive estates in the Island of

76TH HIGHLANDERS.

Skye and North and South Uist, to Inverness, to be enrolled and serve as soldiers in the 76th Regiment. The men on their arrival were attested by a justice of the peace, and received his Majesty's bounty of five guineas. By these means the ranks were soon filled up, and although they contained about 100 Irish and nearly double that number of Lowlanders, in addition to the fine-looking, healthy young Highlanders from Lord Macdonald's estate, yet the regiment had as great a proportion of the natives of the mountains as most others denominated Highland corps. John Macdonnell of Lochgarie, then serving as major in the 71st, or Fraser Highlanders in America, was promoted to be lieutenant-colonel-commandant, and Captain Donaldson, from the 42d, or Royal Highland Regiment, to be first major. The lieutenant-colonel being taken prisoner while returning to Europe, the command devolved on Major Donaldson, a most intelligent, excellent officer, who had served a long time in the 42d, was perfectly acquainted with the character of the Highlanders, and spoke the Gaelic language most fluently. Under this officer the regiment was formed, and a code of regimental regulations established for the conduct of both officers and men, which tended greatly to keep up that regularity and good conduct for which the regiment was remarkable during the whole period of its existence.

The corporation of the City of Edinburgh having

10   MEMOIR OF GENERAL GRAHAM

made an offer to Government of raising a regiment for his Majesty's service, it was accepted, and the 80th or Royal Edinburgh Regiment was raised under the patronage of the magistracy of the city. It consisted of 1000 Scotch Lowlanders, divided into ten companies, with the usual proportion of officers and non-commissioned officers. Most of the officers were recommended by the magistrates, but each officer was obliged to furnish his quota of men, and through their own activity and the influence of the corporation, recruiting went briskly on, and the ranks were filled, or nearly so, in a very short time. Sir William Erskine, then serving in America, was appointed colonel-commandant, and Lieutenant-Colonel Thomas Dundas lieutenant-colonel, and Captain James Gordon first major. The headquarters were at Edinburgh, or in its neighbourhood, in the low country. The regiment being formed under the orders of so excellent a lieutenant-colonel, assisted by captains, most of whom were serving in regiments of the line when promoted, soon began to assume a good military appearance.

The 76th Regiment soon after its formation was sent into Fort-George, a most convenient quarter for the perfecting of a newly-raised corps. It so happened that few of the non-commissioned officers who understood the drill were acquainted with the Gaelic language, and as all words of command are given in English, the major

directed that neither officer nor non-commissioned officer
ignorant of the former language should endeavour to
learn it. The consequence was that the Highlanders
were behindhand in being drilled, as they had, in addition to their other duties, to acquire the knowledge of a
new language. The first duties performed by the regiment were therefore done by the lowland and Irish
recruits, but very great anxiety and zeal were shewn by
the Highlanders, and uncommon pains were taken by the
major to explain to them the articles of war, and the
nature of the duties required of them in Gaelic ; and
they very soon became fit for the performance of their
duties, and evinced a natural talent for the profession of
a soldier. So exact were they in the discharge of their
duties, that, upon one occasion, Colonel Campbell, the
lieutenant-governor, was seized and made prisoner by
the sentry posted at his own door, because the man conceived a trespass had been committed on his post, nor
would the sentinel release the colonel until the arrival
of the corporal of the guard

Fish was plentiful at times in this quarter, but the
major found it necessary that the soldier should have a
certain allowance of meat also, to enable him to undergo
the fatigues of the drills, which were incessant, and for
this purpose he made a contract for sheep, directing
that a certain quantity of mutton should be distributed
to each mess on particular days. The Highlanders did

12   MEMOIR OF GENERAL GRAHAM.

not approve of this, as a certain moiety of their pay was
stopped for payment, and, for the first time, some mur-
muring began.   The officers' commissions having all
arrived, and the colonel's being unfurled, the major
harangued the regiment in Gaelic, explaining to them
the powers of the commanding officer in this and other
respects, and calling upon any of the men who still refused to eat mutton, to come forward and say so.   One
unfortunate did so, whom the major ordered to be tried
by a drum-head court-martial summoned on the spot.
The man was found guilty, and sentenced to receive
corporal punishment, which was immediately inflicted ;
that done, the major next inquired of the whole corps
whether any of them still objected to mutton, an inquiry
which was listened to in silence, and never afterwards
were any complaints heard from them on that subject.
The regiment having remained some time in this quarter
several companies were detached to the sea coast of the
Moray Firth, and in the end of the year the headquarters
were removed to Aberdeen.   In February 1779 they
moved to Perth, and early in March, the regiment being
assembled at that place, was reviewed and inspected by
a general officer, and reported fit for service.

The 80th Regiment had also been detached to the
coast of the Firth of Forth during the winter, but being
assembled, and inspected, and reviewed by a general
officer, was reported fit for service.   The two regiments

EMBARKATION FOR JERSEY. 13

were embarked on board transports, the one on the north, and the other on the south side of the Futh, on the 17th March 1779. Major Donaldson's health not permitting him to go abroad, the 76th were therefore commanded by Lord Berriedale, second major, but Lieutenant-Colonel Dundas commanded the troops. The fleet sailed for Portsmouth, and in a short time anchored at Spithead. While waiting there for the assembling of a fleet with reinforcements of men and stores for the army in North America, an order was received for the two regiments to set sail for the Island of Jersey, the enemy having made an attempt on that place. Being then one of the captains of the 76th Regiment, and having the command of the *Apollo* transport, with about 200 men on board, mostly Highlanders, I was summoned by signal on board the ship of the commanding officer of the regiment to receive orders in case of disembarkation. I was told that the soldiers were to land with the musket and bayonet, only leaving behind the half basket-hilted sword, which formed part of their equipment, but this order was not to be communicated to the men until the signal for landing was actually made. Lord Berriedale also recommended to the officers to land in small clothes and boots, as it was probable the regiment might be obliged to lie out at night. Having returned to my transport, I communicated the major's suggestions to the officers respecting their dress,

14 MEMOIR OF GENERAL GRAHAM

and having given other necessary orders in case of being called upon to land during the night, I retired to my cabin. In the course of the night, the soldiers got possession of a whetstone belonging to the vessel, and employed themselves sharpening their swords , and in the morning early, having entered the cabin, I was surprised to see one of the officers, a most respectable gentleman and of one of the most ancient families of the Macdonalds, dressed out in the full Highland costume. " Sir," I said, " you certainly heard me communicate to the officers the major's wishes respecting their dress" " I did so, indeed," he replied , "but as it was not an order, and as this is the dress in which I am determined to die, I have put it on " *

* STEWART'S HIGHLANDERS, VOL. 1

Page 354 —On the 10th April 1776, the 42d Regiment being reviewed by Sir Adolphus Oughton, was reported complete, and so unexceptionable that none were rejected.

Hostilities having commenced in America, every exertion was made to teach the recruits the use of the firelock, for which purpose they were drilled even by candle light. New arms and accoutrements were supplied to the men ; and the colonel of the regiment, at his own expense, supplied *broad swords and pistols*

Page 387 —The pistols were of the old highland fashion, with iron stocks. These being considered unnecessary except in the field, were not intended, like the swords, to be worn by the men in quarters When the regiment took the field on Staten and Long Island, it was said that the broadswords retarded the men by getting entangled in the brushwood, and they were therefore taken from them and sent on board the transports.

SAILS FOR AMERICA. 15

The troops did not land, and the fleet returned to Spithead. Having waited there until the assembling of all the ships with stores, and recruits for the different regiments serving in North America, we set sail with a large fleet under the orders of Admiral Arbuthnot, and being convoyed by the grand fleet to the Land's-End, we

Admitting that the objection was well founded so far as regarded the swords, it certainly could not apply to the pistols. In a close woody country, where troops are liable to sudden attacks and surprises by a hidden enemy, such a weapon is peculiarly useful. It is, therefore, difficult to discover a good reason for laying them aside. Neither does there appear to have been any objection to the resumption of the broadsword when the service alluded to terminated. The marches through the woods of Long Island were only a few miles. whereas we have seen that the two battalions of the 42d, and Fraser's and Montgomery's Highlanders, in the Seven Years' war. carried the broadsword on all their marches through woods and forests of many hundred miles in extent. In the same manner the swords were carried in Martinique and Guadaloupe islands, intersected with deep ravines, and covered with woods no less impervious than the thickest and closest woods of America. But on that service the broadsword, far from being complained of as an incumbrance, was on many occasions of the greatest efficacy when a decisive blow was to be struck, and the enemy were to be overpowered by an attack hand to hand. I have been told by several old officers and soldiers who bore a part in these attacks, that an enemy who stood for many hours the fire of musketry, invariably gave way when an advance was made sword in hand. It is to be regretted that a weapon which the Highlanders could use so well, should, together with the pistol, which is peculiarly serviceable in close woody countries, have been taken from the soldiers , and, after the expense had been incurred, sent to rust in store. They were never restored,

16 MEMOIR OF GENERAL GRAHAM.

arrived at New York on the 27th August. The two regiments were encamped on Long Island at Bedford, surrounded by the orchards of the Dutch inhabitants; the recruits and draughts for the army were cantoned in the contiguous villages.

and the regiment has had neither swords nor pistols since It has been said that the broadsword is not a weapon to contend with the bayonet. Certainly, to all appearance it is not, yet facts do not warrant the superiority of the latter weapon. From the battle of Culloden, when a body of undisciplined Highlanders, shepherds, and herdsmen, with their broadswords, cut their way through some of the best disciplined and most approved regiments in the British army (drawn up, too, on a field extremely favourable for regular troops), down till the time when the swords were taken from the Highlanders, the bayonet was in every instance overcome by the sword.

MAJOR GORDON. 17

CHAPTER THE THIRD.

Iajor Gordon—Surrender of Charleston—Battle of Camden—
Partizan Warfare—Major Andrè—Various Incidents in the
War.—1780 to 20th May 1781

.IY brother, a lieutenant in the 64th Regiment, being
ent over from New York by his lieutenant-colonel,
he Hon. Major-General Leslie, to inspect and report
.pon the recruits for that regiment, met with such
reatment in the execution of this duty, as to oblige
um to demand satisfaction from another officer. Hav-
ng told me the circumstances, I was preparing to do
he needful upon the occasion, but having mentioned
he affair to my friend and brother officer, Captain
Montgomery Cunningham (known by the name of
Mont Blanc), that officer undertook the business ; and
he matter being settled to the satisfaction of all parties,
ny brother and I were immediately visited by Major
Tames Gordon, of the 80th Regiment, who addressed us,
saying that he had heard of a recent occurrence, and as
ie had served in the same regiment with our father, the
115th or Royal Scotch Lowlanders,* and should ever

* Raised in Paisley in 1761, disembodied about 1763

B 2

18 MEMOIR OF GENERAL GRAHAM.

entertain a great regard for his memory, he insisted that if it ever again happened that either of us stood in need of advice or a friend, we should apply to him, although he had not seen us since our infancy From that moment my intimacy with this most excellent man commenced, and terminated only with his existence. At this period Major Gordon appeared to be about or above middle age, cheerful and lively, active and zealous in his profession, although his person had a tendency towards "en-bon-point."*

During the time of the encampment the army fired a "feu-de-joie" for the repulse of the French army under the orders of the Count d'Estaing, at Savannah in Georgia For our success on that occasion the country is much indebted to the activity and exertions of the late Hon Lieutenant-Colonel Maitland of the 71st or Fraser Highlanders That gallant officer, penetrating

* When the Chevalier arrived in Scotland in 1745, he was hospitably entertained in Linlithgow Palace by Major Gordon's mother, Mrs Glen Gordon her brother, Governor Glen, being at that time keeper of the palace

At a subsequent period, when fortune turned against the arms of the Chevalier, a troop of Hawley's dragoons took possession of the palace, and made fires on the floors, and committed other excesses ; Mrs Glen Gordon remonstrated with Hawley on the conduct of his men, but the only redress she obtained was an intimation that she might leave the palace if she did not relish the presence of the troops It is related of her that she retorted by saying (in allusion no doubt to the battle of Falkirk), " I can run *from fire* as well as any of you," and then quitted the palace

CAMPAIGN IN AMERICA. 19

through morasses and swamps almost impassable, succeeded in entering the town with a reinforcement of troops, and thus decided the victory. Unfortunately for the service, he was soon afterwards carried off by a fever, brought on by his exertions in that unhealthy country.

About this time also the British garrison was withdrawn from Rhode Island, and the troops brought to New York. The flank companies of each of the young regiments were ordered to join the battalions of light infantry, and grenadiers composed of the companies of his description of force of all regiments of the line, and commanded by distinguished officers The encampment broke up in November, and the two regiments went into winter quarters

His Excellency Sir Henry Clinton, the commander-in-chief, having resolved to attack Charleston in South Carolina, gave orders for a large body of troops with stores, artillery, etc., to be put on board ship for this purpose, and embarking himself in command, set sail with a large fleet under the orders of Admiral Arbuthnot about Christmas, leaving the command of New York and its dependencies to General Knyphausen, a Hessian commander of the foreign troops The fleet encountered heavy gales and bad weather on their voyage to the southward, which greatly retarded the intended operations of the army. At New York the frost was so severe

20   MEMOIR OF GENERAL GRAHAM.

as to induce a large body of Americans under the orders
of a general they called the Earl of Stirling to cross over
upon the ice to Staten Island, where they remained for
some days, but did not venture to attack the British
posts under the orders of Colonel Stirling of the 42d
Regiment, a Brigadier-General. Part of the 76th
Regiment was sent over from New York to that island
at the time, but returned soon after on the departure of
the enemy. Major Lord Berriedale, commanding the
76th, having succeeded to the Earldom of Caithness, was
permitted to go to South Carolina to wait upon His
Excellency, and while acting as aid-de-camp to the
Commander-in-Chief was badly wounded on a reconnoitring party, and obliged to return to Europe, and
never again joined the regiment.

The 76th was now left without a field officer, nevertheless they bore a good character, owing to the steadiness and sobriety of the men, and they improved in the
performance of their military duties by mixing with
other troops

General Knyphausen thought proper to cross over to
the Jersies by a bridge of boats with a considerable body
of men in the month of April, and marched in the direction of the army of General Washington ; but could not
prevail upon the Americans to quit their stronghold,
although some sharp skirmishing occasionally took place
Charleston surrendered to His Excellency Sir Henry

CAMPAIGN IN AMERICA. 21

Clinton on the 18th May 1780, and as that part of the country seemed to be brought into a state of tranquillity after this capture, Sir Henry returned to New York, taking with him the élite of his army, and leaving Earl Cornwallis in command of the troops to the southward. Part of these troops, on their arrival at New York, were sent over to join the army of General Knyphausen in the Jersies, but as the enemy declined to leave their post, the army was withdrawn and cantoned in the three islands.

On the 11th July, a French fleet, commanded by M. Ternay, having a large body of troops on board under the orders of the Count de Rochambeau, appeared on the coast of America, having escaped from Brest Harbour, and anchored off Rhode Island. Whether the news of this circumstance produced an effect on the people of South Carolina, or that their apparent return to their allegiance to the British Government in taking out protections from the commanders, had been an act of dissimulation, is known only to themselves; at all events, their minds apparently underwent a sudden change. Earl Cornwallis, who had been employed in selecting proper places for the frontier defences of the state of South Carolina, with a view to moving into North Carolina, was suddenly called at this time to Charleston, and left Lord Rawdon in command on the frontier, whose active mind and military knowledge enabled him

22 MEMOIR OF GENERAL GRAHAM.

to carry out the Earl's wishes to their fullest extent, of which ample proof was afterwards given at the posts of Camden and ninety-six. His lordship was also very successful in obtaining accurate and certain intelligence of the motions of the enemy. Earl Cornwallis's time was much occupied at Charleston in consequence of the discovery of a conspiracy to an alarming extent, in which many of the principal inhabitants were implicated; and it became necessary to arrest above thirty of them, but such was the lenity shewn upon the occasion by Sir Henry Clinton, that these people were only sent out of the country to St Augustine in Florida, and their estates sequestrated for the time to pay the expenses of the war.

The American army, under the command of General Horatio Gates, the victor of Saratoga, was now sent from the north into Carolina. Of this movement Lord Rawdon got early intelligence, which he communicated to Earl Cornwallis at Charleston. His lordship also made every preparation in case of an attack, putting his troops in the best possible state of efficiency, and on being informed that the advance of the enemy under the command of Baron de Thalbe, a foreign officer, were moving towards him, he sent an express to Earl Cornwallis, who arrived at Camden on the 13th August. On the 15th, in the evening,* the Earl ordered the

* Camden, South Carolina, 120 miles north-west of Charleston, was the scene of two actions in this war.

CAMPAIGN IN AMERICA. 23

:oops to move out. The right wing consisted of the 3d and 33d Regiments, under the command of Colonel Vebster of the 33d. The left wing consisted of the 'olunteers of Ireland, Lord Rawdon's corps, afterwards 1e —— Regiment of the line, and two other provincial attalions (troops raised in America), the whole being immanded by Lord Rawdon. It also contained the ifantry of the British Legion, or Tarleton's corps. The iserve included a battalion of the 71st Regiment and 1e cavalry of the British Legion, under Lieutenant-'olonel Tarleton. The enemy also marched out of his antonments on the evening of the 15th for a similar urpose, and the two armies, feeling one another in the ight, halted until daybreak of the 16th, when a con-ict took place, in which the Americans sustained a lost signal defeat, losing their baggage and artillery. he enemy, in a state of the utmost disorder, were pur-ied twenty-two miles from the field of battle. His iidship, in his despatch, pays the highest compliments) Lord Rawdon, Colonel Webster, Lieutenant-Colonel 'arleton, and all the officers, and praises the discipline nd gallantry of the different corps. Our loss was not ery great considering the immense superiority of the nemy in numbers. Baron de Thalbe died of his wounds.

At New York, after the arrival of the French fleet, ; was at one time proposed to embark a body of troops nd attack them in the harbour of Rhode Island, but

24 MEMOIR OF GENERAL GRAHAM.

this scheme was abandoned, and Admiral Arbuthnot blockaded the harbour by anchoring with the British fleet in Gardner's bay. Independent of the movements of the regular army, a predatory kind of warfare had for some time been carried on by the loyal refugees, who, making use of whale boats, landed on the Jersey shore, carried off cattle, and inflicted other damage on the enemy. For the protection of these parties, a block-house had been constructed on the brink of the Hudson's or North River. Their conduct at length became so daring that General Wayne, one of the famed American officers, was induced to attack this block-house with his brigade. The refugees fought with such obstinacy and determined courage that he was obliged to retire after some loss. A song appeared in the *New York Gazette* descriptive of this rencounter. It was attributed to the pen of the Adjutant-General, Major André, and the concluding stanza (supposing him to be the author) was too prophetic of his most unfortunate fate—

> And now I have finished my Epic strain,
> I tremble as I shew it,
> Lest some warrior drover Wayne
> Should ever catch the poet.

The 76th and 80th Regiments were now again brought together under the orders of Lieutenant-Colonel Dundas, being employed in garrisoning the lines at Kingsbridge, where a stream runs, separating New York from the

HESSIAN OFFICER. 25

mainland and forming an island. The 80th had the advantage in being commanded by such officers as Lieutenant-Colonel Dundas and Major Gordon, yet the 76th, although without a field officer, maintained a good character The highlanders had made great progress in acquiring the English language and began to lose that feeling of jealousy which too often subsists betwixt highlanders and lowlanders. A considerable space of ground outside the lines was unoccupied by the real inhabitants, and had got the name of neutral. The loyal refugees had taken up their abode in the deserted farm-houses, from whence they continually sent out foraging parties, and for their protection a redoubt, called No 8, was kept up, being one of a chain constructed for the defence of the army when encamped on this ground A captain and 100 men were sent from the lines to defend the place in case of the enemy's coming down on the refugees, a duty which lasted forty-eight hours, and as it was necessary to shut up the work at nightfall, and man the parapet during the whole night, one half standing to their arms and the other half reposing, the soldiers thus acquired a good idea of their duty. Foraging parties also often went out sometimes under the orders of Hessian field officers, who spoke English indifferently. On one of these occasions the charge of an old redoubt which happened to be on the road was entrusted to a subaltern's party, while the rest marched forward : as it was on the

C

26 MEMOIR OF GENERAL GRAHAM.

flank, the officer naturally asked for orders, the Hessian field-officer immediately replied, " I give you order , you and your men die here while we go forward," meaning, that in case the enemy should come on the flanks they were to defend the work to the last extremity. These and other incidents tended greatly to improve the soldiers

It was about this time that a correspondence commenced betwixt the American General Arnold and the British General Arnold was entrusted by the enemy with the command of a most important post high up the North River, a second Gibraltar, and commanding the intercourse betwixt the northern and southern parts of America To facilitate the business, the *Vulture* sloop of war was sent up the North River, having on board Colonel Beverley Robinson a loyalist gentleman whose property was situated in that district Major André accompanied this officer, and when at anchor in a particular place they were boarded by a boat from the shore in which Major André chose to embark and go on shore where he met General Arnold; but owing to circumstances he could not get on board again, and having a passport from that American General, he attempted to pass into the British lines at Kingsbridge by land, but was intercepted and made prisoner at Tarrytown, and the circumstance being reported to General Washington, his case was referred to a board of general officers, of which General Green was president,

MAJOR ANDRÉ. 27

and the Marquis la Fayette a member, and he lost his life. The story is too well known to be detailed here, but the following passage in the letter from that unfortunate officer to General Washington, wherein he discloses himself and his purposes, in some degree bears upon this narrative :—"I take the liberty to mention the condition of some gentlemen at Charlestown, who, being either on parole or under protections, were engaged in a conspiracy against us , though their situation is not similar, they are objects who may be sent in exchange for me, or are persons whom the treatment I receive may in some degree affect" This most accomplished, and much to be lamented officer, raised to high rank by his own merit, was put to death on a gibbet erected in front of the American army, on the 2d October 1780, in the 29th year of his age. No British friend attended at his last moments; but in justice to humanity it is pleasing to record the tender attention he received from every American officer intrusted with the security of his person, and the conducting him to the scaffold; nor was there an eye amongst the multitude of spectators who witnessed his execution unmoistened by a tear.*

His Excellency Sir Henry Clinton, immediately on

* The manner of his execution was scarcely justifiable by the sternest rules of international law. It was one of the few acts which can be cited as discreditable to the great hero Washington, and like the case of Asgill (of which hereafter) was the fruit of the proverbial bitterness of a civil war.—*Phillimore*, vol. iii., p. 156.

28 MEMOIR OF GENERAL GRAHAM.

receiving the accounts of the action at Camden, had ordered a detachment of the army to be embarked under the orders of the Hon. General Leslie, and to sail for the Chesapeake Bay, and to land there, making a diversion in favour of Earl Cornwallis, whose orders they were also directed to obey. The Foot Guards and Hessian Regiment de Bosc, with some provincial corps and detachments both of cavalry and infantry composed this force, amounting to nearly 3000 men. They took post at Portsmouth on the Elizabeth River, and were preparing to strengthen themselves, when they received orders from Earl Cornwallis to re-embark and join him in South Carolina. Earl Cornwallis moved to the northward with the troops who had fought at Camden after receiving stores, etc., about the 8th September, penetrating North Carolina, where it was supposed the majority of the inhabitants were friendly to Great Britain. This State is much intersected with rivers and creeks, and at that period abounded also in swamps and morasses. In many districts also where settlers had located themselves the country was extremely barren. His lordship, however, persevered, and took the road to Salisbury, having Lieutenant-Colonel Tarleton's corps on his left flank, and Major Ferguson's corps still more to the westward. This last most enterprising officer was employed on the outposts of the army, with about 150 provincial troops and a considerable number of loyalist militia

MAJOR FERGUSON. 29

whom he had trained to his mode of warfare, and he
and Colonel Tarleton had been extremely useful to the
army, having repeatedly defeated the partizan officers of
America, who came out of their swamps like locusts and
were very troublesome Major Ferguson united genius to
gallantry, having introduced improvements both in the
construction and in the method of using the enemy's own
weapon the rifle His lordship had great confidence in
this officer, and employed him in endeavouring to collect
a body of loyal militia in these settlements, in which he
was progressing satisfactorily when intelligence arrived
of the failure of an attack on our post at Augusta, by a
Colonel Clark, a refugee from Georgia, who had got together about 700 men, and attacked that post in the
hope of getting possession of the presents sent by the
British Government to the Indians, Augusta being the
place in which they were distributed. Major Ferguson,
on being apprised of the failure of Clark's attack, formed
a plan to intercept him. Unfortunately, several corps
of riflemen from Kentucky, the Eastern part of Virginia
and South Carolina, had also been assembled by their
leaders like Clark's force, with a design on Augusta ;
these parties fell in with Clark after his defeat, and
were persuaded by him to attempt the capture of Major
Ferguson's corps Having united their forces, the whole
moved off in their usual rapid manner, being all
mounted, and carrying nothing but their ammunition,

30 MEMOIR OF GENERAL GRAHAM.

rifles, and bags of provisions. Major Ferguson took post on King's mountain, and was there attacked by these people in three columns; their first onset was repulsed in the most gallant manner, but they again assaulted his position *en masse*, and he himself and many of his men having been killed, and many more wounded, the remainder, after a short resistance, were overpowered and compelled to surrender.

Earl Cornwallis, advancing towards Salisbury, on receiving intelligence of this disaster, took the resolution of retrograding, and accordingly about the 14th of October he left Charlotte, retiring in a southerly direction. The rainy season having set in, the roads were now saturated with water; sickness began to prevail amongst the troops, and his lordship being attacked with the prevailing malady, the command devolved upon Lord Rawdon. The retreat was harassing on account of the water courses, which had been swelled by the rain, while provisions were scarcely to be obtained. However, after fourteen days' marching the army arrived at Winnsborough. There his lordship intended to remain until the arrival of General Leslie from Virginia.

The enemy were not idle; General Gates, after his defeat at Camden, took post at George Town, where he exerted himself to collect his scattered troops, and received reinforcements from the north. Three very active partisans at this time hovered on the frontiers of

PARTIZANS.
31

South Carolina, Sumpter, Marion, and Pickens. These men, notwithstanding various defeats and attacks from our troops, were very troublesome, retiring when hard pressed into the swamps and morasses, accessible only to themselves and the beasts of the field; and reappearing, when opportunity offered, like locusts, interrupting even the communication betwixt Charlestown and Camden.

His Excellency General Clinton, having appointed General Arnold a brigadier in the British army, with power to raise a regiment of Provincials for his Majesty's service, upon learning that the Honourable General Leslie's troops had been ordered to re-embark and join Lord Cornwallis in South Carolina, directed another embarkation of troops to be sent to Virginia under the orders of Arnold. This force consisted of the 80th Regiment complete (the flank companies having again joined), under Lieutenant-Colonel Dundas, the Queen's Rangers, a corps which had seen much service, under Lieutenant-Colonel Simcoe, a corps of Provincials, under Lieutenant-Colonel Robertson, some Yagers and Artillery. They were put on board without delay, and sailing up the Chesapeake, landed and destroyed stores and magazines at Richmond, in Virginia, and on the 5th of January 1781 re-embarked and sailed to Portsmouth on the Elizabeth river, where they landed and took post. The Militia having been ordered out by the ruling powers in Virginia, in consequence of this and

32 MEMOIR OF GENERAL GRAHAM.

the former debarkation, came down to the neighbourhood of the British post in considerable numbers, and
frequent skirmishes took place with the foraging parties.
General Washington now used all his influence to per-
suade Count de Ternay to send a fleet with a body of
French troops to the Chesapeake, but that foreign officer
deemed it prudent first to despatch a ship of war. The
ship anchored at the mouth of the Elizabeth river, and
sent a summons into Portsmouth in the name of her
commander, and that of the officer commanding the
Militia, desiring the garrison to surrender. This demand
not being complied with, the French ship took her departure, sailing for Rhode island, where the naval officer
who had been employed made such a report, that an
embarkation of troops immediately took place under the
orders of Baron Vismesnil, and part of the fleet was
ordered to convoy them; the British fleet, however, being
on the watch, this expedition did not venture out. In
the meantime, the Commander-in-chief at New York
ordered another embarkation of British troops for Virginia, intrusting the command to Major-General Phillips,
a most excellent gallant officer, who had served as
second in command to General Burgoyne at Saratoga.
It consisted of the two battalions of Light Infantry of
the Line, under Colonel Robert Abercromby, the elite of
the British army, and who had led in almost every action
during the war, the 76th Regiment of Highlanders, a

GENERAL ARNOLD. 33

Hessian Regiment (Prince Hereditaire) with detachments of artillery and stores. This reinforcement left New York as soon as it was known that the sea was clear of the enemy, and entered the Chesapeake about the end of March—Admiral Arbuthnot's fleet being then at anchor in Lynnhaven Bay, a little to the south of the entrance to Elizabeth River.

A number of boats had been constructed, under the superintendence of General Arnold, for the navigation of the rivers, most of them calculated to hold 100 men. Each boat was manned by a few sailors, and was fitted with a sail as well as with oars. Some of them also carried a piece of ordnance in their bows. In these boats the light infantry, and detachments of the 76th and 80th Regiments, with the Queen's Rangers, embarked under the orders of Major-General Phillips and Brigadier-General Arnold, leaving the remainder of the 76th and 80th, with the Hessians, to garrison Portsmouth. The detachment of the 76th which embarked consisted of 1 major, 3 captains, 12 subalterns, and 300 men, commanded by the then Hon. Major Needham, now Earl Kilmorey. The 80th had Lieutenant-Colonel Dundas and Major Gordon, and the Queen's Rangers Lieutenant-Colonel Simcoe. The troops proceeded up the James River, a noble stream, and landed in several places, burning and destroying warlike stores and shipping on the stocks, as well as barracks and foundries.

34 MEMOIR OF GENERAL GRAHAM.

Many incidents occurred on these occasions. At Williamsburg a picquet guard of the 80th was posted at a point on the high road where two roads branched off , on one side of the road was a tavern with a piazza in front, on the other a ditch from which the earth had been thrown out, forming a parapet and serving as a fence to the college garden. At the fork where the picquet was posted, the ground was covered with trees except where they had been cleared away to form the road. As usual at out-picquets, a large fire was made, round which the soldiers not on duty as sentinels were lying. It had begun to rain, and the lieutenant in command of the 80th ordered the men to stand to their arms, and had just moved them to the shelter afforded by the piazza, when a volley was fired in the direction of the blazing fire from the brushwood under the trees— a company of young men, students at the university, composing a volunteer corps, having managed to creep into the thicket unobserved. The lieutenant, with great presence of mind moved his picquet across the road, leaping the ditch and forming them behind the parapet, he fired in the direction from whence the shots came, but whether any of the young men suffered is unknown, but not a British soldier, not even any of the sentinels, who manfully kept their posts, were hurt.

While a British column was crossing a road which ran into the main one, two carriages, each with four

A WEDDING TRIP.

horses and outriders, happened to come in contact with
it, a gentleman jumped out of the leading carriage, and
mounting an outrider's horse, dashed into the wood , a
shot or two was fired after him by the troops, but he
escaped. A lady remained in the carriage seemingly
much agitated. The carriages were detained until the
arrival of the General When the General came up he
immediately recognized the lady, having become acquainted with her when detained as a prisoner of war
on parole in this part of the country. On asking her
who the gentleman was, she replied, "He is my husband—we are just married." The General said, "It
was foolish in him to run the risk he did by trying to
escape, for it was not possible that he could long do so."
"And if you get him," she said, "what will be done to
him?" "Madam," said the General, "he shall be sent
immediately back to you, that you may enjoy the honey-
moon." As soon as the column had passed, the carriages
were allowed to proceed, not a horse being touched, although our artillery horses had not recovered from the
effects of the sea voyage

The army being again collected, we sailed up James
River, and landed at City Point The enemy did not
offer much opposition, although they appeared in con-
iderable number ; next day we moved through Blan-
ord to Petersburgh (25th April). At the last-named
place, the enemy made some show of resistance, but

36   MEMOIR OF GENERAL GRAHAM.

could not withstand the intrepidity of the light infantry, and fled in all directions, cutting down the bridge on the Apamattœ River to prevent pursuit. They were commanded by Baron Steuben and General Mahlenburg. We found a great quantity of tobacco in the warehouses of Petersburgh ,* it was the staple commodity with which they procured warlike stores. Orders were given to roll the hogsheads out of the storehouses, and they were burnt, as we had no means of carrying them away —many thousands were thus consumed

Brigadier Arnold moved to Osborne's on James River, with two field-pieces and a small detachment, and took a fleet at that place, a State ship of war, and another armed vessel, with a number of merchant ships loaded with tobacco. The enemy had set fire to several of their vessels before abandoning them, but the troops succeeded in extinguishing the flames in most of them —the Brigadier displaying much activity and intrepi-· dity on the occasion.

After making some other excursions in the neighbourhood, destroying stores of arms, and burning barracks, we received orders to march to Bermuda Hundreds, opposite City Point, where we embarked on the 2d May, and on the 5th and 6th dropped down the river.

Some of the vessels had got as far down as Hay

---

* Petersburgh, a post town of Virginia on the south-east bank of the Appamatœ River, twenty miles south of Richmond.

LA FAYETTE.

Island, when despatches were received from Lord Cornwallis, which occasioned our immediate return. After relanding we made a forced march in the night, and again took possession of Petersburgh (on the 10th May). During our absence, an aide-de-camp and several staff-officers of the Marquis la Fayette had arrived from the northward with a detachment of continental troops, by whom our motions were closely watched. The Major-General was by this time so unwell that a carriage was obtained for him, and he was lodged in the house of Mrs. Boland. The Marquis la Fayette brought some field-pieces to the opposite banks of the river, and cannonaded us, directing his fire principally against Mrs. Boland's house, in which the General lay dangerously ill. A cannon-ball passed through his bed-chamber, but no further damage was done than killing a black woman, a slave of Mrs. Boland's. General Phillips expired on the 12th May, and was buried at Petersburgh.

38 MEMOIR OF GENERAL GRAHAM.

CHAPTER THE FOURTH.

Lord Cornwallis' movements after the retreat from Charlotte—
The Cowpens—Battle of Guildford—Second Battle of Camden—Lord Cornwallis' force joins the corps at Petersburgh
after the death of General Phillips.

THE bar at Charlestown proved a great impediment to
the troops under General Leslie, and the badness of the
roads, owing to the rains, retarded very much his movements after landing. Lord Cornwallis, who, as stated in
the last chapter, had retreated from Charlotte after Major
Ferguson was killed, and taken up a position at Wins-
borough to await the arrival of Leslie, was consequently
unable to attempt re-entering North Carolina until the
15th January. Finding then that Leslie was approaching,
he left the defence of Camden, to Lord Rawdon, and prepared to move. General Gates had by this time replaced
General Green in the command of the American army,
and Colonel Morgan, an active officer, intrusted with the
light troops, was pushing forward in the direction of
the British posts. Lord Cornwallis directed Lieutenant-
Colonel Tarleton, with his legion, a battalion of the 71st

COWPENS. 39

egiment, some light companies, and also the 7th Fusiers (a regiment mostly composed of recruits, which was n its way to reinforce one of the outposts), to watch nd look after Morgan. Tarleton, by the celerity of his movements, soon came up with Morgan, and an action ook place (at Cowpens), in which the British sustained severe loss, as almost all the infantry engaged were ther killed, wounded, or made prisoners. Lieutenant-olonel Tarleton, with some officers and a party of the 7th Light Dragoons, behaved most gallantly, and so aggered the enemy's cavalry, commanded by Colonel Vashington, that a party of men under Ensign Frazer f the 71st, in charge of the baggage, got safe into the ritish camp. Morgan, knowing too well the nature of is prize, left the officers and wounded on the field with flag of truce, and moved off with his prisoners to the orthward, being well acquainted with the country. he greater part of the cavalry reached the British camp rat night and the following day. This was a severe low to the army, as the light companies, the 71st, and gion infantry had always formed the advance, and had sen much service, but his lordship, being joined by re troops under General Leslie, determined to persevere n entering North Carolina even at this season of the ear, being indeed the only chance he had of procuring absistence for his army in this barren country.

His lordship before commencing his march had

40 MEMOIR OF GENERAL GRAHAM.

directed that a detachment of troops from Charlestown should be embarked and sent up Cape Fear River to Wilmington.* These troops were commanded by Major Craig of the 82d (afterwards General Sir James H. Craig). On the 25th January his lordship halted for two days, and recommended to the army to equip themselves as light troops, and set a noble example by causing all his superfluous baggage to be destroyed, in which he was promptly and cheerfully followed by the whole army; all the wheeled carriages were rendered useless, except such as were necessary for the transport of ammunition, salt, and the hospital. Thus lightened, the army made rapid marches in pursuit of General Morgan and his prisoners, but the wily Virginian escaped into his own province without being overtaken. On the 1st February the British army crossed the Catawba river, breast high in water, the Foot Guards, under General O'Hara, leading ; the enemy in force on the opposite bank, and keeping up an incessant fire ; the column advanced without returning a shot, led by their light company. As soon as they reached the opposite shore their gallant captain, Lieutenant-Colonel Hall, unfortunately fell ; but that circumstance did not restrain their impetuosity, for their lieutenant (the late

---

* A port of entry, North Carolina, on the east side of Clarendon river, 76 miles south-east of Fayetteville ; 127 miles north-east of Charlestown, South Carolina

GREEN'S MOVEMENTS. 41

General Francis Dundas) at once assumed, the command, and charging with the bayonet, drove the enemy from their ground, and killed their general. The army made a rapid advance, but the enemy retired precipitately, crossing the Dar river about the 15th February into Virginia. The noble Earl did not think the force under his command sufficient to warrant his following them into that extensive State; he therefore marched by easy stages to Hillsborough, where he raised the King's standard, calling upon the inhabitants to return to their allegiance. The enemy soon left Virginia, and reappeared in North Carolina; and about the end of February a body of loyalists, amounting to betwixt 300 and 400 men, under Colonel Pyle, meeting with Lee's legion, forming part of their light troops, and mistaking them for Tarleton's corps, was nearly annihilated. About the same time, General Green having received reinforcements, returned with the remainder of his troops, recrossing the Dar.

The army was without information as to the movements of the enemy for several days, owing to the activity of the enemy's light troops; and want of stores, forage, etc., obliged his lordship to move in the direction of Wilmington on Cape Fear river, having received information that the stores he had ordered from Charlestown, and a reinforcement of troops, the 82d, under Major Craig, had arrived there. On the 14th March

c 2

42   MEMOIR OF GENERAL GRAHAM.

his lordship having learnt that General Green was at Guildford Court-house, where he had assembled his whole force, amounting to nearly 7000 men, immediately set off for the purpose of attacking him, although the British troops under his command did not amount to more than 2000 infantry and 200 cavalry. Having detached his waggons he moved with the army towards the enemy on the morning of the 15th. About four miles from Guildford Lieutenant-Colonel Tarleton, with the advanced guard, came upon the enemy's outposts, and driving them back, took some prisoners, who could give no information about the main body of the army, having been for several days with the advance. The enemy's line, however, soon became visible, drawn up on the skirts of a wood near the Court-house. His lordship, on coming in sight of this position, directed Lieutenant (now General) M'Leod, with his field pieces, to cannonade their centre, and made his dispositions for the attack. General Leslie, with the 71st Regiment, and Hessian Regiment de Bose, supported by 1st Battalion of Guards, formed the right wing. The left consisted of the 23d and 33d Regiments, under the command of Lieutenant-Colonel Webster, supported by the Grenadiers and 2d Battalion Foot Guards, under Brigadier-General O'Hara. The Yagers and light infantry of the Guards remained on the left of the guns, and the cavalry on a road, ready to act. The action commenced

BATTLE OF GUILDFORD. 43

about half-past one P.M., and the guards being brought into line to the right of the Hessians, soon defeated everything before them. Colonel Webster was equally fortunate in the repulse of the force immediately in his front, and then finding the left of the 33d Regiment exposed to a heavy fire from the right wing of the enemy, he changed front to the left and completed the route of the enemy's right. The Grenadiers, and 2d Battalion of Guards had moved forward to occupy the ground left vacant by Colonel Webster's movement, and the whole line was now in action; but the woods were so thick, that the enemy, although defeated, was enabled to keep up a desultory fire on the British line, in front, flank, and rear. The Grenadiers, and 2d Battalion of Guards, continuing to advance, were the first to gain the cleared ground, near Guildford Court-house, where they met with a body of Continentals, whom, though superior in numbers, they instantly attacked and defeated, taking two six pounders ; but being thrown into confusion by the heavy fire they encountered, and at the same time attacked by Washington's dragoons, they were forced to relinquish the ground they had taken. The enemy's cavalry, in turn, were driven back by Lieutenant M'Leod's guns ; and the 71st and Grenadiers coming up in support, the 2d Battalion of Guards was rallied, and returned to the charge, through the spirited exertions of Brigadier O'Hara, who had at the

MEMOIR OF GENERAL GRAHAM.

time received two wounds ; while the 23d Regiment appearing on the left, and Colonel Tarleton advancing with part of the cavalry, the enemy were once more put to flight, leaving the two six pounders in our hands, together with two other guns of the same calibre, and two ammunition waggons, being all the artillery they had in the field. The 33d and light infantry of the Guards, overcoming many difficulties, had completely routed that portion of the enemy opposed to them. The 23d, 71st, and part of the cavalry were ordered to pursue. Lieutenant-Colonel Tarleton and the remainder of the cavalry proceeded to the right, and put an end to the firing which still continued in that quarter. The militia dispersed in the woods, and the continentals went off by the Reedy Fork, beyond which it was not possible to follow them, as their cavalry had suffered but little, while our men were excessively fatigued from the severity of the action, and the time it had lasted The want of provisions, and the state of the wounded, dispersed over an extensive piece of ground, also prevented his lordship from following them next day ; so, after leaving about seventy of the worst cases at the Quaker meeting-house, he proceeded to Bell's Mills, approaching towards Wilmington

His lordship extols the conduct of General Leslie, Brigadier O'Hara, Colonel Webster, Lieutenant-Colonel

MARCH TO CROSS CREEK. 45

Tarleton, Major de ———* of the regiment De Bosc, Lieutenant M'Leod of the artillery, also of Governor Martin and Brigadier Howard of the Guards, who were volunteers. Colonel Webster died of his wounds, as did Captains Schultz and Maynard of the Guards, and two Hessian officers. Nearly a third of the force of the army was killed or wounded. The night succeeding the day of battle was very wet, the dead lay unburied, the wounded unsheltered; and the victorious army being without tents and without food could not alleviate their sufferings. The ensuing morning was spent in burying the dead and providing comfort for the wounded, in which duties his lordship was equally attentive to friends and foes. After remaining two days on the field, the army moved for New Garden, where they met with the rearguard and baggage. Leaving the worst cases with a flag, his lordship moved on the 18th, by easy marches, to Cross Creek,† a Highland settlement convenient to Wilmington, then in possession of Major Craig. The enemy, although they retreated a considerable distance, seem to have rallied as their light troops were seen in the neighbourhood of the army; but this part of the country is so exceedingly barren and thinly settled that his lordship moved on to Wilmington, where he arrived on the

---

* Illegible

† Cross Creek, now "Fayetteville," a flourishing town of North Carolina

46　　　MEMOIR OF GENERAL GRAHAM

7th April. His lordship, after the battle of Guildford, issued a proclamation calling upon the loyalists to come forward; and he states in his despatch that many of them rode into the camp and took him by the hand, expressing joy at the defeat of General Green, but went no further. In short, either from timidity or change of sentiment, not one appeared in arms for his Majesty's Government.*

About this period General Green moved to the southward, hoping to make himself master of Camden and the British posts in South Carolina. Earl Cornwallis being apprized of his intention, sent off intelligence of it to Lord Rawdon, but such was the state of the country, and the dispersion of the enemy's light troops, that none of the messengers succeeded in reaching Camden, Lord Rawdon had, however, himself obtained information of Green's design six days before its execution was

---

* The lukewarmness of our friends, and the distresses of the army, compelled me to move to Cross Creek; but meeting there with no material part of the promised assistance and supplies, I was obliged to continue my march to Wilmington, where hospitals and stores were ready for us. Of this move I sent information by several expresses to Lord Rawdon, but unfortunately they all failed. My intention was, as soon as I should have equipped my corps and received part of the expected reinforcement from Ireland, to return to the upper country, in hopes of giving some protection to South Carolina, and of preserving the health of the troops until new measures could be concerted with the Commander-in-Chief.—*Lord Cornwallis' Pamphlet*

SIEGE OF NINETY-SIX.

attempted, and on the 25th he moved out of Camden with little more than 800 men — the 63d Regiment, Volunteers of Ireland, King's American Regiment, and New York volunteers (the three last provincial corps)— and attacked and defeated General Green's army, sustaining, however, a loss of 250 men in killed, wounded, and prisoners. This is called by the enemy the battle of Hobkirk's Hill, and by the British the second battle of Camden.

After this defeat General Green made a move to the southward, and having made himself master of the smaller posts on the frontier, sent his light troops to the southernmost one, called Fort Augusta, and succeeded in taking it also. He next set himself down for the attack of 96, a post defended by Lieutenant-Colonel Cruger, a provincial officer, with about 300 provincial troops and some loyalist militia. Lord Rawdon's messengers shared nearly the same fate as those sent by Lord Cornwallis to himself, not one of them succeeded in reaching his destination. Lord Rawdon had directed the lieutenant-colonel to evacuate the post and retire in the direction of Charlestown ; but Cruger not having received any of the messages, determined to defend his post to the last extremity, and did so for a considerable period, displaying great gallantry and perseverance in holding out until the arrival of Lord Rawdon.

His lordship having evacuated the post at Camden,

48   MEMOIR OF GENERAL GRAHAM.

had gone to Charlestown, and taking with him a reinforcement of troops, principally composed of the flank
companies of the newly arrived regiments from Ireland,
3d, 19th, and 30th, he by rapid marches, and notwithstanding the heat of the weather, came up in time to
save the lieutenant-colonel.

General Green, on the 19th June, raised the siege,
and proceeded to the southward, apparently evincing no
inclination to meet his lordship again in the field.

Earl Cornwallis, while at Wilmington on the 23d
April, got intelligence of General Phillips' expedition,
and immediately decided on moving to Virginia to effect
a junction with him, and having given instructions to
Major Craig at Wilmington, and also to Lieutenant-
Colonel Balfour at Charlestown for their conduct, in case
of failure he set out with the army towards Halifax
upon the Roanoke river, a district less barren, sending
Lieutenant-Colonel Tarleton in advance, and the lieutenant-colonel having crossed the river into Virginia at
this place without anything very material happening,
information was received at Petersburg of the event,
when Brigadier Arnold, with the Queen's Rangers, immediately moved off in that direction to meet him,
and on the 20th May the two armies formed a junction
at Petersburg.*   Words can ill describe the admiration

* Sir Henry Clinton, after the war, issued a pamphlet in
justification of his own conduct as Commander-in-Chief, in which

ARRIVAL AT PETERSBURG.

49

in which this band of heroes was held by the two Scotch regiments, and even by the battalions of light infantry, the "élite" of the army who had fought and generally led in every action during the war. The gallant earl and his brave officers who had shared with him in his long and arduous marches, as well as in his laurels, were almost idolized. Their numbers were —

he animadverts on Lord Cornwallis' march into Virginia, and declares that it was " a measure determined on without his approbation, and very contrary to his wishes and intention." Lord Cornwallis' reply vindicates the measure, and explains the grounds upon which it was undertaken " I could not remain (his Lordship says) at Wilmington, lest General Green should succeed against Lord Rawdon, and, by returning to North Carolina, have it in his power to cut off every means of saving my small corps, except that disgraceful one of embarkation, with the loss of the cavalry and every horse in the army From the shortness of Lord Rawdon's stock of provisions, and the great distance from Wilmington to Camden, it appeared impossible that any direct move of mine could afford him the least relief In the attempt, in case of a misfortune to him, the safety of my own corps might have been endangered, or if he extricated himself, the force in South Carolina when assembled, was, in my opinion, sufficient to secure what was valuable to us, and capable of defence in that province I was likewise influenced by having just heard that General Phillips had been detached and placed under my orders, which induced me to hope that solid operation might be adopted in that quarter, and I was fully persuaded that until Virginia was reduced we could not hold the more southern provinces, and that after its reduction they would fall without much resistance, and be retained without much difficulty"

D

50 MEMOIR OF GENERAL GRAHAM.

Brigade of Guards . . 387 ⎫
23d Regiment . . . 194 ⎪
33d Regiment . . . 209 ⎬ British.
71st Regiment (2 battalions) . 175 ⎪
82d Regiment, light company . 36 ⎭
Regiment de Bosc . . 228   Hessian.
British Legion (Lieut.-Col. Tarleton's) 173 ⎫
North Carolina Volunteers . 33 ⎭ Provincial.

Total . 1435

AMERICAN CAMPAIGN.

CHAPTER THE FIFTH.

American Campaign continued — Action at James City — Siege and Surrender of York Town.

PREPARATIONS were at once made for moving towards the Marquis la Fayette, who had been reinforced by troops from the north, as well as by the militia from the neighbourhood of Richmond. Another detachment from New York joined the British army about 26th May in James River, consisting of two battalions of the troops of Anspach Brandenburg, the 17th and 43d British Regiments. The German regiments and the 17th, being weak in numbers, were sent to join the garrison of Portsmouth, General Leslie was sent to take the command at that post, and Brigadier Arnold went to New York. The 43d Regiment was kept with the army, and, with the detachments of the 76th and 80th, formed a brigade for Lieutenant-Colonel Dundas. Here I had daily opportunities of being with my friend Major Gordon, whose military ability was justly appreciated by Lord Cornwallis, at the same time that it somewhat excited his surprise, as his lordship had known him twenty years before in the gay circles of

52 MEMOIR OF GENERAL GRAHAM.

London. Our encampments were always chosen on the banks of a stream, and were extremely picturesque, as we had no tents, and were obliged to construct wigwams of fresh boughs to keep off the rays of the sun during the day. At night, the blazing fires which we made of the fence rails illuminated the surrounding scenery, which, in this part of America, is of the most magnificent description. There was but one wish in the army, which was to come up with the marquis. At parting with my friends in the evening, it was always "Prælium pugnatum est." The marquis moved to the westmard, keeping about twenty miles off; we marched as far as Jefferson's Plantation, and Lieutenant-Colonels Tarleton and Simcœ were detached, and destroyed tobacco and stores of various descriptions. The former officer came upon the Assembly of Virginia at Charleville by rapid marches, and made prisoners of several members. The army began to move towards Williamsburgh Neck for the sake of health at this season of the year, as well as because there was no chance of coming up with La Fayette's corps; we arrived there on the 25th June. On this march the Queen's Rangers, forming a rear-guard, were assailed by an American corps under Colonel Butler, which had followed close in their rear for several days. After some sharp fighting, in which Lieutenant Jones greatly distinguished himself until he fell, the enemy retired.

ACTION AT JAMES CITY. 53

A few days afterwards, his lordship, wishing to approach the shipping at Portsmouth, had occasion to cross the James River to Cobham, and having made choice of James City Point as a proper place for crossing, he apprised the naval authorities of his intention, and our baggage, bât horses, and the Queen's Rangers crossed over on the 5th July. The rest of the army still remained at James City. La Fayette, with Wayne's brigade, was completely deceived respecting this movement, and supposing that all the army had crossed over except the rear-guard, came down to James City on the 6th, moving by a narrow road across the Green Springs leading to a spot of cleared ground on the bank of the river which was immediately in front of Colonel Dundas's brigade. The British army was drawn up in two lines, the brigade of Colonel Dundas forming the left of the front line, the light infantry the right, the Guards, 23d, 33d, and Hessians formed the second line. The picquet-guard of Colonel Dundas's brigade, consisting of men of the 76th Regiment commanded by Lieutenant Balneaves, an officer of the 80th Regiment, was ordered to resist as long as possible, which they did for a length of time. The lieutenant was killed, and Lieutenant Alston of the same regiment, having taken the command, was severely wounded, and after him Ensign Wemyss of the 76th was also wounded, when the picquet received orders to retire; and the

54 MEMOIR OF GENERAL GRAHAM.

enemy, advancing with great boldness, having a six-pounder on each flank, fronted when the head of the column reached the bank, and advancing in line on the open ground, fired their field-pieces. The troops were then ordered to their arms, and the 76th, under the orders of the Hon. Major Needham, the 80th under Major Gordon, and two companies of the 43d under Captain Cameron (the rest of that regiment being in the wood), advanced under their gallant brigadier, Lieutenant-Colonel Dundas. The enemy kept a good countenance for a short time, returning our fire from their field-pieces and muskets, but the noble Earl coming in the rear of the 76th, called out to charge, which order not being heard on account of the noise, he made a motion with his cane, touching a Highlander on the shoulder, which being repeated, they rushed on most rapidly. The 80th in the centre still continuing to fire, Major Gordon, mounted on a very tall horse, dashed out in front and stopped them, when several Edinburgh men of this regiment were heard to cry out, " Brigadier ! will you no luk at the major, we canna get shooting for him ; he's aye rinnin' in the gate." A general charge took place which soon put an end to the combat. The enemy disappeared in an instant, as if removed by magic, abandoning their field-pieces and their wounded Opposite to our left, where my post was, the enemy left a six-pounder loaded with grape shot. The noble lord,

YORK AND GLOUCESTER. 55

in his despatch, is pleased to make use of these words—
"but the 76th and 80th, on whom the brunt of the
action fell, had an opportunity of distinguishing themselves particularly, and Lieutenant-Colonel Dundas's
gallantry and good conduct deserve the highest praise."*
Thus fortune in her frolics seemed to render these two
corps somewhat worthy of their companions in arms,
but all were soon destined to taste of her frowns. The
enemy's loss was considerable, particularly in wounded,
many of whom, I afterwards ascertained from their officers, were wounded in the lower extremities, a proof that
the young soldiers had taken good aim. The army
crossed the river unmolested, next day proceeding towards Portsmouth.

The light infantry and some regiments embarked
about the beginning of August, and sailed for York
River. Brigadier-General O'Hara was left with the
remainder of the forces at Portsmouth, with orders to
destroy the works, embark the troops and stores, and
follow the main body as soon as possible York† and
Gloucester were taken possession of by the troops of

---

* There are officers now living who remember to have heard
eye-witnesses speak of the distinguished gallantry of Captain
Graham of the 76th in this action

† York or York Town, a port of entry and post town of
Virginia, capital of York county, on the south side of York
river, 12 miles E. of Williamsburgh, 15 miles N.W. of Hampton,
57 miles E.S.E. of Richmond.

56 MEMOIR OF GENERAL GRAHAM.

the first embarkation, and about 22d August the whole army was assembled in these places. Working parties both of the army and navy began fortifying Gloucester. As soon as the works were completed, a garrison, consisting of the 80th and Queen's Rangers, with the Hessian Regiment (Prince Hereditaire), under Colonel Dundas, was left for the defence of that post. The rest of the army was employed in fortifying York Town. The York River at this place makes a bend or curve, in the centre of which the town is situated, which consists of a row of houses built on a high bank, with wharfs and warehouses below on a level with the water. On the right of the town there is a considerable ravine, and on the angle of the opposite bank was constructed a pretty strong redoubt with an abatis as a defence on the right flank. The town was then surrounded by a ditch and thick parapet, having a horn work in its centre, in both of which were batteries, the embrasures lined with fascines. The parapet ran to the river on the left flank, having two advanced redoubts with abatis constructed on that flank, one on the brink of the bank over the river, the other advanced, and in a line with the town's parapet and base of the hornwork. The parapet was formed of trees cut in the woods and placed inside; outside it was formed of fascines; and the earth from the ditch, which was sandy and gravelly, was thrown into the space between; it had also a fraise made of fence rails

SIEGE OF YORK. 57

kept in line and projecting by the earth thrown into the opening of the parapet, giving it an appearance of strength which it little merited During the time that the army was employed in these laborious works there was an encampment outside the town, on the edge of the bank projecting over the ravine with which the town was partly surrounded, particularly on its right, and through which several roads entered the town. This encampment was strengthened by redoubts and field works, thrown up for artillery, in various places commanding the country in its front, which was open and level This was called the outward position. While the troops were employed in this manner, working hard both by day and night, one of the frigates sent with despatches to New York suddenly returned, bringing intelligence that the Count de Grasse with the French fleet was in possession of Chesapeake Bay. A line of battle ship and two frigates blockaded the mouth of York river The Hessian field-officer who had caused a sensation amongst the Scotch soldiers, as before mentioned, being asked his opinion of the defences of the Gloucester side, replied, "I no fear de land, but got tamn she," pointing to the ships.

A British fleet under Admiral Graves came off the Cape of the Bay about 5th September, when the French fleet, cutting its cables, stood out to sea, and a partial action took place, after which the two fleets remained in sight of each other for some days, when the British,

MEMOIR OF GENERAL GRAHAM.

finding no entrance to the Bay, stood to the northward The Count de Barras having left Rhode Island on 25th August with a fleet and stores of various kinds entered the Bay at this period, having escaped the observation of the British fleet, and Count de Grasse again entered the Chesapeake, forming a junction with the Count de Barras A body of French troops, commanded by the French General St Simon, was landed at Williamsburgh from the fleet from the West Indies. Count Rocham- beau also having formed a junction with General Wash- ington's army, after crossing the Hudson or North River, and making a feint while in the Jersies of attacking New York, suddenly moved to the southward with the Ameri- can army by forced marches. This corps arriving at the head of Elk was soon transported by the French fleet also to Williamsburgh. Our army continued strengthening their posts as well as they could, felling trees and causing such other obstructions to the advance of the enemy as were in their power, when, on the 28th Sep- tember, information was given by a picquet in front of a working party that the enemy were advancing in force by the Williamsburgh Road The army immediately took post in the outward position. The French and Americans came on in the most cautious and regular order. Some shots were fired from our field-pieces. The French also felt the redoubt on our right flank, defended by the 23d and a party of marines, but did not

SIEGE OF YORK. 59

persist. The two armies remained some time in this position observing each other. In ours, there was but one wish, that they would advance. While standing with a brother captain (Mont Blanc), we overheard a soliloquy of an old Highland gentleman, a lieutenant, who, drawing his sword, said to himself, " Come on, Maister Washington, I'm unco glad to see you ; I've been offered money for my commission, but I could na think of gangin' hame without a sight of you. Come on." On the 29th the enemy made a movement, the Americans moving to the left of our position, leaving the French on our right, so that we were completely invested. On the 30th, a boat with despatches from New York arrived, having come through the French fleet in safety. In the evening of this day the army evacuated the outward position, retiring within the defences of York Town. The river is about 1500 yards wide betwixt the two posts York and Gloucester. On the 2d October, the legion under Lieutenant-Colonel Tarleton was sent over to Gloucester. On the 3d, a foraging party being sent out from Gloucester by orders of Lieutenant-Colonel Dundas, the rear-guard, composed of cavalry, was attacked by the legion of Lauzun, and driven back, until saved by the light company of the 23d under Captain Champagne, who lost several men, and his Lieutenant Moore, a promising officer. Brigadier-General Choisi, commanding on the Gloucester side,

60　MEMOIR OF GENERAL GRAHAM.

being reinforced by a body of marines, the communication with the country was cut off. At York Town our labours were incessant, the French and Americans on their side were not idle, constructing their first parallel within 600 yards of our works. They had constructed a battery of heavy guns opposite the redoubts on our right flank, and on the evening of the 9th they fired an eighteen pound ball into the town as a beginning, which, entering a wooden house where the officers of the 76th Regiment were at dinner, badly wounded the old Highland lieutenant whose soliloquy is before narrated, also slightly the quarter-master and adjutant, and killed the Commissary-General Perkins who was at table.

An incessant cannonade now commenced on both sides, but our batteries and newly constructed works soon began to feel the effects of the powerful artillery opposed to them, and on the 10th scarcely a gun could be fired from our works, fascines, stockade platforms, and earth, with guns and gun-carriages, being all pounded together into a mass. The Hon. Major Cochrane, of the legion who came express from New York through the French fleet, and was appointed to act as an aid-de-camp to Lord Cornwallis, being led by zeal to fire a gun from behind the parapet in the horn work "en ricochet," and anxious to see its effect, looked over to observe it, when his head was carried off by a cannon ball.

On the 11th the enemy began his second parallel.

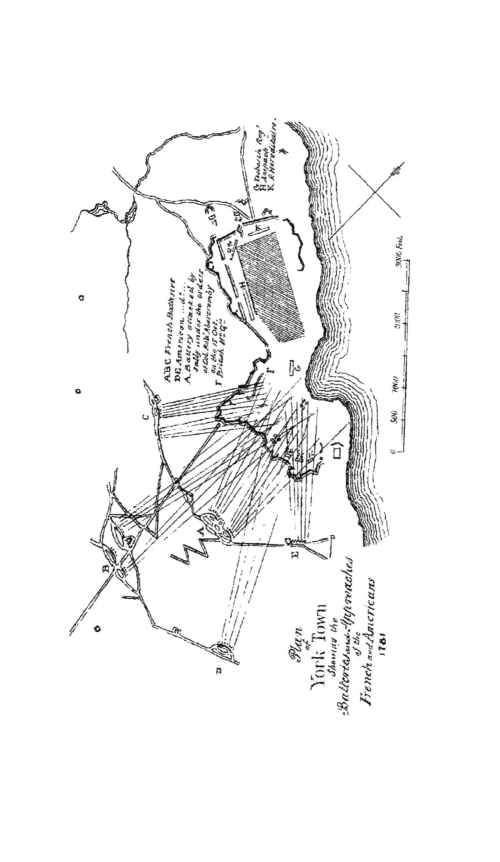

GALLANT SORTIE.

61

)n the 12th Lieutenant-Colonel Dundas, Major Gordon, nd part of the 80th, came over from Gloucester to do uty in the lines of York Town. On the evening of the 4th the two redoubts on our left flank were attacked, nd carried after a gallant resistance ; that next the iver was taken by the Americans, and the other by the 'rench The French general who commanded the at-ick found fault with his aid-de-camp who led for dis-iounting his horse, the works being so much battered nd destroyed The two redoubts were soon included in ie enemy's lines. Early in the morning of the 15th a ortie from our lines, consisting of the grenadiers of the 'oot Guards, and Captain John Murray's company of ie 80th, commanded by Colonel (afterwards Lord) Lake, nd a detachment of Light Infantry, under Major Arm-trong, in all about 350 men, under the immediate rders of Colonel (afterwards Sir Robert) Abercromby, itered the French lines in the most gallant style, killing bove 100 men, and spiking 11 pieces of heavy artillery i one of their batteries almost completed They re-irned without much loss, in face of a large body of 'oops under the Marquis Noailles sent to attack them. his daring enterprise, although it retarded operations ir a short time at that particular spot, had little effect i the general progress of their siege operations, and our ss of men much increasing, the Earl took the resolu-on of crossing over to Gloucester with the most effect-

62 MEMOIR OF GENERAL GRAHAM.

ive of his troops, leaving the rest to surrender the place. His Lordship's intention was to attack Lauzun's Legion at Gloucester and get possession of their horses, and then move rapidly off either to the northward or southward, as circumstances might dictate. Accordingly, an embarkation took place, and part crossed over; but while the next embarkation was on the water, a violent storm of wind and rain occurred, which, driving many of the troops down the river nearly under the enemy's lines, obliged his Lordship to desist from prosecuting his intentions, and recall such troops as had landed at Gloucester. These men suffered a good deal from the enemy's fire while returning on the river.

On the 17th Lord Cornwallis proposed a cessation of hostilities, and Lieutenant-Colonel Dundas and Major Ross (now General) having met the Marquis Noailles and Mr. Lawrence, articles of capitulation were settled. By the 1st the land forces were to become prisoners of war to the United States of America, and the seamen to the naval army of the King of France. By the 3d the troops were to march out with shouldered arms and drums beating to a place where the arms were to be laid down. By the 4th the officers were to keep their private property and wear their side arms. By the 5th the soldiers were to be kept in Virginia, Maryland or Pennsylvania, and to receive provisions as the soldiers of America. A British, Hessian, and Anspach field officer,

PRISONER OF WAR 63

ith other officers, in the proportion of 1 to 50 men,
ere to be allowed to reside near their respective regi-
ents on their parole of honour, and bear witness of
.eir treatment, delivering clothing and necessaries to
.em, for which passports were to be granted on appli-
.tion. By the 8th, the Bonetta sloop of war to be al-
wed to sail to New York with an officer bearing
espatches, and with such other persons as Lord Corn-
allis might think proper to put on board, who are not
. be examined. The ship and crew to be accounted
r, the dangers of the sea excepted. By the 14th
ticle it was stipulated that no *article of this* capitula-
on was to be infringed on *pretence of reprisals*, and if
tere were any doubtful expressions in it, they were to
e interpreted according to the usual meaning and ac-
eptation of the words. The signatures of the Earl
ornwallis, Lieutenant-General, commanding the garri-
ins of York and Gloucester, and of Commodore Symonds, commanding his Britannic Majesty's naval forces
t York River, on the one part, and of his Excellency
eneral Washington, commanding the combined forces
f America and France, his Excellency Count Rocham-
eau, Lieutenant-General Grand Cross of the order of St.
iouis, commanding the auxiliary troops of his Most
hristian Majesty in America, his Excellency the Count
e Grasse, Lieutenant-General, commander of the naval
rmy of his Most Christian Majesty in the Bay of

64 MEMOIR OF GENERAL GRAHAM.

Chesapeake, on the other part, were affixed to the capitulation. On the 19th the garrison marched out betwixt the two lines of American and French troops reluctantly enough, and laid down their arms. A corporal next to me shed tears, and, embracing his firelock, threw it down, saying, "May you never get so good a master." This over, the regiments set about fixing upon the officers who were to remain on parole of honour with the troops. In the 76th this was done by casting lots, which was also the mode followed by the field officers of the British army, and it having fallen upon Colonel (afterwards Lord) Lake, that officer expressed himself in such a manner on the occasion, as induced Major Gordon to say that he would take the duty for him, an offer which was joyfully accepted It fell to my lot to be one of the captains of the 76th detailed to remain with the soldiers in America. Our departure was fixed for the following morning, so that little time was given for preparation, but having a great desire to visit the enemy's works, which we had so long contemplated with feelings understood by human nature, but which language can ill describe, accompanied by a friend I visited the French lines, and met with much courtesy from the French. On the top of the parapet where the guns were placed which had been spiked in the " sortie," they showed me a grave, saying, " Voilà un de vos brave gens." It was that of a serjeant in the Foot Guards who had

POLITENESS OF FRENCH OFFICERS   65

.llen there   Earl Cornwallis also mentions the conduct
' the French officers in making offers of money for our
se.   I have heard of one of them, I believe Le Vicomte
ismesnil, who apologised by saying, " Je n'ai rien à vous
frir.   J'ai eu l'honneur de servir cinquante ans   le
rand Monarque je n' yai gagné que la petite croix et le
rumatisme "*

* In the " New York Packet," December 27, 1781, under
the signature " A Subaltern," there appeared a lengthy comment
n Lord Cornwallis' despatch relating to the reduction of York
he writer charges his lordship with being " No General"—No
ldier—No politician—and no gentleman   For each of these
harges the writer gives his reasons.   The last one, that of Lord
ornwallis being no gentleman, he says " is evident from his un-
rateful silence as to the noble and generous conduct of General
'ashington and the American officers to him and his army after
ie capitulation.

"The magnanimity, humanity, and politeness of the Com-
ander-in-Chief of the American armies would have extorted ex-
ressions of gratitude and respect from an Indian savage, a Tartar,
r a Turk.   A British general and an English nobleman is the
ily human being that could have treated such superlative virtue
ith sullen disrespect."

D 2

CHAPTER THE SIXTH.

Prisoners of war escorted to Winchester—General Morgan as to accommodation for Prisoners—Removed to Little York

THE British prisoners moved out of York Town next day, 20th, in two divisions, escorted by regiments of militia or state troops ; one took the direction of Maryland, the other, to which I belonged, moved to the westward in Virginia. Our guards were all from the upper parts of the state, called backwoodsmen, between whom and the inhabitants of the lower parts there existed no cordiality ; and at night when we halted, they not only allowed, but even encouraged our men to pull down and make fires of the fence-rails, as we had been accustomed to do when we had arms in our hands . and when a proprietor complained they only laughed at him. They did not scruple also to let us make free with a turnip field. We moved on towards the base of the lesser blue ridge of mountains in the direction of an opening or gap called Ashley's Gap, where was a public-house kept by a person of that name. Happening to ride on in front of the

PRISONERS MARCH TO WINCHESTER. 67

column, I asked Mrs. Ashley if she could give two or three of us anything to eat. She stared at my uniform, saying—"A militiaman, I guess." "No," was my reply. "Continental, mayhap;" to which I also replied in the negative. "O ho!" said she, "I see you are one of the sarpints, one of ould Wallace's men; well now, I have two sons, one was at the catching of Johnny Burgoyne, and the other at that of you; and next year they are both going to catch Clinton at New York; but you shall be treated kindly, my mother came from the ould country."

We soon afterwards arrived at Winchester,* the place of our destination. The officers were lodged in the town on parole, the soldiers were marched several miles off to a cleared spot in the woods, on which stood a few log-huts, some of them occupied by prisoners taken at the Cowpens. The guards who had conducted us were relieved by regiments of militia from the neighbourhood. Crowds of the country people came daily amongst the men, inviting them to their plantations. They were not strictly guarded, and as there was not covering for half their number, it was intimated that we should not object, provided they previously made us aware of their

* Winchester or Fredericktown, a post town of Virginia, situated 32 miles S W from the celebrated passage of the Potowmack through the Blue Ridge. It was formerly fortified, but the works have been allowed to crumble into ruins; 62 miles W.N.W. of Washington, 108 miles N.W. of Richmond.

MEMOIR OF GENERAL GRAHAM.

intentions, and gave in the name of the inhabitant ; but that otherwise we should consider them in the light of deserters. The huts were few, and there was a prospect of bad weather. Being senior officer, I therefore applied to the commissary of prisoners for permission to send a certain number of men into the town to occupy a church which was little used, to which request he gave his consent Accordingly, 500 men were brought in, and the huts thus emptied were distributed among the other prisoners. A few days afterwards I got a message from Brigadier-General Morgan, who lived near the town, informing me that the soldiers could not be allowed to occupy the church and remain in the town any longer, and that they must return to the huts I immediately wrote a letter, remonstrating with him, and stating that there was not covering for half of the men at that place, neither had we any money to purchase tools with and erect more, and requesting that the 500 men might be allowed to remain in the town until a statement of their situation could be forwarded to head-quarters. To this I received the following reply :—

"SARATOGA, 28*th November* 1781.

"Sir—I rec^d your letter of this day's date, and am realy surprized at the purport of it two or three days before Christmas our army began to hut at Middle brook, jersey, and had nothing to keep off the inclamency of

LETTER FROM GENERAL MORGAN.

the weather till huts were made. You have time enough, this snow won't last long, it will be gone directly, if your men don't know how to work thay must learn, we did not send for them to come among us, neither can we work for them to build them houses, I have been a prisoner as well as thay, and was kept in close goale five month and twelve days; six and thirty officers and there serv^{ts} in one room, so that when we lay down upon our straw we covered the whole floore, consider this, and your men have nothing to grumble at Col. Holmes had no Right to bring them to town, thay were ordered to the Barrack, and thare thay ought to have continued, Col Holmes, tho a commisary of prsoner, is under controul, you have nothing to do but Hut your men as soon as you can, for that must be the case I have sent to Genl Washington informing him of all matter and of what I had done, and what I intended to do, and am shure it will meet with his approbation, as he has neaver yet found fault with my conduct, Youl conclude from this that Col. Holmes must obay my orders. The sooner your men hut themselves the better, for thay must not stay in Town much longer. I will try to redress every grevence as well as I can, but this I cant look upon as a grevence; if we had barrack to afford you you should have them, but as we have them not your men must cover themselves, at least I would recommand it to them, or they will suffer.

70 MEMOIR OF GENERAL GRAHAM.

I have wrote this letter in a plain, rough stile, that you might know what you had to depend on, at which I hope youl not take umbrage.   (Signed)   DAV. MORGAN, *Brigad^r -Genl*

" To Captain Samuel Graham,
       a Brittish Officer in
           Winchester.
by express "

I lodged with two brother officers in the house of the colonel commanding the militia who guarded the men, and knowing that General Morgan had come to town about some occurrences connected with the prisoners, I waited upon him, and invited him to dinner. He came, and in the course of conversation he asked the Colonel if he remembered a certain person, a most remarkable rifle shot; the latter said he did. He then told him that having been ordered to seize a height contiguous to the British posts at Saratoga; he no sooner did so than his people were driven from it, but having again re-taken the height, he saw an officer on a grey horse advancing, whom he had before observed, he therefore sent this man, who was such an excellent shot, into a tree, with orders to take aim at that officer, which was certainly done, for he did not re-appear, nor was the height re-taken. This was undoubtedly General Frazer, as the story nearly corresponds with the narrative in which General Burgoyne relates the fate of General Frazer, according to that account he fell by a rifle ball. General

GENERAL MORGAN'S ADVENTURES. 71

Morgan also told us that the British still owed him a ash, for in the seven years' war, while quite a youth, he drove a waggon with General Braddock's army, but having committed some gross irregularity, he was tried by a court-martial, and sentenced to receive 500 lashes, of which he had only got 499, as he had counted them himself, and afterwards convinced the drum-major of his mistake.

Major Gordon had remained behind at York, in order to provide for sick and wounded, of whom we had more than 1900 at the time of the surrender; the effectives of all kinds, British and foreign, in the lines at York Town only amounting to 3273, and in Gloucester to 744, including the provincials. Major Gordon's own quarters were fixed at Fredericktown, in Maryland, where the 30th regiment was kept, and soon after his arrival there he visited Winchester. In conjunction with him I made a representation on the subject of our men's rations, as the issue of flour was very irregular, although the men were well supplied with meat. Our joint remonstrances, however, had but little effect, and after staying for two or three days, and making me promise to visit him at Christmas, the major returned to Maryland. According to promise I went to Fredericktown at Christmas, but had not been many days there when orders were given for the Maryland division of British prisoners to march to Lancaster, a town of Pennsylvania, half a mile from

72 MEMOIR OF GENERAL GRAHAM.

Comstoga Creek, and ten miles to the north of the river Susquehannah, and for the Winchester division to move to Little York, a town of the same State ten miles to the south of the same river, and both on the great road leading to Philadelphia.

Nothing very material happened on the march. The weather was intensely cold, and the frost keen. At a small river in Maryland, on the banks of which the division halted in the afternoon of one day, they crossed over on the ice next morning. The officers were badly off for money, and there were not wanting Jews in that part of the world hovering about us, offering money at a most extravagant discount for bills on England, but Major Gordon set his face against this as far as he could, assuring us that a paymaster would soon arrive amongst us. Through the activity of Captain Barclay, paymaster of the 76th, that regiment had been fortunate enough to procure some pairs of shoes for the soldiers, and I was much surprised at an application for a pair from an Irish soldier of the 43d Light Infantry, who had lived with the colonel of militia, in whose house we lodged at Winchester, but to whom none of us ever spoke, as he had quitted his company without giving the requisite notice. I said I was much surprised at his impudence, when he knew our sentiments regarding his conduct; his answer was—"Your honour, ask the Guardsmen, ask your own soldiers, if ever they have been in want of

PRISONERS' CAMP. 73

tobacco since I entered the colonel's store, and your honour knows we have had no money to buy it ; no, no, Patt Sullivan is no deserter, but I had my *raisins* for not telling my officers; and there was no great harm in taking a few more hogsheads of tobacco and giving it to my starving comrades"

At Lancaster the soldiers were kept in a tolerable barrack, surrounded by a high stockade, and strictly guarded. At York they were kept in huts newly constructed, also surrounded by a high stockade, and were also strictly guarded. At a little distance from, but in sight of, our men's huts, upon a rising ground were situated a number of huts occupied by soldiers of General Burgoyne's army, also prisoners of war, but without stockade or guard. Our men named their own camp "Security," and the other camp "Indulgence." Major Gordon having been directed to take charge of the prisoners at Camp Indulgence, and having received but indifferent accounts respecting them—most of them having married in the country—generally selected bad weather to visit them, when very few appeared. About this time *Herman Ryland* arrived from New York to reside with us as paymaster-general, some necessaries for the men were also received, but as some of our fellow-prisoners, who had been long in the country, had enlisted with the enemy and appeared as guards upon their countrymen, wearing the necessaries they had re-

E

74   MEMOIR OF GENERAL GRAHAM.

ceived, it required great circumspection in the distribution of them. The major therefore took every precaution to save the public money, and allowances only were given to such men as resided in the huts. I remained some time at Lancaster with Major Gordon. In March 1782, a Lieutenant Cunningham of the 80th died there. One of his friends applied to Mr Ottley, commissary of prisoners, for permission to bury him in the churchyard in his ground; at first it was refused, but the commissary afterwards consented, and even implored. "No," said Major Gordon; "you see that spot near the barracks where so many British soldiers have been buried, that is the place where I myself should wish to lie were I to die, and there will we deposit the remains of this British officer; for you know that officers and soldiers should not be separated, and at the last day the soldiers would be greatly surprised if they saw no officer." He was accordingly buried there.

CHAPTER THE SEVENTH.

)rrespondence relative to the selection of an Officer to be Executed, as a measure of retaliation—Lots drawn.

*/*HILST hostilities were carried on in America, there as a board at New York styled the Board of Loyalists, ho managed all matters relating to that unfortunate ass. The warfare carried on betwixt these people and ie American republicans has been already alluded to being almost distinct from that of the two armies. was also characterised by the exercise of cruelties of any kinds on both sides. The following corresponnce took place at this time, arising out of an occurnce in this irregular warfare :—

[o His Excellency Sir Henry Clinton, Commander-in-Chief, etc., etc.

"Sir—The enclosed representation of the inhabitants Monmouth, with testimonials to the fact (which can corroborated by other unquestionable evidence), will ring before your excellency the most wanton, cruel, id unprecedented murder that ever disgraced the arms

76   MEMOIR OF GENERAL GRAHAM

of a civilized people. I shall not, because I think it altogether unnecessary, trouble your excellency with any animadversions on this transaction. Candour obliges me to be explicit, to save the innocent I demand the guilty. Captain Lippencot, or the officer who commanded at the execution of Captain Huddy, must be given up, or if that officer was of inferior rank to him, so many of the perpetrators as will, according to the tariff of exchange, be an equivalent. To do this will mark the justice of your excellency's character; in failure of it, I shall hold myself justified in the eyes of God and man for the measures to which I shall resort. I beg your excellency to be persuaded that it cannot be more disagreeable to you to be addressed in this language than it is for me to offer it, but the subject requires frankness and decision. I have to request your speedy determination, as my resolution is suspended but for your answer

(Signed)   "G. WASHINGTON.

" Head-Quarters, 21st April 1782."

(Reply)

" To His Excellency General Washington.

" Sir—Your letter of the 21st instant, with the enclosed testimonials of Captain Huddy's execution, was delivered to me yesterday ; though I am extremely concerned for the cause, I cannot conceal my surprise and

SIR H. CLINTON TO GENERAL WASHINGTON. 77

displeasure at the very improper language you have made use of, which you could not but be sensible was totally unnecessary. The mildness of the British Government does not admit of acts of cruelty and persecuting violence, and as they are notoriously contrary to the tenor of my own conduct and disposition, having yet never stained my hands with innocent blood, I must claim the justice of having it believed that if any such have been committed by any person under my command, they could not have been warranted by my authority, nor can they ever have the sanction of my approbation. My personal feelings, therefore, need no incitement to urge me to take every proper notice of the barbarous outrage against humanity which you have described to me the moment it came to my knowledge; and accordingly, when I heard of Captain Huddy's death, which was only four days before I received your letter, I instantly ordered a strict inquiry to be made into all its circumstances, and shall bring the perpetrators of it to an immediate trial. To sacrifice innocence under the notion of preventing guilt in place of suppressing, would be adopting barbarity and raising it to the greatest height, whereas, if the violators of the laws of war were punished by the generals under whose power they act, the horrors which these laws were formed to prevent would be avoided, and every degree of humanity war is capable of maintained. Could violations of

78   MEMOIR OF GENERAL GRAHAM.

humanity be justified by example, many from the parts
where your power prevails, that exceed and probably
gave rise to this in question, could be produced. In
hopes that the mode I mean to pursue will be adopted
by you, and prevent all future enormities, I have the
honour to be, sir, your excellency's etc., etc., etc.,

(Signed)   "HENRY CLINTON.
"New York, 22d April 1782."

His excellency Sir Henry Clinton having embarked
on his return to England, Lieutenant-General Robertson,
on whom the temporary command devolved, addressed
General Washington on this subject, and received the
following reply :—

"HEAD QUARTERS, 5th May 1782
"Sir—I had the honour to receive your letter of the
1st instant. Your excellency is acquainted with the
determination expressed in my letter to Sir Henry
Clinton, of the 21st April. I have now to inform you,
that so far from receding from that resolution, orders are
given to designate a British officer for retaliation ; the
time and place are fixed, but I still hope the result of
your court-martial will prevent the dreadful alternative.

(Signed)   "G. WASHINGTON.
"To his Excellency General Robertson."

His Excellency Sir Guy Carleton having arrived at

New York, as successor to Sir Henry Clinton, wrote to General Washington :—

> "NEW YORK, *7th May* 1782.

"Sir—I am much concerned to find that private and unauthorized persons have on both sides given way to their passions, which ought to have received the strongest and most effectual control, and which has begot acts of retaliation, which, without proper preventions, may have an extent equally calamitous and dishonourable to both parties, though, as it should seem, more extensively pernicious to the natives and settlers of this country. How much soever we differ in other respects, upon this one point we must perfectly concur, being alike interested to preserve the name of Englishmen from reproach, and individuals from experiencing such unnecessary evils as can have no effect on general decisions. Every proper measure that may tend to prevent these criminal excesses on individuals I shall ever be ready to embrace ; and as an advance on my part, I have, as the first act of my command, enlarged Mr. Livingston, and have written to his father in New Jersey, desiring his concurrence in such measures as even under the conditions of war, the common interests of humanity require (Signed) GUY CARLETON.

"To his Excellency General Washington."

80   MEMOIR OF GENERAL GRAHAM.

(Reply.)

" HEAD QUARTERS, *9th May* 1782.

" Sir—I had the honour this evening to receive your excellency's letters of the 7th instant, with the several papers inclosed. Ever since the commencement of this unnatural war my conduct has borne invariable testimony against these inhuman excesses, that in too many instances have marked its various progress. With respect to a late transaction I have already expressed my fixed resolution—a resolution formed on the most mature deliberation, and from which I shall not recede.

(Signed)   " G. WASHINGTON.

' To his Excellency Sir Guy Carleton '

Although the above letters were published in the Philadelphian newspapers, yet we had not an opportunity of seeing them at that time; but in all the papers we observed many inflammatory paragraphs calling upon General Washington and Congress to retaliate for cruelties exercised upon the Americans. I remained at Lancaster till about the middle of May with Major Gordon, and then returned to Little York, where the 76th lay, and had been there only a few days when I was surprised by a visit from the major. He appeared to be labouring under some affliction, being greatly depressed in spirits. He begged of me not to ask him the cause, as he had pledged his honour not to divulge what

CAPTAINS ASSEMBLE AT LANCASTER.

had been communicated to him, but said that he had
brought an order from the commanding officer at Lancaster, directing the officer in command at Little York
to order all the British captains on parole there to repair
to Lancaster next day. The major also requested that
I would advise them each to take a servant, with spare
necessaries, and that he expected to see them at his
quarters next day soon after their arrival Accordingly,
having received the order from Colonel Gibson, I communicated the major's wishes to the captains, and on
Sunday, 25th May, five lieutenants of the Foot Guards,
one captain 23d Regiment, and two of the 76th Regiment, set off for Lancaster, crossing the Susquehannah,
and arrived there about three in the afternoon. We repaired to the major's quarters, where we were soon
joined by one captain 17th, one captain 33d, two of the
80th Regiments, and one of the Queen's Rangers, in all
thirteen The major addressed us in a most feeling
manner, acquainting us that orders had arrived to send
on one of us as a subject of retaliation for the murder of
a Captain Huddy, said to have been put to death by the
refugees. He assured us that no exertion should be
wanting on his part to save the life of the unfortunate
person, be he who he may, and read us letters which he
had sketched out, expressed in the strongest terms to
General Washington, to the President of Congress, to
Count Rochambeau, and to the Chevalier de Lucerne,

82 MEMOIR OF GENERAL GRAHAM.

French consul at Philadelphia and also one to Sir Guy Carleton at New York, acquainting him of the transaction. "Moreover," said he, "Gentlemen, I beg leave to tell you, that I am determined to accompany the gentleman, whoever he may be, to the place of his destination, having obtained the general's promise to be allowed to do so. We parted, not a little consoled by the thought of being accompanied by this excellent man ; and having been summoned to assemble next morning at nine o'clock at the Black Bear, on passing through the yard of that inn to the room we were directed to, we there saw a Dragoon officer and twenty dragoons, already mounted. In the room we met Brigadier-General Moses Hazan, the officer in command, Captain White, his aid-de-camp, and Mr. Witz, commissary of prisoners. The thirteen captains were—

Lieuts. Eld,			Killed at Dunkirk.
„ Perryn,		Foot Guards	Died a brig.-gen. in West Indies
„ Asgill,			Died a lieut.-gen. and a baronet.
„ Ludlow,			Earl Ludlow, and a general officer.
„ Greville,			Quitted the army.

Captains Lawford Mills, 17th Reg., served afterwards in militia.
    „   Saumarez, 23d Reg., now Sir Thomas, and lieut.-general
    „   Ingram, 33d Reg., died in the service.
    „   Graham, 76th Reg., a lieutenant-general.
    „   Barclay, 76th Reg., served in 54th Reg., since dead.
    „   Arbuthnot, 80th Reg., died in the service in W. Indies.
    „   Hathorn, 80th Reg., died on half-pay
    „   Whitelocke (Queen's Rangers) settled in Nova Scotia,
and accompanied by Major Gordon. After the usual

GENERAL WASHINGTON'S ORDERS 83

salutations, the Brigadier-General, with much feeling, proceeded to read us the following letters, the Dragoon officer entering at the same time :—*

* In 1782, after the capitulation of Lord Cornwallis, many loyalists urged Sir H Clinton to threaten vengeance for injuries inflicted on those who had joined the royal standard but he declined issuing a proclamation, and was deterred by the advice of the principal refugees from establishing the civil government, which would have permitted the trial of captive continentals as rebels. While he was engaged in projects of defence, and while commissioners appointed by him and General Washington were negociating for an exchange of prisoners, one Joshua Huddy, a captain in the service of Congress, was taken by a party of loyalists, and after being conveyed to several prisons, and confined some days, delivered with two others to a Captain Lippencott, for the ostensible purpose of being exchanged , but Huddy was hung on a tree, with a label on his breast, denoting that his fate was a retaliation for that of one White, an associator. Sir Henry Clinton, highly resenting this disgraceful outrage on humanity, and insult on himself as commander, arrested Lippencott, and with the concurrence of a council of war, ordered him to be tried for murder. But the Americans were not appeased by this act of justice. The inhabitants of Monmouth County urgently entreated General Washington, as the person in whom was lodged the sole power of avenging their wrongs, to bring a British officer of the same rank as Huddy to a similar end

Acting with great promptitude on this requisition, the American commander wrote to the British general demanding that the murderers of Huddy should be given up to him

Clinton expressed surprise and displeasure at the imperious language in which this communication was couched. The board of loyalists stated circumstances relating to the execution of Huddy, in which, though Lippencott had exceeded his authority and their orders, he had merely adopted the precedent shewn by the Americans in the case of White. Washington's letter was

MEMOIR OF GENERAL GRAHAM

84

" To Brigadier-General Moses Hazan, Commander at
" Lancaster.

" HEAD QUARTERS, 5*th* *May* 1782.

" Sir—The enemy persisting in that barbarous line
of conduct they have pursued during the war, have
lately most inhumanly executed Captain Joshua Huddy
of the Jersey State troops, taken prisoner by them at a
post on Tom's River , and, in consequence, I have written to the British commander-in-chief, that unless the
perpetrators of this horrid deed were delivered up, I
should be under the necessity of retaliating, as the only
means left to put a stop to such inhuman proceedings.
You will therefore immediately, on receipt of this, designate by lot for the above purpose, a British captain
who is an unconditional prisoner, if such a one is in our
possession ; if not, a lieutenant under the same circumstances from amongst the prisoners at either of the posts

accompanied with depositions showing that Huddy was not concerned in the murder of White , but, on the other hand, Huddy
confessed to his own activity in murdering associated loyalists.
Lippencott was tried by court-martial ; he pleaded that he
was not subject to martial law, and by common laws could not
be tried in New York for an offence committed in another state,
New Jersey. These objections were overruled by the Chief-
Justice and Attorney-General, but as it appeared that Lippencott
acted under the orders of a board he was bound to obey, he was
acquitted. Then the barbarous edict of retaliation was ordered
to be enforced —" *Phillimore*" *on International Law*

GENERAL WASHINGTON'S ORDERS. 85

in Pennsylvania or Maryland As soon as you have fixed upon the person, you will send him under a safe guard to Philadelphia, where the Minister of War will order a proper guard to receive and conduct him to his place of destination For your information respecting the officers who are prisoners in our possession I have ordered the commissary of prisoners to furnish you with a list of them It will be forwarded with this I need not mention that every possible tenderness that is consistent with the security of him, should be shewn to the person whose unfortunate lot it is to suffer

(Signed)   " G WASHINGTON"

" To Brigadier-General Moses Hazan, Commander at
" Lancaster

" HEAD QUARTERS, 13th May 1782

" Sir—It was my wish, for the purpose of retaliation, to have taken an officer who was an unconditional prisoner of war, but being informed by the Secretary at War that none of that description is in our power, I am under the disagreeable necessity to direct that you immediately proceed to select in the manner before prescribed, from amongst all the British captains who are prisoners either by capitulation or convention, who is to be sent on as soon as possible under the regulations and restrictions contained in my former letter to you

(Signed)   " G. WASHINGTON"

86   MEMOIR OF GENERAL GRAHAM

Having finished, he again addressed us, saying that it was much his wish that we should settle amongst ourselves who the unfortunate was to be; but we unanimously declined, protesting against this breach of a solemn treaty, by which we had come into their power. Major Gordon also added, that these gentlemen were but a small portion of the captains of the army which had surrendered at York Town, and that if such a deed was to be done, the whole ought to be called upon, being certain that no one officer, let him be where he might at the time, would decline to take his chance. The brigadier replied that his instructions limited him to those only present. The major then said that there was another captain, he believed, now in Virginia, not yet arrived, belonging to the 43d Regiment, and wished to have the decision put off. But the brigadier stated that his instructions particularly mentioned such as were in Maryland and Pennsylvania, and as he was directed to forward the unfortunate person directly, being himself a servant, he was obliged to comply. The brigadier then turning to his aid-de-camp, and to the commissary, the two latter left the room, and in a short time returned, each with a hat in his hand, and accompanied by a drum-boy. In one hat were the names of the thirteen captains, written on separate slips of paper; in the other were thirteen slips of paper of the same size, upon one of which was marked *unfortunate*. A drum-boy

LOTS DRAWN. 87

hrew a name, while the other drew the ship, until the
eleventh, when the ship bearing the word came up, after
hat of Captain Asgill. The brigadier immediately
addressed the dragoon officer, saying—"This gentleman,
ir, is your prisoner ;" but Major Gordon prevailed upon
him to delay the departure till next day, and also obtained leave to despatch an officer to New York without
delay.

The meeting then broke up, and there being a vast
crowd of persons assembled, their observation was—
'What odd people these Britishers are ! they went in
ill cheerful and chatting before they knew which of
them was to suffer for our good friend Captain Huddy ;
but now when they know, they all come out in tears,
except the young man himself who has been selected"
The Hon. Captain Ludlow having procured a swift
horse, was furnished with Major Gordon's letter to Sir
Guy Carleton at New York ; also with proper passports
from General Hazan, and lost not a moment in setting
off. The brigadier likewise promised to send off the
major's letter to General Washington, which was accord-
ngly written out nearly in these words —

'To his Excellency General Washington, Commander-in-
"Chief, etc , etc , etc

"Sir—As field officer of the British prisoners of war
at this place, I have the honour to inform your excel-

88   MEMOIR OF GENERAL GRAHAM

lency that Captain Charles Asgill of his Britannic Majesty's Regiment of Foot Guards, a prisoner of war, on his parole of honour, in terms of the capitulation at York Town, whereof your excellency is a principal, with the Counts Rochambeau and De Grasse on one part, and the Earl Cornwallis and Commodore Symonds on the other, has been selected and put in close confinement by your excellency's orders, as an object for retaliation for a murder said to have been committed in New Jersey by a banditti, styling themselves refugees, in direct violation of that solemn treaty, the fourteenth article of which expressly stipulates that no article shall be infringed on pretence of reprisals ; and if there are any doubtful expressions in it, they are to be interpreted according to the usual sense and meaning of the words. I do therefore demand, in the name of his most sacred Majesty George the Third, King of Great Britain and Ireland, my royal master, that you cause the said Captain Asgill to be set at liberty, and admitted to his parole, in terms of the capitulation, as you shall be hereafter responsible.   (Signed)   JAMES GORDON."

A letter was written to the minister-at-war at Philadelphia, and to the Chevalier la Lucerne, French ambassador ; and a friend having informed the major that the Count Rochambeau was in Virginia, another was written to him, calling upon him to interfere ; and a messenger

MEANS TAKEN TO DELAY THE ESCORT. 89

was found who delivered the letter into his own hands
The major being also informed that the party of dragoons who formed the escort had regular stages on the
road, where forage was issued, and finding that the dis-
tances between each was considerable, a circumstance
which would enable them to reach Philadelphia in a
short time, and delay being most desirable on such an
occasion, to give time for the letters to reach their destination, prevailed upon the general to allow him to
choose his own stages, provided he furnished forage to
the dragoons Accordingly he lengthened out the journey several days ; but deeming this to be a service
of a public nature, he directed Mr. Ryland, paymaster-
general, to be prepared with £500 in money, to be carried with him next day for that and other purposes

E 2

90　　MEMOIR OF GENERAL GRAHAM.

CHAPTER THE EIGHTH.

Captain Asgill leaves Lancaster—Arrives at Philadelphia—
Exertions of Major Gordon—Further Correspondence—
Release of Captain Asgill.

ON Tuesday morning the 27th, the hawkers were selling
in the streets an account of the action of the 12th
April, wherein the Count de Grasse had been made
prisoner in the "Ville de Paris." I got a copy and
gave it to Major Gordon, who said that the news was
too good not to be made use of. About eleven o'clock
on Tuesday 27th, Captain Asgill and Major Gordon left
Lancaster, escorted by the officer and party of dragoons.
The brigadier also accompanied them for several miles,
and at parting, gave strict orders to the party to obey
such orders as Major Gordon should give them. They
arrived at Philadelphia (70 miles) in a few days, and
the major lost not a moment in finding the French
ambassador, urging him in strong terms to interfere,
now that the Count de Grasse was in our power, but
without effect. He also found out some members of
Congress, and applied to them ; in short, he tried every
possible means which he could think of or devise. On

going out he left Captain Asgill in a hotel, and gave strict orders to the sentinel over him (one of the dragoons) not to allow any person to enter the room in which he was confined. The major had just returned disconsolate and without hope, and entered an adjoining room to compose himself, when he heard the footsteps of some person as if approaching the prisoner's room. Rushing out, he encountered a solemn-looking man in black in the passage, and sharply demanding what he wanted, received for a reply, "I am the chaplain to the Congress of the United States, and have come to give a word of advice to the young man who is about to suffer for one of our good friends" "You have no right to come here, sir," said the major, "be you who you may;" and seeing him to the door, reproached the sentinel on duty, who said in his defence that he durst not deny admission to the chaplain of Congress. It is supposed that several persons in power at Philadelphia did interest themselves in favour of Captain Asgill, whether through the instigation of Major Gordon or not is uncertain, but an order was given for his being sent to Chatham, in New Jersey, and placed in charge of Colonel Elias Dayton, of the 2d New Jersey troops The following letter to the colonel, dated head-quarters, 4th June 1782, has been published :—

"Sir—I am just informed by the secretary at war

92 MEMOIR OF GENERAL GRAHAM.

that Captain Asgill, of the British Guards, who is destined to be the unhappy victim to atone for the death of Captain Huddy, has arrived at Philadelphia, and would set off for the Jersey line, the place assigned for his execution. He will probably arrive as soon as this will reach you, and will be attended by Captain Ludlow, his friend, who he wishes to be permitted to go into New York with an address to Sir Guy Carleton in his behalf You will therefore give permission to Captain Ludlow to go by the way of Dobb's Ferry into New York, with such representations as Captain Asgill may please to make to Sir Guy Carleton ; at the same time I would wish to intimate to the gentleman, that though I am deeply afflicted by the unhappy fate to which Captain Asgill is subjected, yet that it will be to no purpose to make any representation to Sir Guy Carleton which may serve to bring on a discussion of the present point of retaliation, that on the stage to which the matter has been suffered to run, all argumentation on the subject is precluded on my part My resolutions have been founded on so mature deliberation, that they must remain unalterably fixed. You may also inform the gentleman, that while my duty calls upon me to make this decisive determination, humanity dictates a tear for the unfortunate offering, and inclines me to say that I devoutly wish his life may be spared This happy event may be attained, but it must be effected by the

GENERAL WASHINGTON'S ORDERS 93

British commander-in-chief, he knows the alternative which will accomplish it, and he knows that this alternative only can avert the dire extremity from the innocent, and that in this way alone the 'manes' of the murdered Captain Huddy will be best appeased. In the meantime, while this is doing, I must beg that you will be pleased to treat Captain Asgill with every tender attention and politeness consistent with his present situation, which his rank, fortune, and connections, together with his present state, demand.

(Signed) "G. WASHINGTON"

The following is another letter to Colonel Dayton, dated

"HEAD QUARTERS, 11*th June* 1782.

" Sir—You will inform me as early as possible what is the present situation of Captain Asgill, the prisoner destined for retaliation, and what prospect he has of relief from his application to Sir Guy Carleton, which I am informed he has made through his friend Captain Ludlow. I have heard nothing yet from New York in consequence of his application. His fate will be suspended until I can hear of the decision of Sir Guy, but I am impatient lest this should be unwarrantably delayed. The enemy ought to have learnt before this that my resolution cannot be trifled with.

(Signed) "G. WASHINGTON."

94 MEMOIR OF GENERAL GRAHAM.

The following are other letters from General Washington to Colonel Dayton, but without dates.

" Sir—I was informed that Captain Asgill is at Chatham without a guard, and under no restraint. This, if true, is certainly wrong, 1 wish to have the young gentleman treated with all possible tenderness consistent with his present situation, but until his fate is determined, he must be considered as a close prisoner and be kept in the greatest security. I request, therefore, that he may be sent immediately to the Jersey Line, where he is to be kept close prisoner in perfect security till further orders.

(Signed) " G. WASHINGTON."

" Sir—I have received your two letters of the 17th and 18th inst. The only object I had in view in ordering Captain Asgill to be confined to the huts, was the perfect security of the prisoner ; this must be attended to, but I am very willing, indeed wish, that every indulgence be granted him that is not inconsistent with that. When I ordered on an officer for retaliation, I mentioned my willingness that he should make every application to the British commander-in-chief, in whose power alone it lay to avert the destiny ; but I, at the same time, desired it to be understood that I should receive no application, nor answer any letter upon the

ESCAPE OF ASGILL PLANNED.

subject which did not inform that satisfaction was made
'or the death of Captain Huddy. I imagine that you
were not informed of this circumstance, or you would
have prevented Major Gordon's application on the sub-
ect.　　　　(Signed)　　" G. WASHINGTON."

I never saw any other letter of Major Gordon's to
General Washington, except the one sent off from Lancaster; but I know that his exertions were unceasing
at this period, and that he even applied to the widow
and family of Captain Huddy, who resided not far off,
and induced them to intercede for Captain Asgill
Moreover, I know that through the friendship of
females at the place, he had laid a plan for the escape
of the captain, in case an order had been given for his
execution, and that his escape would have been effected,
and that the major intended to have avowed his partici-
pation and concern in the affair; I know also that a
confidential servant of Captain Asgill's went into New
York, and returned more than once during their stay at
Chatham. On the 5th August, General Washington
wrote to the honourable Captain Ludlow, at New York,
as follows :—

" Sir—Persuaded that your desire to visit Captain
Asgill at Chatham is founded on motives of friendship
and humanity only, I enclose you a passport for the

96   MEMOIR OF GENERAL GRAHAM.

gratification of it. The enclosed letters for that gentleman came to me from New York in the condition you will receive them; you will have an opportunity of presenting them with yourself. Your own letter came under cover to me, *via Ostend.*

(Signed)   " G. WASHINGTON."

(Copy of the Passport.)

"Captain Ludlow, of the British Guards, has my permission (with his servant) to pass the American posts at Dobb's Ferry, and proceed to Chatham. He has liberty also to return to New York the same way.

(Signed)   " G. WASHINGTON."

On the 25th August, General Washington in a postscript of a letter to Colonel Dayton, directed that Captain Asgill be left on his parole at Morristown till further orders. The annexed letters are from General Washington to Captain Asgill.—

" HEAD QUARTERS, *7th October* 1782.

" Sir—I have to acknowledge your favour of the 27th September. The circumstances which produced in the first instance your unfortunate situation, having in some measure changed their ground, the whole matter has been laid before Congress for their directions, and I am now waiting their decision. I can assure you, I shall be most happy, should circumstances

GENERAL WASHINGTON'S LETTERS. 97

1able me to announce to you your liberation from your
isagreeable confinement.

(Signed)   " G. WASHINGTON."

" HEAD QUARTERS, 13th November 1782.

" SIR—It affords me singular pleasure to have it in
y power to transmit to you the enclosed copy of an
t of Congress of the 7th instant, by which you are re-
ased from the disagreeable circumstances in which you
ave been so long. Supposing that you would wish to
) to New York as soon as possible, I also enclose a
assport for that purpose. Your letter of the 18th Octo-
r came regularly to my hands I beg of you to
lieve, that my not answering it sooner did not proceed
om inattention to you, or a want of feeling for your
tuation, but I daily expected a determination of your
se, and I thought it better to await that, than to feed
u with hopes that might in the end prove fruitless.
ou will attribute my detention of the enclosed letters,
hich have been in my possession a fortnight, to the
me cause. I cannot take leave of you, sir, without
suring you, that in whatever light my agency in this
pleasant affair may be viewed, I was never influenced,
rough the whole of it, by sanguinary motives, but by
hat I conceived to be a sense of my duty, which loudly
lled upon me to take measures, however disagreeable,
prevent a repetition of these enormities which have

F

98 MEMOIR OF GENERAL GRAHAM.

been the subject of discussion, and that this important end, so likely to be answered without the blood of an innocent person, is not a greater relief to you than it is to, sir, your humble servant,

(Signed)   " G. WASHINGTON."

(Copy of the Act of Congress enclosed.)

" By the United States, in Congress assembled, 5th
" November 1782.

"In the report of the committee to whom was referred a letter of the 19th August, from the commander-in-chief, a report of the committee thereon, and motion of Mr. Williamson and Mr. Rutledge, relative thereto, and another letter of the commander-in-chief of 25th October, with a copy of a letter from the Count Vergennes, dated July 29th last, interceding for Captain Asgill—Resolved, that the commander-in-chief be directed, and he is hereby directed, to set Captain Asgill at liberty.

(Signed)   " C. THOMSON, Secretary."

Copy of the letter from Count de Vergennes, alluded to
in the Act of Congress.

" VERSAILLES, 29th July 1782.

" Sir—It is not in the quality of a king, the friend and ally of the United States, though with the knowledge and consent of his Majesty, that I now have the honour to write to your excellency. It is as a man of sensibility, and a tender father, who feels all the force of

COUNT DE VERGENNES.

99

rental love, that I take the liberty to address your cellency my earnest solicitations for a mother and nily in tears. Her situation seems the more worthy notice on our part, as it is to the humanity of a nation war with her own, that she has recourse for what she ght to receive from the impartial justice of her own neral. I have the honour to enclose your excellency copy of a letter which Mrs. Asgill has just written me. I am not known to her, nor was I acquainted th her son, now the unhappy victim destined by lot to piate the odious crime that a formal denial of justice liged you to revenge. Your excellency will not read is letter without being extremely affected. It had at effect upon the King and the Queen, to whom I mmunicated it. The goodness of their Majesties' arts induces them to desire that the inquietude of an fortunate mother may be calmed, and her tenderness issured. I feel, sir, that there are cases where humity itself requires the most extreme rigour; perhaps e one now in question may be of the number,* but

* "The clearest evidence of the absolute necessity of self-pre-vation is required to palliate any infraction of the rights of a soner of war. A prisoner who has yielded under *conditions*, inot be injured as long as he fulfils his part of the conditions' *Phillimore on International Law*

In the same work, the case of Henry the Fifth, after the ttle of Agincourt, and of Anson and the Acapulco, are given as tances in which an infraction of the rights of prisoners were tifiable.

100   MEMOIR OF GENERAL GRAHAM.

allowing reprisals to be just, it is not the less horrid to those who are the victims; and the character of your excellency is too well known for me not to be persuaded that you desire nothing more than to be able to avoid the disagreeable necessity. There is one consideration, sir, which, though it is not 'decisive, may have an influence on your resolution. Captain Asgill is, doubtless, your prisoner, but he is amongst those whom the arms of the King contributed to put in your hands at Yorktown. Although this circumstance does not operate as a safeguard, it however justifies the interest I permit myself to take in this affair. If it is in your power, sir, to consider and have regard to it, you will do what is very agreeable to their Majesties; the danger of young Asgill, the tears, the despair of his mother, affect them sensibly; and they will see with much pleasure the hope of consolation shine out for these unfortunate people. In seeking to deliver Mr. Asgill from the fate which threatens him, I am far from engaging you to seek another victim. The pardon, to be perfectly satisfactory, must be entire. I do not imagine it can be productive of very bad consequences—if the English general has not been able to punish the horrible crime you complain of in so exemplary a manner as he should, there is reason to think he will take the most efficacious measures to prevent the like in future. I sincerely wish, sir, that my intercession may meet success. The senti-

LADY ASGILL. 101

ent which dictates it, and which you have not ceased
manifest on every occasion, assures me that you will
ot be indifferent to the prayers, to the tears of a family
hich has recourse to your clemency through me. It is
ndering homage to your virtues to implore it I have
e honour to be, sir, with the most perfect consider-
ion, (Signed) " De Vergennes.'
To his Excellency General Washington."

opy of Lady Asgill's letter to the Count de Vergennes.

" London, 18*th July* 1782.

" Sir—If the politeness of the French Court will per-
it the application of a stranger, there can be no doubt
at one in which the tender feelings of an individual
n be interested will meet with a favourable reception
om a nobleman whose character does honour not only
his own country but to human nature. The subject,
r, in which I presume to implore your assistance is too
eart-piercing for me to dwell upon, and common fame
is most probably informed you of it, it renders there-
re the painful task unnecessary. My son, sir, an only
n, as dear as he is brave, amiable as he is deserving
be so, only nineteen, a prisoner by the capitulation
York town, is now confined in America, an object of
taliation Shall an innocent suffer for the guilty?
epresent to yourself, sir, the situation of a family

102   MEMOIR OF GENERAL GRAHAM.

under these circumstances, surrounded as I am by objects of distress, distracted with fear and grief, no words can express my feelings or paint the scene. My husband given over by his physicians a few hours before the news arrived, and not in a state to be informed of the misfortune ; my daughter seized with fever and delirium, raving about her brother, and without one interval of reason save to hear alleviating circumstances. Let your own feelings, sir, suggest to plead for my inexpressible misery. A word from you, like a voice from heaven, will save me from distraction and wretchedness ; I am well informed that General Washington reveres your character, say but to him you wish my son to be released, and he will restore him to his distracted family and render him to happiness. My son's virtue and bravery will justify the deed. His honour, sir, carried him to America. He was born to affluence, independence, and the happiest prospects. Let me again supplicate your goodness, let me respectfully implore your high influence in behalf of innocence, in the cause of justice, of humanity, that you would dispatch a letter to General Washington from France, and favour me with a copy of it to be sent from hence. I am sensible of the liberty I take in making this request, but I am sensible, whether you comply with it or not, you will pity the distress which suggests it ; humanity will drop a tear on the fault and efface it. I will pray that

CAPTAIN ASGILL. 103

heaven may grant you may never want the comfort it is in your power to bestow on, etc., etc., etc.

(Signed) " T. ASGILL "

Captain Asgill, after his liberation, lost no time in going to New York, where he embarked for England by the first opportunity.

104 MEMOIR OF GENERAL GRAHAM.

CHAPTER THE NINTH.

Death of Colonel Gordon.

AFTER the release of Asgill, Major Gordon returned to Lancaster quite an altered person, having lost much of that liveliness of disposition which had always seemed so natural to him. The whole of the British prisoners being assembled at Lancaster, we remained there till June 1783, when orders were given for our march to New York, in consequence of peace. We moved off in divisions, passing through Philadelphia, where a British general officer, Sir Alured Clarke, had been permitted to reside during the period. Being senior captain, I moved with the first division, Major Gordon remained till the last, in which the men from Camp Indulgence were included. The soldiers received marching money daily, and the clothing not delivered out was carried in waggons. Numerous applications were made to us on the road to give away part of our stores. On our arrival at Staten Island we found transports in readiness, and all the men whose regiments were in Europe, and who embarked,

COLONEL GORDON.

105

were settled with for pay and clothing, and sailed for England. The others were quartered in New York and its dependencies. Major Gordon and the 80th were sent to Kingsbridge, his quarters were in Morris's house. The 76th remained at Staten Island. Shortly after our arrival, Major Gordon got the brevet of lieutenant-colonel, and was named to be president of a court-martial at New York, of which I was also a member. It continued several weeks, and a great number of cases came before it, many of them relating to inhabitants of the Jerseys, who had petitioned the commander-in-chief that their claims or disputes might be submitted to the decision of the court of which Lieutenant-Colonel Gordon was president, so much was he esteemed during his stay in that neighbourhood with Captain Asgill, even by the enemy. The court on that account protracted its sittings for a length of time. On Saturdays, I always accompanied Colonel Gordon to Morris's house, where we remained till Monday morning. Language fails me to describe the beautiful scenery spread out before us on these occasions. The house itself occupies an elevated situation betwixt the North or Hudson's river, and the East or Sound, commanding an extensive view of that noble stream, with its high and rocky bank on the Jersey shore, clothed with wood from the water's edge to the summit. There may be seen the dark pine rearing its lofty head in the midst of deciduous trees of

106   MEMOIR OF GENERAL GRAHAM.

every description, not the least conspicuous of which is
that splendid tree, the scarlet oak. The whole contribut-
ing to form a picture of surpassing beauty at this season
of the year, particularly at sunrise and sunset. We continued to spend our time in this manner for several weeks,
until, the court-martial being dissolved, I returned to my
regiment in Staten Island. When I left Colonel Gordon
he was getting rather corpulent, but apparently enjoyed
good health ; I had not, however, returned to my quarters many days when I received an express from Sir
William Nicholson, Colonel Gordon's adjutant, desiring
my immediate attendance at Morris's house, as the
colonel wished to see me instantly, and informing me
that the colonel was in a most dangerous state. I lost
not a moment ; and on my arrival was dreadfully
shocked to find him in a dying state. He said, " I rejoice to see you before I die, there is a letter I got from
England since we parted ; it is from a lady, and you
know I have never been deficient in my respect to the
fair sex. When you go home apologise to her for my
not replying ; you see the state I am reduced to
Another thing, while I have got recollection left, let me
entreat, should chance at any time ever entitle you to
take such a liberty, that you will tell my noble prince,
the Prince of Wales, what a consolation at this moment
is the thought, that my conduct in Asgill's affair has
been approved of by so high-minded, so truly honour-

COLONEL GORDON 107

able and exalted a personage I am told that he has been pleased to speak in high terms of what I thought my duty at the time."

The colonel did not survive many hours after this. His body was carried to New York, and there buried with military honours

The eloquent remarks by General Burgoyne, on the death of General Frazer, may appropriately be transferred to the memory of my lamented friend Lieutenant-Colonel Gordon :—

"To the canvas, and to the faithful page of a more important historian, gallant friend, I consign thy memory. There may thy talents, thy manly virtues, their progress, and their period, find due distinction, and long may they survive—long after the frail record of my pen shall be forgotten."—*General Burgoyne on the death of General Frazer.*

Copy of Lady Asgill's letter to Lieutenant-Colonel Gordon, delivered to me by him on his deathbed.

"Sir—If distress like mine had left any expression but for grief, I should long since have addressed myself to you, for whom my sense of gratitude makes all acknowledgment poor indeed , nor is this the first attempt ; but you were too near the dear object of my anguish to enter into the heart-piercing subject I earnestly prayed to heaven that he might not add to his

108 MEMOIR OF GENERAL GRAHAM.

sufferings the knowledge of ours. He had too much to feel on his own account, and I could not have concealed the direful effect of his misfortune on his family, to whom he is as dear as he is worthy to be so. Unfit as I am at this time, by joy, almost as unsupportable as the agony before, yet, sir, accept this weak effort, from a heart deeply affected by your humanity and exalted conduct, as heaven knows it has been torn by affliction. Believe, sir, it will only cease to throb in the last moment of life with the most grateful and affectionate sentiment to you. But a fortnight since I was sinking under a wretchedness I could no longer struggle with. Hope, resignation, had almost forsaken me. I began to experience the greatest of all misfortunes, that of being no longer able to bear them. Judge, sir, the transition, the day after the blessed change takes place—my son is released, recovered, returned, arrived at my gate, in my arms! I see him unsubdued in spirit, in health, unreproached by himself, approved of by his country, in the bosom of his family, and without anxiety but for the happiness of his friend, without regret but for having left him behind Your humane feelings that have dictated your conduct to him, injured and innocent as he was, surely must participate in every relief and joy his safety must occasion. Be that pleasure yours, sir, as every other reward that virtue like yours, and heaven can bestow. This prayer is offered up for you in the

LADY ASGILL. 109

heat of transport as it has been in the bitterness of my anguish ; my gratitude has been soothed by the energy it has been offered with ; it has ascended the throne of mercy, and is, I trust, accepted. Unfit as I am, for nothing but sensibility so awakened as mine could enable me to write, exhausted by too long anxiety, confined at this time to a bed of sickness and languor, yet I could not suffer another mail to go without this weak effort. Let it convey to you, sir, the most heartfelt esteem and gratitude of my husband and children You have the respect and esteem of all Europe, as an honour to your country and to human nature, and the most zealous friendship of, my very dear and worthy Major Gordon, your ever affectionate and obliged servant, (Signed) " T. ASGILL."

110 MEMOIR OF GENERAL GRAHAM.

CHAPTER THE TENTH.

Anecdotes—Campaign in Holland, 1793.

UPON the return of the 76th Regiment to England from America, in February 1784, the promotion of Captain Graham took place from the captain-lieutenancy of the regiment to a company, and very shortly afterwards the regiment was disbanded, and he was reduced to half-pay.

An old friend, still living, remembers to have heard him say that he was the first person who appeared in Edinburgh in the highland costume after the act prohibiting the use of that dress was repealed, at the instance of the Duke of Montrose. This must have been about this period, and after he was placed on half-pay, and considered himself a civilian, as the prohibitory law never applied to officers and soldiers on duty.

Another anecdote which has been preserved, but without a date, relates, in all probability, to this period. An officer of one of the regiments stationed in the Highlands was detached from his regiment to an outpost, in a part of the country where he received great attention

OLD HIGHLAND CUSTOMS

111

from the resident gentry in the neighbourhood, all of whom were in the habit of obtaining annually a supply of stores from France, such as brandy, wine, and other articles, the produce of that country. Their practice was to join in freighting a vessel, and an opportunity was taken to land the cargo at some convenient moment when the custom-house agents were engaged elsewhere. During the time that the officer in question was quartered at this highland outpost the annual vessel was signalled off the coast; but on this occasion the time had not been well chosen, and a requisition was made by the custom-house authorities upon the officer himself, as commandant of the troops, for a party of soldiers to protect them in *seizing* the cargo whenever it might be landed

The officer's duty left him no alternative but to furnish a party, in compliance with the requisition ; but, as might be expected, he felt not a little perplexed at finding himself obliged to be aiding and abetting in the confiscation of the property of those kind friends whose hospitality he had so long enjoyed. In this dilemma he hit upon a device, by which he was enabled to rescue his friends' property from the claws of the custom-house myrmidons, without compromising himself, in the execution of his duty, as an officer. He paraded the party of soldiers as required, and marched them off at the time appointed, but with his drummer leading the way, and making as much noise as a vigorous application of

112 MEMOIR OF GENERAL GRAHAM.

the drumsticks could produce. The exciseman remonstrated, but in vain. He was told that he should not have called for an officer's party; that an officer was entitled to the honour of being preceded by a drum; a double rat-tat-too followed, and the alarm thus created by the drum was such, that timely intimation was given to the master of the vessel to choose some other point for landing.

In April 1786, by paying the difference between full and half-pay, Captain Graham was appointed to the 19th Foot; and in 1787 joined the regiment in Jamaica. He remained in the West Indies until 1789, when he was sent home, and employed on the recruiting service until the return of the regiment to England in 1791. He then rejoined the corps on its arrival at Portsmouth.

Amongst the general's memoranda relating to his service with the 19th after the return of the regiment from the West Indies, he notes that the regiment was reviewed by his Majesty in Hyde Park in February 1792. The appearance of the troops of the line in London, is so far memorable, that it is a sight of rare occurrence even in these days, when troops must occasionally be transferred from one railway to another on the transit through London. When the Emperor of Russia was in this country some years ago, he expressed a particular wish to see some of the line regiments; and on that occasion, two regiments, the 47th and 59th, were brought to

WAR WITH FRANCE. 113

London expressly to appear before the Emperor ; and singular as it may appear at the present day, no regiment, except the Buffs, can march through the city without a special permission from the Lord Mayor. Even the Guards require to obtain his lordship's sanction.

The price of provisions at the review in Hyde Park in 1792 is not stated by General Graham ; but in the "Annual Register" for 1792, it appears that at a review before the King at Bagshot, a mutton chop and pint of bad wine were charged 18s., and a cup of coffee and slice of bread and butter, 5s.

At the opening of Parliament in 1792, the King congratulated the House and the country on the peaceable aspect of political affairs, and the prospect of reductions in the naval and military establishments of the country; but before the close of the year his Majesty was obliged to address his people in very different language ; and after directing the attention of Parliament to the alarming indications of an intention on the part of France to propagate revolutionary doctrines, subversive of the existing constitutions of states, his Majesty, in conclusion, intimated to the House the necessity of an augmentation of the forces of the country.

On the 1st February 1793, France declared war against England. The result of this declaration was the embarkation of the Duke of York, with 10,000 men, for Holland, where his force was augmented by a rein-

F 2

114   MEMOIR OF GENERAL GRAHAM.

forcement of 25,000 Hanoverian, Hessian, and Brunswick troops.

The first events of this campaign were most encouraging, and at one time 130,000 men might have been assembled to march upon Paris—a movement which would probably have brought the war to a satisfactory termination. History can only now point to the campaign as a monument of the fatal influence of cabinets in war. England, over-elated at the first successes, and more attentive to her maritime interests than to the general objects of the war, insisted on his Royal Highness laying siege to Dunkirk, the possession of which was much coveted. This unfortunate resolution sealed the fate of the campaign. A force, which in one mass was capable of achieving great things, was thus fractioned into parts, exposed to ruin in detail. The national indignation of the French was roused at the bare idea of the soil of France being touched by foreign hosts; and in the national enthusiasm thus created, the rival parties which had risen out of the revolution, overlooked their party animosities, and united in the most energetic measures to resist the invasion of their country.* The

* "The state of public feeling in the early part of 1794 exemplifies the erroneous conclusions to which men's minds are liable to be led, in judging of the means and resources of neighbouring nations. The enormous exertions which had been made by republican France were looked upon by many politicians as certain to exhaust the energies of the nation; whereas the mili-

ARMY IN HOLLAND 115

fearfully disorganized state of society at that time was also highly favourable to the morale of the French army, by introducing into its ranks great numbers of a superior class ; the profession of arms, strange to say, being one which offered more security than any other General Foy, in describing the mode of fighting of the republican armies, says—" Sometimes, in the midst of a shower of balls, an officer, or a soldier, or a representative of the people, would sing the hymn of victory , the general displayed his hat, with its tricoloured plume, on the point of his sword, as a rallying point · whilst the men advanced at the charge, their drums beating, and their voices rending the air with cries of ' Forward, forward ; success to the republic !' (*Vive la République*).

Captain Graham accompanied his regiment, the 19th, to Holland at this time, but before they arrived, the allied army under the Duke of York had raised the siege of Dunkirk, and fallen back upon Menin.

The appearance of the army at this time is thus depicted in Sir H Calvert's journal —" It is a very great amusement to me to inspect and examine the manners and dress of the different corps we are acting with—the

tary enthusiasm had at that time attained to such a pitch, that the nation was prepared to make any sacrifices in vindication of the principles they had adopted and introduced into their country."—*Court and Cabinet George Third ; Duke of Buckingham*

116 MEMOIR OF GENERAL GRAHAM.

drawings which Captain Cook brought home from the South Seas are nothing to some of our friend's. Their dress is fully as extraordinary, and their countenances, by continued exposure to the elements, have the true Indian dye ; but they are the bravest, hardiest soldiers I ever saw."

General Stewart, in his "Highlanders," says—

"The enemy on this occasion took advantage of the variety of uniforms in the British army, and frequently dressed parties in a similar manner for the purpose of deceiving our troops, an artifice which sometimes succeeded."

The German officers were described by General Graham as such inveterate smokers, that at guard-mounting it was part of the drummer's duty to keep the captain's pipe alive while the old and new guards went through the usual compliments ; the customary forms being finished, the drummer wiped the mouth-piece of the pipe on his sleeve, and returned the pipe to the captain.

The 19th, 37th, and three companies of the 42d joined the Duke about the middle of September.* From

---

* There is a letter from Watson, the commissary-general—dated Furnes, 8th September 1793—which seems to confirm the intended retreat, and says that he has provisions, etc , in the rear of the army —Lord Grenville to Marquis of Buckingham, 11th September 1793.

RELIEF OF NIEUPORT. 117

this time until the middle of October nothing of any importance appears to have taken place except an affair of outposts—the enemy availing themselves of a dense fog to attack the advanced post at Warwick—when twenty men were killed and wounded, and fifty taken prisoners. On the 11th October, the 19th, 27th, 42d, and 59th Regiments were ordered to march from Menin to Ostend for the purpose of embarking to join the army under Sir Charles Grey, destined for the West Indies.* On arriving at Ostend, and while in the harbour, Sir Charles Grey detached the 42d Regiment and some light

---

* The good accounts from Flanders are overbalanced, I fear, by the bad. These checks were, in my opinion, to be expected whenever the French took the resolution to leave the sieges on the side of Hainault to their fate in order to break in upon the line of communication. This must have happened equally if the combined armies had remained together and undertaken a joint operation ; and the proposed plan had the advantage of being the only one whose success would have remedied this inconvenience resulting from the nature of an attack from an open country against such a barrier.

It must be left to military decision what is precisely the best point of attack, combined or separate, which now remains ; but the loss of Menin as a post of communication does not tend to lessen the difficulties of any plan, and I am averse to anything which shall hazard the delaying of the West Indian expedition.

A few towns more or less in Flanders are certainly not unimportant ; but I am much mistaken in my speculations if the business at Toulon is not decisive of the war.—Lord Grenville to Marquis of Buckingham, 15th September 1793.

118   MEMOIR OF GENERAL GRAHAM.

companies, amongst others that of the 19th, then commanded by Captain Graham, to the relief of Nieuport,* then besieged by the enemy.

The enemy, whose numbers were computed at 8000, kept up a brisk fire during the right of the 28-29th, and took one of the towers near the place, but their fire was well answered by the garrison, and the reinforcement under General Dundas, thus seasonably

---

* Nieuport forms the extreme right of the frontier line of the Netherlands. This town is distant about one and a half mile from the sea, with which it communicates by the Iser river, navigable for small vessels up to the town, and only fordable on the sea-beach at the time of extreme low water

Nieuport does not command any chaussée from France by which this country might be invaded, but derives much military importance from the circumstance of its harbour communicating with the three canals of Bruges, Ypres, Furnes, by means of the sluices of which, a very considerable inundation of the adjacent country with fresh water may be effected ; and if the sea water be also admitted at spring tides, the inundation would extend to the neighbourhood of Ypres, and towards Mont Cassel in France.

To secure the means of so efficient though destructive a mode of defence of a considerable portion of the frontier must be an object of importance in every scheme of defensive war in this country

The enceinte of Nieuport, which is nearly of a square figure, consists of an ancient wall flanked by small towers, in addition to which a few general flanks have been obtained by throwing out some irregular works on the angles of the body of the place The whole is surrounded by a good wet ditch, excepting on one side where that part of the river which forms the harbour serves as a ditch.

NIEUPORT RELIEVED. 119

received on the morning of the 29th, enabled the brave governor to hold out. In the night of the 30th, the enemy raised the siege and retreated, leaving behind four twenty-four pounders and two mortars, as well as a quantity of shot and shells and intrenching tools.

Sir Charles Grey, in his despatch of the 30th October, thus expresses himself :—" I feel that much is due to the zeal and intelligence with which Major-General Dundas undertook and executed the service intrusted to him after his arrival at Nieuport."

On Nieuport being relieved, Captain Graham returned with his regiment to England.

120   MEMOIR OF GENERAL GRAHAM.

CHAPTER THE ELEVENTH.

Campaign in Holland, 1796—Lord Moira's Orders.

In June 1794 the 19th Regiment was again embarked
for Flanders with the army, under the Earl of Moira.*
On this occasion Captain Graham embarked as aid-de-
camp to General Crosbie, on the staff of Lord Moira.

The force under his lordship's command consisted
of the 19th, 27th, 28th, 40th, 42d, 54th, 57th, 59th, 87th,
and 89th Regiments, amounting in all to about 7000
men. They landed at Ostend on the 26th June. On
their arrival the enemy was in possession of Ypres,
Bruges, and Thoront, and was advancing on Ghent.

Ostend, famous for its resistance to Spinola in the

---

* Upon the subject of the arrival of Lord Moira's force :—
The Marquis of Buckingham to Mr T Grenville

Aug. 31, 1794.

If the object had been to exhaust the enemy by protracting
the war, in that case " the war would have been defensive, and
co-operation settled to that object, instead of abandoning the
Duke of York to certain ruin, if the winds and the circumstances
of this country had not permitted Lord Moira's army to arrive
just (and only just) in time to cover their retreat and communication."

LORD MOIRA AT OSTEND. 121

seventeenth century, when the Archduchess Isabella made a vow not to change her chemise until it was taken, was not now deemed in a defensible state ; but irrespective of that circumstance, the state of affairs in the country was such on the arrival of Lord Moira, that his lordship, who was restricted by his instructions to the defence of Ostend, thought he could not honestly confine his attention to the defence of that place After glancing at such plans as suggested themselves for the employment of the force under his command, his first step was to communicate with Generals Clairfayt and Walmoden, proposing a junction of their forces, in order to act from Bruges by Thielt upon the left wing of the French General Clairfayt eagerly adopted the idea, but made it a condition that Lord Moira should singly possess himself of Bruges before he (General Clairfayt) should move.

With this object in view, Lord Moira moved out of Ostend on the 28th June.

In Alison's history of Europe, a degree of supineness and indolence, highly reprehensible in any commander or military body, is attributed to Lord Moira and his corps on their arrival at Ostend. Fortunately for their memory, the reflection thus cast on them cannot be sustained by facts

A mere examination of the dates of occurrences at this stage of the campaign is sufficient to convince any

122 MEMOIR OF GENERAL GRAHAM.

impartial mind that the historian has, by some means, been led to very inaccurate conclusions in his desire to trace out the causes of events, and that he has thus been prompted to pass a most unmerited censure on his countrymen.

The passage referred to occurs in the second volume of Alison's work.* It is there insinuated that the defeat of Clairfayt is partly to be ascribed to the inaction of 30,000 Austrians at Tournay, and 6000 *English "reposing from the fatigues of the sea voyage at Ostend."* We leave the Austrians to answer for themselves, but with regard to the charge against the English, we would ask the historian to explain how the defeat of Clairfayt, which took place on the 25th June,† could have been

---

* Chap. xv., p. 387.

† His Royal Highness the DUKE of YORK to the Right Hon. HENRY DUNDAS.

Renaix, *June* 28

Sir—Having received intelligence, on Tuesday night (24th June), that the enemy had moved forward in great force upon General Clairfayt's position, and that they had detached a corps to attack Oudenarde, I found it absolutely necessary, for the defence of the Scheldt, to march immediately to this place, as from hence I could, with greater facility, support that place, and move upon any point at which they might attempt to force a passage

The enemy obliged General Clairfayt to abandon his position at Deynse, and to fall back upon Ghent, on Wednesday (25th June), where they again attacked him the next day, but were fortunately repulsed.

LORD MOIRA'S STRATAGEM.

123

averted by Lord Moira and his corps, who were that day on board their transports on the passage from England, and did not reach Ostend until the following day, the 26th?

Owing to the advantages gained by the enemy on the 25th and 26th June, it was necessary for Lord Moira both to preserve the utmost secrecy with regard to his movements, and to mislead the enemy as to his real intentions and the strength of the force under his command.

With the latter object, the burgomaster of Bruges, who was a French partizan, was called upon to furnish rations for 15,000 men, being, it was stated, *part* of the British force just landed at Ostend. This information

This retreat of General Clairfayt rendered it impossible for General Walmoden to support himself with so small a body of troops as he had under his command at Bruges. He therefore found it necessary to abandon that place on Thursday, and to fall back to Landmark, and join General Clairfayt's right flank.

The consequences of these movements, though necessary, are extremely unpleasant, as all immediate communication with Ostend is cut off.

Yesterday the enemy made another attempt upon Oudenarde, which they cannonaded the whole day, and even carried in the afternoon the fauxbourg, but were driven back again in the night, and have now retreated to a small distance.

Yesterday evening I received the disagreeable intelligence of the Prince of Cobourg's having failed in his attack upon the French army at Gosselies and Fleurus, as well as of the surrender of Charleroi.—I am, &c   FREDERICK.

124 MEMOIR OF GENERAL GRAHAM.

was of course immediately communicated to General Vandamme at Wingham by the burgomaster, who was much commended for his zeal in obtaining and forwarding intelligence ; and Vandamme, who had 20,000 men under his orders, believing the intelligence he had received as to the strength of his enemy to be correct, instead of attacking the earl, lost no time in getting out of his way.

Lord Moira marched through Bruges on the evening of the 29th to Malle, four miles on the opposite side, and in the course of his march received important despatches from the Duke of York and General Clairfayt, which caused an alteration in his plans.

The Duke, anxious for his assistance, but looking upon it as impracticable for him to march by the ordinary road, urged his joining him by Sluys and Sas de Gand. Clairfayt, on the other hand, declared it to be impossible for him to fulfil any engagement with his lordship, in consequence of the Prince of Coburg's defeat, and farther stated that he expected to leave Ghent in a few hours.

It was then that Lord Moira resolved to push forward by the route of Ecloo and Ghent to join the Duke of York, although he had no longer any assurance of co-operation.

In order to favour his movement, he requested General Walmoden to create an impression on the

MARCH OF LORD MOIRA'S CORPS, 125

enemy of an impending attack, and he himself took every possible measure to promote a belief in the exaggerated account which had been already circulated of the strength of his force.

On the 30th Lord Moira's force came into communication with that under General Walmoden, within three miles of Ghent.*

On the 6th the rear-guard was attacked near Alost. On the same day, H. R. H. the Duke of York, retreating from Grammont in the direction of Antwerp,† reached

---

* On the same day, an occurrence took place on the march, attended with rather serious consequences, but affording a very useful lesson to the young soldiers in the earl's army. A false alarm was given by a sentinel firing at an ass, and one of the regiments in the rear, on turning out, fired on its picquet.

† Lord GRENVILLE to Marquis of BUCKINGHAM, St. James' Square.

9th July 1794.

The retreat to Antwerp has been decided, not by opinions here, nor even by those of the Duke of York and Lord Cornwallis, but by the necessity consequent on the Austrian movements. Whether those movements were right, I am not enough of a soldier, nor enough informed as a statesman, to pretend to form an opinion. The immediate effect of them is not necessarily the abandoning the towns taken last year, which are in a state to maintain themselves long, and to impede many of the operations of the enemy. Nor, as long as the Austrians maintain their line from Louvain to Namur, is the possibility of succouring them considered desperate. What I most fear in the present moment is the effect of despondency here and abroad. It would have been a flattering and glorious thing to have terminated the war by a successful offensive campaign in Flanders; but if that

126 MEMOIR OF GENERAL GRAHAM.

Asche. On the 9th, the duke marched through Malines, and there met with Lord Moira's column, which halted till the duke passed

Head-quarters were fixed that day at the Chateau of Contich, and the corps under the Earl of Moira formed the first line in front of the village of Waerloos.

The Hessians occupied Malines, under the command of Lieutenant-General Dalwig

Lord Moira's corps had at this time undergone uncommon fatigues. Owing to the secrecy preserved on their leaving Ostend, the officers left all their clothing and camp equipage behind, thinking they were merely moving to an encampment outside the walls of the town, and therefore neither officers nor men had shifted, or had

has failed, I am far from thinking it a reason for abandoning a cause in the issue of which our existence is implicated

If we listen to the ideas of peace, it is a confession we are unable to carry on the war, and such a confession is a bad security against the events which must follow in Flanders, in Holland, and, by a very rapid succession, in this island

Lord GRENVILLE to Marquis of BUCKINGHAM, St James' Square

19*th July* 1794.

Lord Cornwallis is returned speaking highly of the Duke of York, and far otherwise of the Austrian generals, to whom he and all mankind in Flanders impute all that has happened It is a whimsical circumstance, and hardly to have been foreseen, that, in a war which we carry on conjointly with Austria, the great want which we experience should be that of Austrian generals of capacity sufficient to command the excellent troops which are acting in the Netherlands

CAMP AT ALOST. 127

the covering of a tent or house from the time they landed. Water was scarce, and in consequence of the dryness of the season, and the soil in this part of the country being of a light sandy nature, they were almost smothered in their encampment with clouds of dust.

Amongst the papers left by General Graham, some orders issued by the Duke of York and Lord Moira during this campaign are so suggestive and interesting to military men, even at the present day, that the following extracts have been made :—

HEAD QUARTERS, Alost,*
Saturday, 5th July 1794.

After Orders, half-past six o'clock.

Lord Moira is exceedingly distressed by the complaints which have been made to him from inhabitants plundered by the British soldiers. He calls upon the officers commanding regiments, by every sense they have of military discipline or national credit, to exert themselves in suppressing a conduct so disgraceful to the army. On his part, he must subject the troops, in consequence of this irregularity, to restrictions which, out of a view of their convenience, he could wished to

---

* Some of the proper names and names of places in these orders are probably not quite correct, being in the orthography of the orderly sergeant who copied the orders.

128 MARAUDING.

have forborne. A captain's guard is immediately to be mounted at the bridge leading into the town, and no soldiers (officers' servants or others) are to be permitted to enter the town, unless under the care of a non-commissioned officer, who is to be responsible for the man or party. No officer is to absent himself from his battalion but by the special leave of his commanding officer for a time limited. The provost-marshal has orders to patrol in the environs of the camp, and to punish on the spot every man who shall be found committing the smallest outrage. Should these enormities hereafter take place, it will be strictly inquired how such a want of vigilance existed in the regiment to which the offenders may belong, as to have given the individuals the opportunity of committing the offence.

B. O.

When the brigade halts a time that their packs and accoutrements are put off—their packs to be put down regular by the arms, and their accoutrements hung upon them, that every man may be able to get his own without any confusion.

HEAD QUARTERS, Camp on the Heights of Alost,
Sunday, 6th July 1794.

Returns to be immediately made out for two days' bread, forage, and fuel, for the 6th and 7th inclusive.

AFFAIR NEAR ALOST 129

Communications to be immediately made by the different regiments on their front and flanks.

HEAD QUARTERS, Camp near Alost,
Monday, 7th July 1794.

The detachment of the 8th and 14th Dragoons will put themselves under the command of Lieutenant-Colonel Churchhill immediately.

A return of killed and wounded of the different regiments in the skirmish of yesterday to be given in immediately.

HEAD QUARTERS, After Orders, *7th July.*

All wheel-carriages, of every denomination and description whatsoever, belonging to the different regiments and detachments, are immediately to be loaded and assembled on the road leading to Malines. A person will be appointed to conduct them, and to give further instructions.

The shameful marauding in the neighbourhood of the camp having continued, Lord Moira positively orders that no soldiers shall be permitted to leave their corps under any pretext, except in parties headed by a non-commissioned officer.

As soon as the regiments get their meat, they are to cook provisions for to-morrow as well as to-day.

A return to be immediately given in of the number

130 ORDER OF MARCH

of loaves wanting by the different regiments and detachments to complete them to two days—this day and to-morrow included.

Tuesday, 8th July,
Camp at Thisselt on the Canal.

After Orders.

The baggage to be loaded immediately, and proceed by way of Leest to Malines It will enter Malines by the gate of Ghent, and will quit the town again by the gate of Antwerp, proceeding to Waerloos where it will halt.

The brigades of Brigadier-General Graham and Hunter will march from the right at twelve o'clock this night, pursuing the road above directed for the baggage. An officer will meet them at Waerloos, and point out the ground on which they are to encamp Two pieces of cannon will move at the head of the column, and four in the rear

Wednesday, 9th July,
Camp at Waerloos

For to-morrow Brigadier-General Hunter, Major Lord Blaney and Major B. Vassel. Brigadier-General Hunter's brigade gives the ordinary guards and orderlies this day; and to-morrow Brigadier-General Graham's brigade and 87th Regiment will furnish detachments—

CAMP AT WAERLOOS.   131

to consist of 2 captains, 4 subalterns, 6 sergeants, 12 corporals, 2 drummers, and 138 privates, for the post at the village of Duffel, on the left of the line

Two days' bread and forage to be issued to the troops immediately at the commissary's stores in the village of Waerloos, for this day and to-morrow, for which returns are to be sent to the adjutant-general's office. States to be given in to-morrow morning by ten o'clock, from the brigades and the different regiments, and detachments not brigaded accounting for all casuals since last states.

Lord Moira's corps encamped at Waerloos is not to be included in the detail, it is to have a separate one of its own.

A morning and evening gun to be fired from the British park, or any place more convenient, to be appointed by Lieutenant-Colonel Congreve

It is his Royal Highness the Commander-in-Chief's express order that no forage be ever cut down without directions; and he particularly desires the generals and officers commanding regiments to be most pointed in their attention that no more damage be done to the corn or country than what the situation of the camp renders indispensable. He likewise desires to observe that the late instances of plundering which have occurred, events the necessity of frequent rolls calling at unexpected hours, as also of patrolling in the villages round the camp.

132 BAD BREAD.

Reports having been sent to the adjutant-general by Major-General David Dundas's brigade, of unserviceable bread issued to them yesterday, the army has notice that the commissary-general will replace all bad loaves which may be sent to him this evening. Mr. Matses' quarters are at a public-house, about the middle of the main street in Contich.

Lord Moira's corps will send in a major of brigade at twelve o'clock every day, for orders. It will likewise send to the adjutant-general's an orderly dragoon every evening at gun firing.

N.B.—The way which has been practised of issuing spirits is for the officers commanding regiments to purchase it for their men, and it is re-paid by the quartermaster-general's order.

HEAD QUARTERS,
Thursday, 10th July 1794.

Communications to be immediately made between the corps.

Lord Cathcart's brigade gives the guards and orderlies to-morrow; a picquet to mount at the village of Waerloos, till further orders, consisting of one corporal and six dragoons; one sergeant, two corporals, and eighteen privates from the infantry, to receive their orders from the deputy adjutant-general.

Two days' bread and forage to be issued to-morrow morning, for the 11th and 12th inclusive. In future,

CAMP AT WAERLOOS. 133

all returns for bread, forage, and wood are to be made and sent to the commissary-general the day previous to the issuing.

Camp at Waerloos, *Friday,* 11*th July.*

Lord Moira's Orders.

Captain Dawling, provost-marshal, is desired to patrol the camp of Lord Moira's army, and see that all nuisances be removed, if he finds any, he is to apply to the officer commanding the nearest regiment, who will give him every assistance in removing them. A number of dead horses have been seen near the camp, which ought to be buried immediately, and the provost-martial will take care it is done

Lord Moira's After Orders.

The picquet at the village of Waerloos, consisting of one corporal and six dragoons ; one sergeant, two corporals, and eighteen privates, is taken off till further orders.

Three days' bread, forage, and wood, will be issued the day after to-morrow for three days, viz, the 13th, 14th, and 15th, inclusive.

The quarter-masters of the different regiments and detachments, are to send in their returns to the assistant-commissary-general at Waerloos by half-past six o'clock to-morrow evening.

134 BAT HORSES.

HEAD QUARTERS, Contich,
12th July 1794.

His Serene Highness the Landgrave, having called Lieutenant-General Wurmb, has been pleased to appoint Lieutenant-General Dalwig to have the command of his troops, serving in the army under the command of his Royal Highness the Commander-in-Chief

The regiments and departments are to include, in their general return for bread and forage, every person belonging to them who is at, or in the neighbourhood of, Antwerp, requisitions coming from individuals will not be attended to

Lord Moira's Orders.

Every officer commanding a company is to provide, with as much expedition as possible, four bât horses for the service of that company, for the purchase of each of which eighteen guineas will be allowed by government; the horses to be purchased are the property of government, and the officers commanding companies are answerable for them

HEAD QUARTERS, Contich,
Sunday, 13th July

The corps under Lord Moira to send in returns, to Major-General Fox, quarter-master-general, of their strength, in order to regulate the issue of wood and

HEAD QUARTERS, CONTICH. 135

straw, after which returns of wood to be sent in every fourth day, and returns for straw every seventh, previous to each subsequent delivery.

HEAD QUARTERS, Contich,
Monday, 14th July 1794.

Earl of Moira's Orders.

Returns for 200 days, bât and forage money from the different regiments and departments to be immediately made out and sent to the quarter-master-general.

The different brigades and regiments will immediately apply to the park of artillery for their ammunition, to complete them to sixty rounds, agreeable to returns which are to be sent in to the adjutant-general's office.

The horses ordered to be furnished by captains of companies, are to be paid for by the paymaster of their respective regiments, and charged to their agents.

Two additional bât horses to be provided by each regiment, one for the purpose of carrying the surgical and medical apparatus, the other for carrying the quarter and rear-guard tents; these horses to be paid for by the quarter-master-general.

136 ORDNANCE DRIVERS.

Camp at Waerloos,
Tuesday, 15*th July* 1794.

Returns to be given in this evening for two days' bread and forage, for the 16th and 17th instant, to the assistant commissary-general at Waerloos, who will fix the hour for the waggons to assemble to-morrow morning on the chaussée leading to Antwerp, and a person will be appointed by the quarter-master-general to attend and conduct them to and from the magazines.

Each regiment of the three brigades is to send to the artillery park this forenoon three men to serve for the present as drivers for the ordnance ; such men are of course to be chosen as would be least useful in the ranks. The 87th Regiment will send 13 men for the same purpose ; 5 temporary conductors will also be requisite, but as it will be a station desirable from the pay attached to it, Lord Moira wishes to appoint deserving sergeants for that service ; he therefore requests Lord Cathcart to have the goodness to recommend two such from his brigade, General Graham two from his, and Brigadier-General Hunter one.

B. O.

Head Quarters, Contich, 15*th July.*

Lord Moira's Orders.

Duffel, *Wednesday,* 16*th July* 1794.

HEAD QUARTERS, Contich,
Thursday, 17th July.

The women of the army to receive flour in room of bread, till further orders.

Lord Moira's Orders.

A grand guard to mount immediately at the barrier near the windmill, consisting of 1 captain, 1 subaltern, 2 sergeants, 1 trumpeter, and 50 privates, from the dragoon guards.

Brigadier-General Hunter's brigade will relieve General Graham's brigade at the different posts in and near the village of Duffel, this day after dinner. It will take this duty for two days.

Returns of bread and forage for three days, 18th, 19th, and 20th inclusive, to be given in from the different regiments and departments to the adjutant-general at head-quarters this afternoon. Receipts for the waggoners to be taken at the same time for the bread and forage by the quarter-master of regiments to the assistant commissary at Antwerp to-morrow morning.

The orderly time will in future be at 11 o'clock.

After Orders, 17th July.

A detachment, to be commanded by Major Malcolm, 78th Regiment, is to parade at the great church in Duffel at five o'clock precisely; it is to consist of a

G 2

138 DUFFEL.

company from the 87th Regiment, and a subaltern and 20 men from 3d brigade ; two pieces of cannon are to be lent from Lord Cathcart's brigade to this detachment, as the service for which this party is destined is to keep up a communication with the Hanoverians and Dutch outposts ; the men will, of course, take their packs with them

HEAD QUARTERS, Contich,
Friday, 18*th July.*

Camp at Duffel, *Saturday,* 19*th July* 1794.

For the day, to-morrow, Major Harris, Brigadier-General Lord Cathcart's brigade, will relieve Brigadier-General Hunter's brigade at the different posts at and near the village of Duffel this day at four o'clock in the afternoon ; it will take this duty for two days.

The brigadier-general commanding the brigade on this service will continue on duty for that time with his brigade During this service the field-officer of the day will visit the guards and the duty in camp, and the brigadier-general at the advanced posts will appoint a field-officer to do duty there

Lord Moira's Orders.

Duffel, 20*th July* 1794.

An allotment of waggons being made for the general and staff-officers, and respective regiments of the army under the command of Lieutenant-General the Earl of

BREAD AND FORAGE WAGGONS. 139

Moira, as per list, the general and staff-officers, and commanding officers of regiments, will be pleased to make out receipts for the waggons so allotted, and send them, with the requisition for the delivery of such waggons, to Major Pool, waggon-master-general, on the east esplanade near the citadel, Antwerp, where they will be delivered on producing the said receipt. All waggons now in the possession of the staff, or regiments belonging to this army, are to be returned on receipt of the waggons contained in this list, and not suffered to go away as the drivers please.

The weight each waggon should carry is not to exceed 2000 pounds.

The bread waggons to be appropriated solely for the carriage of bread.

Bread for the drivers and forage for the horses to be drawn for by the respective departments and regiments, viz, bread $1\frac{1}{2}$ pounds per day ; forage, 11 pounds hay and 12 pounds oats.

The returns for two days' bread and forage to be given in this evening as usual for the 21st and 22d inst inclusive.

The waggons now with the regiments, for which receipts have not been given, will go immediately to Antwerp to Mr. Mill, assistant-commissary in the Rue Imperiale, who will instruct the different quarter-masters where to get to their waggons on a receipt being given.

140   DUFFEL.

These waggons will load at Antwerp with bread and forage, and the former be delivered up to Mr. Mill.

The continuation of the appointment of Sergeant Evans of the 27th Regiment as deputy provost-martial, not having been in orders since the army left the island of Guernsey, it is hereby confirmed, and his pay will be allowed for that period, he having continued to do duty as such.

A monthly return to be given in immediately for the 1st of July.

Brigadier-General Graham's brigade will relieve Brigadier-General Lord Cathcart's brigade at the different posts in and near the village of Duffel, to morrow afternoon at four o'clock.

Earl of Moira's after Orders, 20th July.

Particular circumstances calling Lord Moira immediately to England,* he is to be relieved at this post by Lieutenant-General Abercromby.

* Sir Harry Calvert, in a letter, dated 14th July, writes as follows —

"The rank of officers of the corps that has joined under Lord Moira promises to be productive of great inconvenience. As yet the two corps are kept distinct, Lord Moira forming the first line *Entre nous*, I believe he intends to return to England very soon."

And again, writing on the 22d July, Sir Harry says :—

"Lord Moira returns to England on account of the disproportionate local rank given him last year, which will always deprive his country of his services on the Continent."

LORD MOIRA'S FAREWELL ORDER. 141

Lord Moira cannot surrender his command without entreating the officers, non-commissioned officers, and men of the corps which accompanied him from Ostend, to accept his warmest and most grateful thanks for the kind and cheerful acquiescence he has experienced from them, and the severe fatigues with which he was obliged to subject them , he has the flattering assurance that he is still to have their support in the service to which they were originally destined.   And that hope lessens his reluctance at ceasing, for the present, to share the honourable dangers of service with them.   He trusts they will believe that no light consideration would have obliged him to quit them, as he persuades himself they are sensible of his having endeavoured to repay the generous attachment they have shewn to him by the most lively interest for their welfare.   For the present he bids them farewell, with the most fervent prayers for their honour and prosperity.

The corps under the command of Lieutenant-General Abercromby are to receive bread and forage to-morrow up to the 25th instant inclusive.

HEAD QUARTERS, Contich,

Monday, 21*st July* 1794.

The several corps of the army march to-morrow morning precisely at half-past three o'clock, except Colonel Stein's corps, which will remain till the Hesse

142 HEAD QUARTERS, CONTICH

Darmstadt troops arrive near Wetrych, when it will proceed and form the head of the column. The different columns will take the routes marked in the distributions which have been sent to the lieutenant-generals.

All the out-posts on the river are to continue to be occupied by light troops of the respective corps till eight o'clock, when they will march upon the same routes as their corps did; all carriages of every sort are to be away this evening at five o'clock; those of the column of H. R. H. the Commander-in-Chief, as well of those of Lieutenant-General Sir William Erskine's and Lieutenant-General Abercromby's, are to rendezvous at that hour on the causeway beyond Contich towards Antwerp, where an officer of the quarter-master-general's department will attend.

The wheel carriages of the other columns to march at the same hour, upon their respective routes. The quarter-masters and camp-colourmen are to assemble and march, so as to arrive to-morrow morning at four o'clock at the following places—those of the British at Bergenhout—those of the* Hessians at Diebeci—the Hanoverians at Winhen. The British to send two camp-colourmen per regiment only, and these ought to be careful and strong men.

The following is the order of march of the column under the immediate command of his Royal Highness :—

Major-General Ralph Dundas's brigade.

CONVEYANCE OF SICK. 143

Reserve artillery.

Brigade of guards

Major-General Fox's brigade.

Remainder of the heavy cavalry.

The bât horses at the head of their respective regiments.

The sick of any who are not able to march to be sent to Antwerp immediately, and a proportion of spring vaggons will be sent to each brigade to convey them.

The quarter-masters and camp-colourmen of the British will assemble at the park of artillery at two o'clock to-morrow morning, where they will be conducted by an officer of the quarter-master-general's department.

General Abercromby's orders.

Duffel, 21st July.

The detail of duty, and the disposition of the outposts to remain the same as ordered by Lieutenant-General the Earl of Moira

The corps under the command of Lieutenant-General Abercromby will march to-morrow morning by the right, and the following order at half-past three o'clock—

Bât horses of the army.

Heavy artillery and spare ammunition horses

5th and 6th dragoon guards

8th, 15th, and 16th light dragoons.

Loyal emigrants.

The infantry by brigade with the battalion guns.

144 DUFFEL.

The brigade under the command of Brigadier-General Graham, with the cavalry now on the advanced posts, and 1 squadron 15th Light Dragoons, will form the rear guard.

The advanced posts will be withdrawn at seven o'clock in the morning, and the whole of the rear guard will march precisely at eight by the same route with that of the column, viz., by Lindt, Bouchaut, Borsbeck, and Duivin. Lieutenant Tinling of the 57th Regiment will this evening point out to the different corps the route by which they are to leave camp to-morrow morning, and will conduct the column.

Brigadier-General Graham will apply to the burgomaster for guides, who will have them in readiness.

Captain Johnston of the corps of engineers, with the artificers, will remain with the rear guard, and as soon as all the advanced posts have been withdrawn, will effectually destroy the bridge.

The battalion gun now on the advance posts, and which is not attached to General Graham's brigade, will join its brigade this evening at ten o'clock. The 87th Regiment will close in the left of the 57th before they march at half-past three o'clock.

After Orders by Lieutenant-General Abercromby, 21st July.

The greatest care to be taken that no huts, straw, or forage be set on fire during the night or before the

NO HUTS OR FORAGE TO BE BURNED. 145

march Officers commanding corps will be pleased to attend particularly to this caution, as the lieutenant-general is determined to make a severe example of any soldier who may disgrace himself by being guilty of that offence

HEAD QUARTERS, *Tuesday*, 22d *July* 1794.

All the wheel carriages of the British are to assemble at Merxim precisely at five o'clock this evening ; they are to go along the Chaussèe through Berginhoute, and behind the glazies of the town ; they are to pass the village of Merxim, and halt on the Chaussèe till put in motion by an officer of the quarter-master-general's department.

H. R. H. the Commander-in-Chief looks up to the general officers and officers commanding brigades for the strict observance of these orders, being determined to take particular notice of any breach of them which he may observe

The artillery are particularly directed to keep no waggons with them that are not absolutely necessary.

B. O.

Brigadier General Graham desires that the above order may be strictly complied with.

After Orders, nine at night

The army will march in three columns in the follow-

146 ORDER OF MARCH.

ing order, the first column under the command of Lieutenant-General Harcourt—

Major-General R. Dundas's brigade—heavy cavalry.
Major-General D Dundas's   do
Major-General White's   do.
Colonel Vyse's   do.

followed by the artillery attached to them

This column will march at three o'clock by its right to Achterbroeck, by the route of Beiginhoute, Merxim, and Cappel.

Second column under the command of Lieutenant-General Sir William Erskine will march from the right

Bntish reserve artillery.

Major-General Stewart's brigade of infantry.
Brigadier-General Lord Cathcart's brigade, 2 5½-inch howitzer British.
Brigadier-General Hunter's brigade
Major-General Balfour's brigade, 2 12-pounders British
Major-General Fox's brigade
Brigadier-General Graham's brigade, 2 5½-inch howitzer British.
Two battalions of Hesse Cassel regiments of Casport.
Two   do.   of   do.   guards
Two   do   of   do   life regiment.

7th and 11th British Dragoons   The British reserve artillery to march as soon as this column has passed the

ORDER OF MARCH. 147

Park, and to proceed to West Vasse by the route of Berginhoute, Merxim, and Bresshet. The remaining part of this column will pursue the same route, and be ready to commence the march at five o'clock.

Third column, under the command of Lieutenant-General Walmoden—

Hanoverian reserve artillery—two long 12-pounders Hesse Cassel Gensd'armes.

Three squadrons Hesse Cassel Carbineers

Hanoverian heavy cavalry

Hanoverian infantry of the line, with six pieces of ordnance from the Hanoverian reserve, to be placed in the column of march as General Walmoden may think proper to direct.

This column to be ready to commence its march from the left by Achterbroeck at five o'clock, and to proceed by the route of Seauten, Chattel, Creigant, and to the Chaussée leading from Antwerp to Breda without entering upon that which leads up from Antwerp to Rotterdam.

The reserve of the army under the command of Lieutenant-General Abercromby will follow the route of this column. Two $5\frac{1}{2}$-inch howitzers, and two long 6-pounders, will be attached to the reserve of the army which will be placed as Lieutenant-General Abercromby may direct. The advance of the army, under the command of Lieutenant-General Hammerston, consisting of two companies of Hesse Cassel light infantry, two companies

148 ORDER OF MARCH.

of Yagers, Hessedarmsted light infantry, 4 battalions Hessian Grenadiers, 4 squadrons Hessedarmsted cavalry, four squadrons Hanoverian light dragoons, 87th Regiment British, loyal emigrants.

Two battalions of Hessedarmsted infantry is to cover the march of the 2d and 3d column in the manner which Lieutenant-General Hammerston may direct.

The quarter-masters and camp-colourmen of the Hessians and British, and Hessians, the former as directed in yesterday's orders, are to assemble in the churchyard at Berginhoute, at four o'clock in the morning, to be conducted by an officer of the quarter-master-general's department.

The quarter-masters and camp-colourmen of the Hessians and reserve to assemble at the same hour at Neheim, to be marched from hence to West Vassel by an officer of the Hanoverian quarter-master-general's department.

G. O.   HEAD QUARTERS, Colmsthout,
Wednesday, 23d July 1794.

The Hessians belong to the left wing. Two battalions infantry, and two squadrons cavalry to be in reserve for each wing.

Lieutenant-General Abercromby will settle the detail for the reserve. The general officer of the day to see the camp picquets posted according to the general instructions.

HEAD QUARTERS COLMSTHOUT.

All wheel carriages in the same manner last night to assemble to-morrow morning at six o'clock at Achterbroeck, to be marched from thence by an officer of the quarter-master-general's department to Rosendal.

A non-commissioned officer and ten men from each of the regiments of heavy cavalry, as also from the 8th and 14th Light Dragoons, with a subaltern per brigade, and a captain from Major-General David Dundas's brigade, to parade at the same time at Achterbroeck to escort the waggons and to assist the quarter-master-general's department, which they are requested to do in enforcing the regulations of the march. The wheel carriages of the Hanoverians and reserve are to assemble at the same hour on the road leading to Breda, and to march then under the conduct of such officers as General Walmoden may appoint. Any wheel carriages which belong to the advanced corps must be sent to one or other of the places mentioned by the above hour.

The army halts to-morrow.

When the army is to take up its ground, the advanced corps and the corps appointed for its support will always receive their instructions from Major-General Hammerston.

British Orders.

The brigades must furnish sentries to the wells which are near them, to prevent any damage to be done to them, or any unnecessary waste of water.

150 INHABITANTS' HOUSES PROTECTED.

The general officers will also be pleased to furnish safeguards to all the houses near their respective brigades.

Those corps that have not received bread for the 25th inst. will receive it this night in camp, the commissary-general having undertaken to deliver it at the head of each regiment so circumstanced. An allowance of wood for the infantry and cavalry of the right wing is ordered to be delivered in front of the camp, between the left of the heavy cavalry and right of the 1st line of infantry, to which place the corps of that wing will send for it. Wood for the brigade of guards, 15th and 16th Light Dragoons, is ordered to be sent to their place of encampment.

HEAD QUARTERS, Colmsthout,
Thursday, 24th July 1794

The army will march to-morrow morning at four o'clock The lieutenant-generals, aide-de-camps, and majors of brigade are to attend this evening at six o'clock for the order of march

It is with the utmost concern that H.R.H. the Commander-in-Chief has perceived the very scandalous height to which plundering and marauding of every species have gotten in the army under his command It is now got to a pass that requires every exertion to suppress it, and reduce the army to that regularity of conduct, without which it can hardly continue to exist.

PLUNDERING.   151

H.R.H. can scarce look up to any other cause for this disgraceful licentiousness, but to the inattention of officers commanding of regiments to enforce the orders and regulations which are issued. For these they are in duty responsible, and H.R.H. will put in arrest the first officer commanding a regiment in which any disobedience or inattention to orders is perceived.

As the situation of the corps late under the command of the Earl of Moira, with respect to provisions, has obliged the men frequently to subsist on the country by picking up such roots and vegetables as would be found in the fields, it is necessary that they should now be warned that that is considered as plundering to all intents and purposes, and the provost-marshal has orders to punish on the spot any man he may detect in injuring any gardens or fields. Two drummers and a trumpeter are constantly to attend the provost guard, to execute such punishment as the due discharge of his duty may oblige him to inflict.

The outlying picquets are to be always posted as ordered by the general regulations, but in future there are to be no inlying picquets—the battalions and squadrons ordered for the reserve being considered in lieu of each, and are consequently to be in constant readiness to turn out in a moment's warning, The outlying picquets of cavalry to be an officer and 30 men per brigade.

H.R.H. the Commander-in-Chief express order that

152 PICQUETS.

no person upon a march be ever sent forward upon any pretence whatever. In the march of an army there is a place assigned to every one, to which he must adhere. Quarters will be marked out for such persons as are entitled to them, and the houses or convenience within a proper distance of the rear of a brigade are to be disposed of by the general officer commanding a brigade

After Orders, eight at night.

The army marches in four columns to-morrow morning; the several columns to march precisely at four o'clock.

The first column consists of the British cavalry of the right wing under the command of Lieutenant-General Harcourt, it will march from the right through Colmsthout to Rosendal to its position The artillery attached to the cavalry to accompany this column.

Second column, under the command of Lieutenant-General Sir William Erskine, consists of the British infantry, and will march by its left; the second line leading through Achterbroeck to its position; the 7th and 11th Light Dragoons close the march of this column; General Fox's brigade will march in the rear of the infantry of this column, and will be shewn where to turn off the road so as to reach the camp destined for it, near Rosendal, by the shortest road. General Balfour's brigade will by this means follow General Graham's brigade.

ORDER OF MARCH. 153

Third column consists of Hanoverian reserve artillery, Hanoverian infantry marching by its left, followed by the Hessian infantry also from its left, and the column to be closed by the Hanoverian and Hessian cavalry of the left wing. This column marches upon Rukveen by the route which will be pointed out to it by an officer of the Hanoverian staff.

The reserve forming the fourth column will march from its left, by the route which will be pointed out by Major Suntock of the quarter-master-general's department. The bât horses march at the head of their several regiments as formerly ordered, the sick, if any, unable to march, must be sent to the rear of the reserve artillery at two o'clock in the morning. Guides will be sent to the heads of the leading regiments of each column, except the third column, which, as already mentioned, will be led by an officer of the Hanoverian staff; an officer from the Hanoverian and Hessian troops to meet Lieutenant-Colonel Bronderick at Thiebeen at five o'clock to-morrow morning.

The quarter-master and two camp colourmen per regiment of British, to be at the British park of artillery at one o'clock in the morning, where an officer of the quarter-master-general's department will attend to conduct them.

Head quarters of the British, Rosendal; Hessian, Rukveen; Hanoverian, Sprundel.

154   ALTERED VALUE OF CURRENCY.

HEAD QUARTERS, Rosendal,
Friday, 25th July 1794.

The army being now in Holland, it is necessary that they should be informed that the money they now have diminishes in its value, and that the weights and measures increase almost in an equal degree. The French crown, which was paid five shillings, and for which they received sixty-five sous and one leier in Brabant, in Flanders, passes only for fifty-six in Holland; this deficiency will be made up to them in the purchase of bread and butcher's meat.

The regiments and departments are to receive two days' bread and forage, for 26th and 27th inclusive, tomorrow. The empty waggons, bread and forage, are to be sent to Oudenbosch this evening, and to be packed for the night in some proper place; requisitions for the above bread and forage must be sent to the inspecting commissary at Oudenbosch immediately.

Morning Orders, *July 26th*, 1794.

A battalion of the line is to relieve the 87th Regiment at the advanced posts immediately; this battalion is to be relieved every fourth day. The first brigade, consisting of the 3d, 63d, and 88th regiments, gives the above battalion, which will march from this to Maaspen, there to receive their orders from Lieutenant-General Hammerston.

SINKING WELLS 155

Saturday, HEAD QUARTERS, Rosendal,
26th July 1794.

British Orders

The cavalry of the right wing to be ordered not to water at any other place than at the river on the right, which cross the road leading from Rosendal to Maaspen

The regiments to report on the probability of sinking wells, in their front or rear, and every attempt to be made to find water by this means.

Application to be made to the quarter-master-general for any materials that may be wanted for this purpose

The front line to make kitchens in front; the second line will make theirs in the rear

The corps to make immediately communications, and level all ruts in front and rear.

Brigade Orders.

Brigadier-General Graham having observed of late some officers of the brigade absent, he desires that in future no leave be granted on any pretence, without having previously obtained his permission

The rolls of the regiments to be called hourly from an hour after reveille, till retreat beating, the officer of the quarter-guard of each regiment to see this duty done.

156 NEW FORMATION OF INFANTRY

Sunday, HEAD QUARTERS, Rosendal,
27th July 1794.

British Orders.

His Royal Highness the Commander-in-Chief orders
the formations of the battalions of infantry of the army
under his command to be in three ranks, but with the
following regulations, which are at all times to be observed —

When the battalion forms for action, the third rank
is instantly to be formed into two divisions, and two
ranks, each under the command of an officer.

When the army or corps to which the battalion be-
longs is in two lines, those divisions will form on the
rear of the centre of each wing of their battalions at
the distance of fifty paces.

When there is no second line, the two divisions
joined together, a captain is appointed to the command
of them ; and being then in one body, it forms a reserve each to its own battalion, at 200 paces in the rear
of the centre ; in this manner these divisions form a
reserve or second line, which may be used either in
lengthening the first line by being carried to either
flank, or as a corps-de-reserve to strengthen any point
may be necessary

When a battalion is ordered to march, the two divisions formed from the third rank will join again as

ISSUE OF BREAD AND FORAGE 157

expeditiously as possible, being always on the march of a column, disposed of as a third rank, unless it be on a short march of manœuvre to right or left, in which case these divisions will move in column in the same directions, preserving their relative situation to the battalion.

As this may require a little practice to render it familiar to the regiments, his Royal Highness desires that the general officers, and officers commanding brigades, will see that they are trained to it at roll-calling, or other occasions or theory of exercise

The regiments which were in the corps lately under the orders of Lord Moira, must take measures for landing their camp equipage and baggage immediately, a proper officer of each, with a non-commissioned officer, to repair to Bergen-op-Zoom this afternoon, when they are to apply to the commissary, who will have directions to procure them boats and other conveniences for this purpose.

The several corps of the army to send in returns this afternoon to the quarter-master-general's office for four days' wood, from 28th to 31st July inclusive

The regiments composing Brigadier-General Lord Cathcart's brigade, Brigadier-General Graham's, and Brigadier-General Hunter's, are immediately to report to the quarter-master-general the state of the commissariat bread and forage waggons, and horses attached to them.

158   REVIEW OF ARMY.

The bread and forage waggons must be constantly
sent to the magazine the day before the issues are made,
and packed by brigade for the night, under the command of their respective officers ; the requisitions must
be sent in at the same time, and the orders on the
magazine prepared, so that the forage of the army may
go through with regularity and without delay.

Pass Orders.

The brigades to send in to-morrow morning as early
as possible, a return of the ammunition necessary to
complete them to sixty rounds per man.

Such battalions as are not provided with ammunition tumbrils, are to send to the artillery park to-morrow
afternoon at five o'clock, where they are each to receive
one.

Monday, HEAD QUARTERS, Rosendal,
28th July 1794.

Orders.

The army to be under arms this evening at five
o'clock at the head of their encampment ; the brigades
to be in order of battle, with no further interval between
the battalions than what is necessary for the field-pieces ;
the ranks to be closed, the cavalry with drawn swords,
and the infantry with carried arms. His Royal Highness the Commander-in-Chief will go along the line,
accompanied by his Serene Highness the Prince of

WAGGONS ON THE LINE OF MARCH 159

Orange. The officers are not to salute, nor is any compliment to be paid. The cavalry trumpets may, however, sound, and the music of the infantry may play.

British Orders.

The corps that have no tents will receive a further supply of straw by applying to the commissary this afternoon

Orders for conducting the regimental bread and forage waggons of the army.

Whenever it moves, the bread and forage waggons, with the forge carts belonging to the brigades of waggoners, are to be kept separate from all other wheel carriages.

A captain of the corps of waggoners will take charge of those of the cavalry, and another of those of the infantry, who will take an account of the periods for which they are carrying bread and forage, and who will wait upon the quarter-master-general to receive instructions where, and in what manner, the waggons are to be unloaded.

When the army advances, the bread and forage waggons are to be the nearest carriages to it, in the rear; when the army retreats, they will be placed in the same situation in its front, no other wheel carriages being permitted to occupy the intermediate space between the troops and their bread and forage.

160 ORDER OF MARCH.

The officers having the charge of the bread and forage waggons, are constantly to receive their orders from the quarter-master-general, of the ground they are to move to, whenever the army marches. An officer of the waggon corps must constantly march at the head of the column to regulate the pace, as circumstances may render necessary, and to prevent the column from halting, except when he receives an order from the commanding officer ; another officer to be placed in the rear, to prevent the waggons from halting and the men from straggling. These officers to be assisted by a front and rear-guard of cavalry ; the rest of the officers to be placed on the flanks, in order to keep the column close and in line, and to prevent every kind of irregularity.

After General Orders.

The heavy baggage of the army is to assemble to-morrow at two o'clock in the afternoon, at the village of Etton, to proceed from thence under the direction of the baggage-master-general, according to a route that will be given to that officer.

General Count Walmoden, and Lieutenant-General Dalwig, will please to give the necessary directions for the assembling and marching of their respective nations to that village, when marching in the general column. It will march by the left, so that the baggage of the Hanoverians leads, followed by that of the Hessians,

ROSENDAL 161

and the column will be closed by that of the British. One squadron of Hanoverian cavalry, and one of British, are to accompany their baggage to Etton, and afterwards to serve as an escort to the column.

The forage and bread waggons to be unloaded to-morrow at daylight, to proceed immediately to Oudenbosch.

British Orders.

The reserve ammunition of the park of artillery, together with the heavy baggage, assemble precisely at twelve o'clock near the gallows upon the left of the reserve.

Major-General Ralph Dundas's brigade furnishes the squadrons for the escort of the baggage.

Rosendal, 29*th July* 1794.

Pass Orders Seven o'clock.

The regiments are desired not to use any of the hay now in the lines, but to provide themselves with green forage in lieu of it, separate requisitions for one day, bread and forage (30th July) ; and for two days, bread and oats for 31st July and 1st August, inclusive, to be sent to the inspecting commissary at Oudenbosch.

(Signed) R. AMHUTH, A. D. A. General

162   ORDER OF MARCH.

29th July 1794

Pass Orders.   Ten o'clock.

Notwithstanding the orders which have already been
given on the subject, it appears that the regiments continue to send men with the baggage, and on other duties,
without subsistence. The commander-in-chief expressly
orders and directs the officers commanding regiments,
to see that this does not occur again.

THOMAS BRINLEY, A. D. A. General.

HEAD QUARTERS, Rosendal,
Tuesday, 29*th July* 1794

The army to march to-morrow morning at four
o'clock in two columns, from its left, in the following
order :—The left column to consist of Hessian and
Hanoverian cavalry of the second line ; the Hanoverian
and Hessian infantry of the same ; two British 12-
pounders ; Major-General Fox's, and Brigadier-General
Graham's brigade, British ; two howitzers ; Major-
General Balfour's brigade, infantry of the reserve, with
their guns ; British cavalry of the second line ; Hessian
dragoons of the reserve.

Right Column.

Hanoverian and Hessian cavalry of the first line,
Hanoverian and Hessian of the same ; two British 12-

CONVEYANCE OF SICK. 163

pounders; Major-General Stewart's brigade, British; Brigadier-General Hunter's do; three 4-pounders; Brigadier-General Lord Catchart's do.; three 4-pounders, two howitzers, three 12-pounders, two howitzers, 1st Brigade Cavalry Artillery; British Cavalry of the first line; 15th and 16th Light Dragoons; 7th and 11th Light do., who will receive orders from Major-General Hammerston. The left column will march through Etton, and be under the command of Lieutenant-General Sir William Erskine; the right column through Sprundel, and be under the command of General Count Walmoden.

General Count Walmoden will place his artillery in the two Hanoverian lines as he shall think proper; an officer of the quarter-master-general's department will be at the head of each of the columns to point out the route.

The quarter-master and camp colourmen of the whole army, to be at Etton this evening at six o'clock, where an officer of the quarter-master-general's department will conduct them.

The officer of the quarter-master-general's department of the Hessians will be informed, on the ground, of their respective head-quarters.

British Orders

A return to be sent in this evening at five o clock

164 NO HUTS TO BE BURNT.

to the quarter-master-general's office, of the number of sick of each brigade who are not able to march to-morrow, they are to assemble in front of the corps-de-reserve at three o'clock to-morrow morning, where waggons will be provided for them; the sick of each corps is to be under the charge of a non-commissioned officer, who is to have five days' subsistence for them, and a surgeon or mate of each brigade is to attend them

Brigade Orders

The brigade will fall in to-morrow morning at half-past three o'clock, and be ready to move off by their left, agreeable to general orders, precisely at four; the bât horses to be at the head of each battalion, with a non-commissioned officer to conduct them.

The greatest care to be taken that no fire be set to any huts or straw during the night or before the march; commanding officers of regiments will please to pay particular attention to this caution

HEAD QUARTERS, Rosendal,
Wednesday, 30th July 1794.

The corps who have not received bread and oats for the 1st of August inclusive, are immediately to send their waggons to Oudenbosch, where it will be delivered.

Morning B. Orders

Brigadier-General Graham will inspect the 89th

CONVEYANCE OF SICK. 165

Regiment to-morrow at eleven o'clock. They will have inspection returns prepared, and be very particular in the state of the arms and accoutrements

The report made out in the evening for the adjutant-general, for the information of his Royal Highness the commander-in-chief, is to be made up from the state of the evening parade, accounting for casuals from the preceding evening.

HEAD QUARTERS, Rosendal,
Thursday, 31st *July* 1794

All the sick in camp are to be sent at three o'clock to the front of the guards, where waggons will be provided to carry them to the hospital; the physicians and surgeons of the park of that department attached to the field hospital, will attend them, to such time as they can be delivered over to the physicians and surgeons of the flying hospital, who are then to take charge of them

A careful non-commissioned officer, with three men from each regiment, is to attend the sick , these men to have their arms, and are to serve at the same time as an escort.

A captain and two subalterns for the hospital duty, to be at the place of rendezvous at the same hour to take the charge and conduct the sick, and the command of the escort. Instructions will be given to the captain on the ground ; the non-commissioned officer of each

DISTRIBUTION OF OXEN

regiment is to have subsistence for six days for the sick, and for ten days for the men of the escort, both are to take with them bread as far as the regiments have received it.

The first brigade of infantry to furnish the officers for that duty.

A detachment, consisting of one captain, two subalterns, and 100 men, from the infantry, with non-commissioned officers in proportion, to march to-morrow morning at five o'clock to Oudenbosch, to relieve the party now on duty there; this detachment to be furnished by Major-General Stewart's brigade.

The commissary-general having provided cattle for the use of the army, in the proportion of two oxen per regiment; those corps that wish to have a supply of meat in this way, will send their quarter-masters, and proper persons to drive them, to-morrow morning to Sprundell, where the cattle will be; the regiments are to pay for the cattle at a value, which is estimated so as that the meat shall not be charged to the soldiers at a greater rate than $3\frac{1}{2}$d. per lb., if the sum paid for the oxen will admit of a less price, of course the soldiers will pay accordingly; and if the weight of the oxen at that price fall short of the sum paid for them, the difference will be returned by the commissary-general on the certificates of the commanding officers of corps.

The regiments and departments are to send their

RETREAT OF DUTCH AND HESSIANS. 167

bread and forage waggons to the magazine at Oudenbosch to-morrow, in order to receive, the following day, three days' bread and forage from the 2d to 4th August, inclusive.

As the sick, and men appointed for the escort, will receive bread on the march, they are to be deducted from the requisition given to-morrow.

HEAD QUARTERS, Rosendal,
Friday, 1st August 1794.

The regiments which have field-pieces attached to them, must furnish the number of additional gunners required for their service; these men must be stout able men, and in every respect fit for the service for which they are destined.

On the 16th July, the general commanding the Dutch troops had retired from his position on the Dyle, and the Hessian General, Dalwig, had quitted Malines, mutually reproaching each other with being the first to quit his position; and the Earl of Moira had made a forward movement with his corps to Duffel, but without attempting the recovery of Malines. On the 20th July, the Duke of York received intimation that his allies, the Austrians, had withdrawn from Drest,

168   MEMOIR OF GENERAL GRAHAM.

and were assembling their forces to march on Maestricht. This is said to have been the result of secret overtures for peace between the Cabinet of Vienna and the French Government.

Alison says the conditions were, that the Austrians should not be disquieted in their retreat to the Rhine, and the Republic should be permitted, without molestation, to reduce the few great fortresses which had been wrested from them in the preceding and present campaign.

In consequence of this treacherous conduct on the part of the Imperialists, the Hereditary Prince of Orange was obliged to fall back from his position on the Greater Neethe, and the left of the Duke of York's position at Liere became completely exposed. In the last campaign it has been seen that the interference of the Government, in prescribing to the Duke of York the siege of Dunkirk, had the effect of neutralizing all the advantages previously gained by His Royal Highness. In the dishonourable conduct of his allies in the present campaign, we may find an explanation of the causes which led to the disasters and sufferings endured in the winter of '94 and '95.

"While the Austrians cast aside all consideration for the welfare of their Flemish subjects, and their allies the Dutch and British—the Prince of Orange not being very popular—his allies and supporters, the British,

FEELING OF THE DUTCH 169

were looked upon with an inimical feeling by the Dutch:
the most obvious means of defending their country were
neglected, the fortifications were not repaired, trust-
worthy intelligence was hardly to be obtained, their
fortresses were feebly defended, they made little resistance to their enemies in the field."*

Let the disadvantages against which the Duke of

---

* Mr. Thos. Grenville to Duke of Portland.

Vienna, August 24th, '94

M. de Thugut, the efficient minister of this court (Vienna)
is personally very much disposed (and long has been so) to the
old project of an exchange of the Netherlands, and though that
project appears to be laid aside for the purpose of conciliating
Great Britain and Holland, yet it is evident that M. Thugut's
opinions are such as lead him to set little value upon the possession of the Netherlands, and therefore that every circumstance,
either of expense or of military enterprise, which looks towards
the acquisition and defence of these provinces, is as much dis-
couraged by him as he can venture to do without openly declaring the whole bias of his mind, and it is very remarkable that,
much as we have made it our business to press this to him in
our conversations, we have never yet been able to draw from
him even a cold assent to the idea of the Low Countries being of
any real value in themselves to the Emperor; though he sometimes feebly admits, that with a considerable addition to them,
they might be made so.

I am aware that part of the indifference which I so much
remark in M. Thugut, may be affected for the purpose of throwing the whole weight of the defence of the Low Countries on the
maritime powers. But if that is his policy, he must mean to
support it by abstaining from vigorous exertion, and the result

170 WAR IN HOLLAND 1794.

York had thus to contend be fairly weighed, and the judgment passed upon him as a General by his countrymen at the time must be very much modified.

The proclamation which was addressed to the Germanic circles by the Prince of Coburg, explaining

will be equally fatal, whether the inactivity arises from feigned or real opinion.

What decision the Cabinet will make on their heavy demands for subsidy I know not, but I know not how to hope that a subsidy will give vigour to their councils, or enterprise to their armies. There is no soul in the bodies of these men—none at least which is alive to the magnitude of all the objects now at stake, or which leads them to share with you, as it ought, the great points of common danger and common interest, and while these mainsprings are wanting, it is in vain to look for such movements and effects as cannot be produced without them.

All M. de Thugut's conversation, even upon the idea of a subsidy, is evidently adverse to the prosecuting of the war in the Netherlands, and even when the danger of Holland is urged as a powerful argument for this course, he very coldly answers that, supposing the French to succeed in Holland for a time, they would be glad enough to relinquish it if the armies of the allies were successful in the interior of France.

I confess that I suspect this disinclination to the defence of the Netherlands to arise not only from a habit of undervaluing them, but partly, too, from a persuasion that the maritime powers must and will, at their own expense, protect them; and partly also, from a narrow and timid view of collecting the whole Austrian force on the German frontier, so as to be more immediately ready for the defence of the Imperial dominions, as well as to have less reason to fear in their jealousy of the intentions of the King of Prussia.

AUSTRIAN PROCLAMATION. 171

the causes which had led to the withdrawal of the Imperial troops, and justifying that measure, is characterised by Colonel Calvert as one of the most impudent papers ever published.

This paper states that the "inexhaustible resources of France, its innumerable cohorts, *the inactivity of a blinded people (the Belgians)*, who would not listen to the paternal voice of their good prince, and the secret practices of some of their ambitious representatives, are the causes which have caused the Imperial armies to retreat."

The proclamation then proceeds to threaten to plunder the country before leaving it, on the grounds of withdrawing *whatever the enemy might find for subsistence.*

On the 4th August, the Duke took up a position near Osterhout, in the hope of securing Bois-le-Duc and Breda, and deterring the enemy from attempting Bergen Op Zoom.

On the 28th of the month a general attack was made on the outposts of the Duke's army, as well as on those of H.R.H. the Prince of Orange ; in consequence of this, a council of war was assembled in the afternoon, at which it was decided that as the object for which the position at Osterhout had been occupied was now attained, it was not desirable to remain there any

172 WAR IN HOLLAND 1794.

longer, and the army marched at night and encamped the next afternoon at Bois-le-Duc.

Valenciennes and Conde having fallen in consequence of the secret understanding between France and Austria, 40,000 men were thus liberated to swell the ranks of Pechigru's army, and the last hope of the allied Dutch and British army being able to maintain itself was cut off.

By the middle of September the allies had retreated to the vicinity of Nimegnen, and the only barrier separating them from the enemy was the Meuse.

The difficulty of obtaining correct intelligence at this time, is thus alluded to in a letter from Colonel Calvert to Lord St. Helens, dated September 13:—" I have waited on General Doughlas, who commands at Bois-le-Duc, by his Royal Highness's order, to represent to him that owing to the change of language and other circumstances, I am apprehensive that our intelligence may be very defective, and to request his assistance in procuring some new channels of information.

" General Doughlas assured me that he was very willing to give us any assistance in his power; but that the disaffection of the people in this part of the country was so great, that it was entirely out of his power to be of any service to us in the present instance.

INTELLIGENCE DEPARTMENT. 173

"I need not represent to you how very essential it is that our intelligence should be good at this time, and, I request the favour of you to be so kind as to interest yourself in procuring us Dutch agents for that purpose, if possible. The neglect of our allies on this subject, renders it more necessary for us to bestow on it the utmost attention."

174   NARRATIVE OF A SPY.

CHAPTER THE TWELFTH.

Narrative of a Spy.

AMONGST the papers of the late General Graham, there is a curious manuscript in the handwriting of a person employed as a spy at this time, which is interesting in connection with the passage thus quoted from the journal of the officer charged with the Secret Intelligence Department.

The writer gives the following account of himself: —" I happened to be in the capital of France when *Brissot*, of execrable memory, ridiculously declared war against the *Sovereign* of Great Britain and Ireland, without including *his subjects!* to them he offered health, fraternity, and good wishes, while he hurled defiance and insult at the prince, whose battles they were bound to fight by every law of nature, by inclination as well as duty! By my writings, which appeared every other day in an esteemed Paris print, I aimed at and obtained the honour of being considered as a royalist; my essays drew upon me (which flattered me not a little) the fixed odium of all factors of insurrection in general, and of all

FLIGHT FROM PARIS. 175

the British in particular, who had fled to Paris from the justice of the offended laws of their native land ; several times was I arrested, either for expressing my detestation of the infamous system pursued by the worse than atheistical rulers of France, or because I was found not armed with a *citizen's card,* which I never could stoop to solicit at my section ; and as often did I escape republican vengeance by my own ingenuity and devices ; but among a people so lively and subtle as the French, it was impossible to think of persisting in the idea of remaining in Paris, though to quit it without a passport was to expose myself to the probable horrors of the guillotine ; all correspondence and intercourse with England, however, was cut off by the declaration of war, and I thought it advisable, in the distressful alternative I then stood, to risk a flight to the army of his royal highness the Duke of York, who was just landed on the continent with his royal father's Foot Guards.

" After an unpleasant variety of ever-succeeding difficulties and hair-breadth escapes from the vigilance of an alert enemy, I arrived at Famars the 24th of May 1793, the day after the allies drove the French from the famous heights of that name, and that British valour shone so conspicuous in the field of trial.

" The Duke of York's head-quarters at that time were at the chateau, and the celebrated Marquis de Bouillé, then with his royal highness, was the first person of con-

176   NARRATIVE OF A SPY.

sequence with whom I had the honour of conversing.
On hearing my account of the state of affairs in France,
and my adventures in making my escape, he expressed
his opinion that *I might make myself very useful to his
royal highness,* and recommended me to Colonel Calvert,
in charge of the secret intelligence department.

"One of Colonel Calvert's first questions was, 'By whom
could I get myself recommended?' My answer was, 'I
conceived my reasoned abhorrence of French principles
was a sufficiently loyal introduction to a chief who was
directing all his exertions against the new-fangled doctrines of unfledged republicans; but that if more was
required, I had reason to think, that in writing to a certain illustrious secretary, and reminding his lordship of
the contents of *four anonymous letters* addressed to him
from Paris (letters not only fully expressive of what
was at that moment machinating against his countrymen
and mine, but greatly portentous of the dire effects which
we, with the astonished universe, have severally witnessed), there was a possibility of my being honoured
with a recommendatory answer from that virtuous nobleman.' I observed at the same time, that my letters
were sent without a signature, because I looked for no
reward for acquitting myself of a sacred duty.

"I know not what, or if any, answer was returned, nor
had I any reason to be over anxious to learn that circumstance, as an opportunity soon presented itself, of

SECRET MISSIONS.   177

which I very eagerly availed myself, and proved beyond the reach of doubt, that as I had the will, so I had the faculty of recommending myself.

"I shall but glance at the first services which I was enabled to render in the short course of a month up to the 21st June. During that time I made various excursions to the close vicinity of Dunkirk; I visited Cambray, and obtained certain information relative to the strength of that place, the quantity of provisions in the garrison, and the state of the public mind, the exact number of regular troops in the place, the number of the new levies, every piece of artillery, with its calibre, and the quantity of arms in the citadel; but above all, the prevailing spirit of the magistrates and inhabitants, who wished to admit a conqueror of any nation that was friendly to the ancient government of France. Posterity will perhaps have to regret that the allies made only a *feint* to sit down before that respectable city, which was ready to open its gates through necessity to the first summons of the conquering general.

"On the 21st June 1793, being sent on a mission not less important than hazardous, I judged it to be in unison with prudence and policy to wait on the Austrian officer who had the permanent command of the extreme outposts, and to solicit his friendly aid and advice towards the completion of the design I had in view,

178 NARRATIVE OF A SPY.

"*Major Baron O'Brady* then had his quarters at Douchy, in the neighbourhood of Bouchain, and more immediately commanded the Tyrolean sharpshooters; as often as the Prince of Saxe Coburg had occasion to send a well-informed officer with a flag to the enemy, so often did Major O'Brady find it his turn to be designated by his Serene Highness the commander-in-chief; and it will appear in the sequel how much the French general, who was acquainted with his military worth, dreaded the splendour of his talents.

"The major, after having looked over the morning reports, shewed me on his map the exact spot on which stood every vidette through the entire chain of posts; the position of all the pickets, the villages which our and the enemy's patrols visited alternately, to which he added every other information I could either solicit or require.

"The Austrian chiefs order secret service better than other chiefs do with whom we are acquainted.

"After having taken leave of my friend, I proceeded towards the enemy's lines, and was overtaken by a strong reconnoitring party of Barco's Austrian Hussars. I had some slight knowledge of the officer who led them on; to him I communicated my intentions in Latin, as he could not speak French, and he, squeezing my hand, uttered these expressions, '*Hic maneas velim dum redeam; noli charissime vel minime progredi.*' I deemed

EXCITING POSITION. 179

it advisable to wait the issue of the expedition, and I waited accordingly at the *ferme de Fleury*.

"It happened that the French General had that very morning issued an order to drum in all our outposts and almost immediately the troops were mounting, and proceeding to carry his will into execution. Both parties met, and after an obstinate and bloody contest, the Austrians, infinitely inferior in numbers, were compelled to fall back, and finally to seek safety in flight. Seeing the Hussars returning, I fondly hoped that victory had declared for them, but the sad reverse proved to be the fact—closely pursued by the enemy, nothing but the fleetness of their horses could have saved them from falling into their hands.

"When I perceived what I most dreaded, I ran back into the farm house, in which I deposited in a paillasse my pocket-book, that contained a general pass signed by the Duke, and another important paper in German bearing the signature of His Serene Highness the Prince of Coburg, either of which instruments, had they been found in my possession, would, by every law of war, have subjected me to certain and immediate death.

"The French dragoons soon rode into the farm-yard, and, on their asking the woman of the house if she had got any of the enemy under her roof, she, who had purchased a great quantity of church lands, and was,

180   NARRATIVE OF A SPY.

through interest as well as perhaps inclination, friendly
to the government of the day, answered in the affirma-
tive, and said there was an Englishman within—in fine,
I was taken prisoner.

"The monsters into whose gripe it was my fate
to fall had nothing human in their composition but
their form. They treated me with a degree of savage
cruelty of refined torture, of which perhaps the most
untutored Indians are incapable. Not contented with
the submission I testified, they struck me repeatedly,
some with the but-ends of their pistols, others with their
sabres ; they then drove me before them through a deep
though narrow river—the Selle—in which I must have
inevitably perished, had I not caught hold of the long
tail of the sergeant's horse, which could swim faster than
any of the others.

"My captors, apprehending no pursuit from the
Austrians, very deliberately alighted, and proceeded to
plunder me systematically. They began with putting
me in the state of nature, and took whatever they
thought valuable from me, nor could I prevail on
them, for the sake of decency, to return me my shirt !
They gave me back my coat and waistcoat, and it was
with the greatest difficulty they would allow me to keep
my pantaloons. Notwithstanding my extremely unpleasant position, I could not help observing with what
joy, not to say ecstasy, they contemplated the golden

UNDER THE GALLOWS. 181

profiles of the ill-fated monarch whom they had helped
to murder by siding with his executioners.

" In this very uncomfortable situation was I conducted to Lieutenant St Arnaud, and to the quarters of
the officer who had command of the outposts. He received me with humanity, gave me one of his own shirts,
ordered a surgeon to dress my wounds, and bathe my
contusions with salt and water—it was then about four
o'clock in the afternoon. An orderly dragoon was commanded to escort me to the quarters of a general whose
name I do not recollect ; but the man mistook his road,
and went five leagues out of his way. At length we
met an officer of the Staff on the road, and he advised
him to take me to *Paillencour*, to the quarters of *Adjutant-General Cherin*.

"The way to Paillencour lay through the famous
Camp de Cæsar. As I was proceeding through the
camp, the soldiers who perceived my black cockade, desired me to take it out and not offend, as they were
pleased to say, their sight with a badge of slavery. I
refused to comply, and told them as it was the *national
cockade* of England, it became them better than it would
me to tear it from my hat. I am free to own the extravagant impolicy of my conduct, which so exasperated
the soldiery that they determined, one and all, to sacrifice me to their detestation of troops sent by foreign
powers to interfere with their internal government, for

182   NARRATIVE OF A SPY.

it was that that Frenchmen argued then as well as now. Already was a picket planted as a gallows—already were the cords prepared, while I looked on the apparatus of death with an unconcern which I conceived did honour to the cause for which I was going to breathe my last.

"Just as I was seized for execution, the officers rushed from their tents, sword in hand, ordered the men in *the name of the law* to desist, and at length, with the greatest difficulty, they succeeded in rescuing me from the fate which seemed to await me. I still had my cockade, and have it to this moment, though I do not wear it. My death was, I believe, reported, and I have heard that H. R. H. expressed his high concern for my fate. If that be so, I can only say I am more indebted to the Royal Duke for his gratuitous uneasiness on that occasion than for any other subsequent favour which H. R. H. has conferred on me.

"Unaffected by any emotion of joy for my providential escape, nor of grief for being about to experience all the horrors to which a prisoner of war is liable, I was escorted to Paillencour.

"There I commenced an acquaintance with Adjutant-General Cherin who was at the head of the intelligence department—a man of acute conceptions, subtle, eloquent, and enterprising, he had full powers from Commanding General to act as he thought proper. The contents of the military chest were at his disposal, and

HOSPITABLY ENTERTAINED. 183

he was considered as the soul of the army. *Secret service* will perhaps never be managed by a man so capable, and when Custine named him to the department he at once proved he was a judge of superior merit, and strongly devoted to the cause for which he fought, and for the true spirit of which he *died*, however contrary to this assertion the general opinion may prove.

"*Spies* are the first acquisition which an able general should aim at. They are his eyes, and without them he is left in utter darkness with respect to the enemy's force, their accurate position, and the designs they have formed against his army.

"*Cherin* received me well, and after a variety of questions which I answered as I thought proper, I begged to know to what part of France it was intended I should be sent prisoner. He replied that there was time enough to think of it, as it was necessary the General, who was then at Lisle, should decide that question. Cherin in the meantime treated me with so much kindness, that had he not been a Frenchman and I a subject of Great Britain, I should have supposed his sentiments to be of a friendly nature towards me; but as we mutually stood, sincerity must be supposed out of the question.

"The third day of my captivity, which in reality had nothing dreadful in it but the name, General Custine,* as I was informed by one of the adjuncts to the staff of

* Appendix D.

184 NARRATIVE OF A SPY.

the army, arrived at head-quarters in Cambray. Cherin, who conceived a much higher notion of me than I in any manner deserved, reported me in such colours to the Commander-in-Chief that he was ordered by the latter to offer me any terms in order to induce me to accept a command in the Republican army, and a brigade of cavalry was actually offered to me!

"I assured *Citizen Cherin* that, however highly the General thought of the talents which he lent me, he could not but condemn me in his heart if I, through any consideration, consented to serve against my native land. I told him that though I had the most respectful regard for several of the French emigrants, I could not bring myself to esteem them as a body of men collectively engaged for the destruction of their country, with several other direct objections which do not for the moment occur to my memory. It was in vain that arguments were used to bring me over to a system which I abhorred; and I finally requested that the unpleasant topic should never more be mentioned to me.

"That I became a prisoner without having the smallest piece of paper, and without even a pocket-book about me, seemed a matter of much surprise to the French, who are ever awake to suspicion ; in consequence of which, and as a proof the General resented my rejection of his offer, he sent a reconnoitring party of 300 men to the farm-house where I was taken, with strict orders to search very minutely whether I had or not deposited any papers in the rooms in which I had been. I heard with pleasure that my pocket-book, which I had every right to call the "Book of Fate," had not been discovered.

"I was particularly indebted to a young officer on the staff, who is still in the service, but whose name my regard for his welfare forbids me to mention. He was bred up in the army, was by principle a royalist, and had not emigrated for two very honourable reasons. Infamy he knew would attach to his character if he acted as a hireling against his country, and he had an aged father living who would become liable to all the horrors of persecution if he quitted his post, which he emphatically termed the "post of religion." This gentleman, who spoke a little English, never failed hinting to me the daily occurrences of the army, and what more particularly concerned myself.

I lived thus for several days at the most luxurious table, and having the most exquisite wines. I always dined with the adjutant-general, and usually supped with some of the superior officers of the staff. Abundance and good humour presided at our board; and, while conviviality prevailed, the main point was not neglected. Service was carried on both with an exemplary rigour and justice that would have done honour to a veteran army.

"At length General Custine sent me his compliments

186 NARRATIVE OF A SPY.

by his freind *Cherin*, and wished to know if I had any objection to see him. Astonished at the question, I replied that the Commander-in-Chief of the enemy's army had only to order a prisoner of war into his presence to be obeyed; and as I had been told that the general would swallow the most nauseous dose of adulation, I added that, to satisfy my curiosity, had Caesar been my contemporary, I would record it as a flattering circumstance of my life to have even the most distant intercourse with that gallant leader.

" *Custine* came down to Paillencour, and on my being introduced to him, he told me that as soon as he was informed I had been his prisoner, he gave orders I should be treated with comfort and distinction. I replied he had been most religiously obeyed, and that I considered myself very much indebted to Adjutant-General *Cherin* for carrying his commands into prompt and cheerful execution. The General then entered fully into the cause of the war, regretted that England should have, by what he termed machinations unworthy of a great people, compelled France to act in a hostile manner against her; he declared, however, that he did not think the British Government in earnest, and that it was merely to feel the pulse of Europe that *Mr. Pitt* made a feint against French liberty ; that that great man was too enlightened not to foresee that, though the French nation might experience a variety of difficulties

TEMPTING OFFER. 187

in rearing their infant freedom to maturity, they would ultimately succeed in the glorious undertaking. He added, I hope like a *pseudo-prophet*, that if his country should, in the actual contest, prevail over the exertions of the combined world, which to him appeared probable in the highest degree, England would ere long be reduced to an ultra-marine department of republican France. The General then came to the object of his visit to *Paillencour*. He lamented, or pretended to lament, that I rejected the splendid appointment to which he was ready to name me, but said though he was so well convinced I cherished liberty in my heart, that he came down with the design of furnishing me with another argument in favour of the idol to which Frenchmen were sacrificing their ease, their lives, and every thing but their national honour. He concluded with making me the solemn offer of 25,000 *livres in specie* per month, if on my return to the Duke of York's head-quarters, I would consent to transmit him every circumstantial detail relative to the allied army, together with 30,000 *livres also in hard cash* if I delivered Baron O'Brady into his hands!

"I requested four and twenty hours to reflect on the important proposition, though at the moment my mind was made up to act in diametrical opposition to what I intended to promise in order to obtain my liberty.

"The four and twenty hours being nearly elapsed, the French general came down to receive my final answer.

188　　　　NARRATIVE OF A SPY.

I promised him everything he wished, and it is equally certain he believed me.

"The General then, with Cherin, continued almost uninterruptedly in the apartment which had been allotted for me. He thought no time was to be lost, and in consequence wrote a letter, which he told me to copy, and which I addressed to Colonel **Harry Calvert**, hoping his Royal Highness would, or the colonels representing the matter to him, kindly, and as my natural protector, claim me as a British subject not carrying arms against France, and of course coming within the regulations established by the contending generals. Custine, in the letter which he caused me to copy and sign as if the dictates of my own free will, set forth I was considered by the enemy in a very suspicious light; that I was kept a close prisoner in the citadel of Cambray, that I was lying upon straw in a dungeon, having only half a pound of bread per day, some small beer and a little broth, and finally that I had experienced extreme difficulty in obtaining the permission to request H. R. H. to exert his best endeavours to rescue me from the fatal end which menaced me

"The French general acted thus politically, under the persuasion that the Duke of York, being informed I was still alive, would lose no time in claiming me, and that then my pledged word would be soon put to the test.

"With the letter here alluded to, General Custine sent

SPY IN DOUBLE CAPACITY. 189

a chief of division, who asked leave from the outposts to deliver it in person, to which H. R.H. consented, on condition of his being blindfolded coming through the allies' camp. The Frenchman objected to the mode, gave the letter to Major O'Brady, who signed a receipt for it; it was immediately forwarded to head-quarters, and I was claimed by H. R. H. in a manner highly flattering to my pride.

"In the meantime General Custine returned me much more money than his soldiers had plundered me of when they took me prisoner. He introduced me to his *spies*, with whom I was to keep up an habitual intercourse. He gave me, in his own handwriting, the detail of important questions, to which he required positive and circumstantial answers. He gave me a letter for the person at Mons, who was, by his order, to pay me 25,000 livres a month, and 30,000 for delivering up Major O'Brady into the hands of the French. He then ordered a guard of dragoons and a party of the *maré chaussée*, with a trumpet, etc. etc., to escort me as far as the Austrian outposts. He hoped I would not take it ill that I should be blindfolded going through the different French camps, as to go otherwise would at once excite the surprise of both armies. I rode a very fine charger of *Custine's* on this occasion.

"The first officer I spoke to was Major O'Brady, who received me with marked attention and friendship. I

190   NARRATIVE OF A SPY.

told him I had a message to deliver to him from his
friend *Cherin,* and that I was to receive 30,000 livres
for putting him into the hands of the republicans.   He
replied undauntedly, ' *If the fellows ever take me, it shall
not be before I am dead.'*

"The major lent me a horse of his own, and sent an
orderly hussar with me to the British head-quarters,
where, as soon as I arrived, I got a small box, into
which I put the money I received from *Custine,* the
papers he gave me for my instructions, the ' *Républicain
Français,'* which he desired me to give the Duke of
York *from him*—all these articles, with a letter from
myself explanatory of the whole, I caused to be delivered
into the hands of Colonel Calvert, for the inspection of
His Royal Highness, who testified his full approbation
of my conduct, and mentioned me with distinction to
the Prince of Coburg, and two days afterwards Colonel
Calvert took down in writing the various observations I
had made during my captivity, in consequence of what
I could collect at table from the very communicative
company whose society I enjoyed.   These observations
were at that time deemed of high importance."

The foregoing record of the services of this spy were
drawn up in consequence of a misunderstanding which
he had in the sequel with Colonel Calvert and His
Royal Highness the Duke of York on the subject of

GENERAL CHAPUY. 191

remuneration for his services. In addition to his loyalty, evinced in the instance just narrated, he asserts that it was through his correspondence with the French generals, *Custine* and his successor *Hochard*,* that the enemy never once interrupted the blockade of Condé, or attempted to raise the siege of Valenciennes, and he contrasts his own conduct with that of other people employed on secret service for the British army, who were, he states, *Frenchmen*, who abhorred the English name, who gave to the enemy every information they could wish to obtain against the allied army, and concealed every important object from the British.

Upon the merits of this case it is impossible to form an opinion at the present date, but the statement of the impediments which the British encountered in obtaining correct information seems to accord very well with the observations in various passages of Colonel Calvert's correspondence.

There is a discrepancy between the narrative of the Spy and Colonel Calvert's memoirs, in relation to the circumstances under which the French General Chapuy fell into the hands of the Allies. In Calvert he is stated to have been taken prisoner; in the other narrative it is stated that he deserted to the English on 26th April 1794.

* Appendix E.

192   MEMOIR OF GENERAL GRAHAM.

CHAPTER THE THIRTEENTH.

Campaign in Holland continued.*

AT the end of September General Clairfayt found himself obliged to abandon his position behind the Roer. This movement rendered the position of the British and

* Mr. THOMAS GRENVILLE to Lord GRENVILLE.

VIENNA, *Sept* 1, 1794.

From this letter it would appear that Austria wished to obtain a loan of two millions, secured upon the revenues of the low countries

The following is a curious picture of the tortuous policy of Austria and Prussia —

"They (the Austrians) dwell certainly upon the difference which they state between loan and subsidy, and wish to prove to us that their offer of security upon the revenues of the Low Countries should, at least by us (who always insist on those territories remaining in the House of Austria), be accepted as a good and ample mortgage for the repayment of the sums which they want for this year and the next ; but if it is true that they do not feel interested at heart in these possessions, or if they think us so earnest in our wishes on this subject that thay may safely throw the whole weight of it upon us, their offer of a *hypothèque* on those possessions takes a much more suspicious character; nor is it perhaps an unreasonable jealousy on my part to apprehend that they may wish you to have a mortgage of two millions on the Netherlands, as an inducement to you hereafter to give up

EXPOSED SITUATION OF LEFT FLANK. 193

Hanoverians no longer tenable, their left being unco-
vered, while the enemy appeared also in considerable

some of your French acquisitions in the West Indies, in order to
recover for them a country in which you will have a large pecu-
niary stake, added to the ordinary course of political observations

"Much, at least, of M. Thugut's conversations would seem to
tally with this view of the matter It is observable that he perpetually recurs to its being a settled point that, *de façon ou
d'autre*, the Netherlands will be secured to Austria at the peace,
and yet he never seems (in his view of the military operations
to be pursued) to consider them as a main object of defence, and
is so little disposed to make them so, that he expresses much
reluctance at the idea proposed of engaging Austria to furnish so
large an army to *act in that country*, which he thinks might be
better employed elsewhere. Add to this his remarking that
England might be satisfied by the irrevocable detriment done to
the navy and commerce of France ; and his contrasting the difference in point of acquisitions made by Great Britain with the total
failure on the side of Austria ; and it is no great refinement to
suspect the whole of this to lead to an expectation that we may
better buy back the Netherlands for them than put them to the
expense of defending them or regaining them , and that we
should have an additional motive for sacrificing some of our con-
quests to this object, if we have two millions of money mort-
gaged upon it.

"If the Emperor's personal character had steadiness enough
to influence the Government, his disposition to the true principles of the war would be a great security to us , at present,
however, it is of little or no avail.

"With respect to the ministers, Thugut is certainly the most
efficient minister here ; very diligent and laborious in his office.
What *we*, however, miss in him is either the disposition or the
capacity to see the present great crisis of Europe upon the large
scale on which it should be looked at by the leading Minister of

194 MEMOIR OF GENERAL GRAHAM.

force on their left. Accordingly, the Duke found it advisable to prepare to pass the Waal. With this object in view, he placed the reserve on the right bank this empire ; instead of which we see a cold, narrow, and contracted view of this subject—many discouraging tokens of that total want of manly energy and direct dealing, without which all co-operation must necessarily be languid or feeble , always taking merit for having sent the most distinct orders to try the relief of Valenciennes, yet never taking the obvious mode of satisfying us by communicating these orders to us ; maintaining as an argument for the loan, that without it the army cannot move, yet, at the same time, resisting our objections of the delay of waiting for answers from M. de Marcy, by stating this movement as being actually in great forwardness, and not depending on the loan for its execution ; acquiescing in the change of command urged by us, and yet, ever since that event, reminding us that, in his opinion, this very change may defeat the operation which we wished to assist by it ; gratifying our impatience at one time by counting up the days to the probable time of the desired movement, and then again stating that Clairfayt's army may be weakened too much to attempt it by his detaching, perhaps considerably, towards the side of Treves ; complaining that the Austrians had been prevented from sending Blankenstein's corps towards Flanders, as they wished, by the Prussians having engaged it in their line of defence, and yet refusing to us a corps much more inconsiderable and not involved in the objection—I mean the corps of Condé—a corps, too, which, as I have before observed, from their own statement of their want of money, they should have been glad to have seen transferred to the pay of another country

" These and many other such traits of inconsistency I advert to only as being descriptive of the very unsatisfactory manner in which our business is discussed, always providing, on their side, apologies for future failures, instead of means of success and projects of vigour and enterprise "

EVACUATION OF NIMEGUEN.

opposite St. Andrè, a strong corps in Nimeguen, and the rest stretching away from thence to Emmerick.

The position was strengthened by batteries erected at intervals upon the dyke, which ran along the river, and a road was made behind the dyke for the passage of guns, carriages, etc. The Hessians and Hanoverians were on the British left, and the Dutch were on their right, extended as far as Gorcum.

On the 4th November, the enemy having formed a trench and a work within 500 yards of the British position, it became evident that Nimeguen must be evacuated, as the Dutch, notwithstanding repeated representations, had neglected to put the place into a defensible state. To favour this movement, the troops, without firing a shot, entered the enemy's entrenchment and put all they found to the bayonet , and the cavalry sweeping round the flanks made great havoc amongst the fugitives

Nimeguen was entirely evacuated on the 9th ; in this operation, the enemy having brought some guns to bear on the bridge, a random shot cut a cable, by which part of the bridge swung round to the enemy's side, and about 800 Dutch were taken prisoners.

In a journal of this war, by a most intelligent man, Corporal Brown of the Guards, the above entry on the subject of the loss of 800 Dutch is followed by the pithy remark—" The loss would not be great if they were all taken."

196   MEMOIR OF GENERAL GRAHAM.

Amongst other stories current in the army with regard to our Dutch allies, it was said that a Dutch general, who had an excellent billet in a house where there was some very good wine with a yellow seal in the cellar, had not long enjoyed his good fortune when an order arrived to move his brigade immediately. He called for his A.D C. and asked him how much of the yellow seal remained in the cellar? On receiving a reply, he said, How long will it take us to finish it? Oh, till to-morrow afternoon, was the answer. Very well, then, give out an order to march at 2 o'clock to-morrow.

About the middle of November a severe frost set in, but before the end of the month a change took place, and by the thaw the roads, except on the dykes, became almost impassable, and the sickness amongst the British increased to such an extent that thirty or forty men died daily in the hospitals.

Early in December, in consequence of the return of the Duke of York to England, Count Walmoden succeeded to the command of the allied army, and under him Lord Harcourt took command of the British contingent.*

---

* The transfer of the command of the army to other hands had been for some time in contemplation. Such a measure had been proposed to the king in the month of August, and ministers at the sametime recommended that Lord Cornwallis should be appointed the Duke's successor. His Majesty consented to Mr Wyndham's being despatched to the Continent to propose this

FRENCH CROSS THE WAAL. 197

On the 11th December the enemy crossed the Waal near the point of separation of that river and the Rhine, and spiked some guns, but two Hanoverian battalions

measure to the Duke, merely observing that, in his son's place, he should prefer to return home if the command should be given to Lord Cornwallis, although he should not object to its being given to General Clairfayt.

Lord Grenville, writing to his brother Mr Thomas Grenville, from London, August 29, 1762, thus refers to the proposed transfer of the command of the army in Holland —

"The Austrian government is already prepared for your proposal respecting the giving to Lord Cornwallis the command of the whole combined force, as Count Staremberg is apprised of it, having indeed, himself, in a great measure, suggested the measure, on some general hints which I threw out to him to try the ground For the moment the great point seems to be to bring them to acquiesce in the virtual command, which his rank of field-marshal will give him over Clairfayt, and to send positive orders to the latter to that effect , and, if there should be any difficulty in Clairfayt's submitting to this, then to let Clairfayt absent himself for the moment, and leave the Austrian troops under the command of some officer whose standing will occasion no difficulty in this respect. You will observe that, by virtual command, we mean precisely the same deference as the Duke of York has shewn to the Prince of Coburg, not extending to any of the points of military etiquette by which command is usually rendered ostensible, but going to the effect of complying with his suggestions respecting the mode of executing the operations agreed upon in concert, when the instructions of his court do not interfere with such suggestions Before you receive this letter, Lord Cornwallis will probably be on the spot , and it is, therefore, urgent, to prevent the first beginning of dissension, that no time should be lost in making the Austrians give their orders to Clairfayt."

198   MEMOIR OF GENERAL GRAHAM.

arriving, they were driven out of the battery and obliged to retreat.

Hitherto the army had expected to go into winter quarters, and the Duke would appear to have been under the impression that he had left the troops in a secure position for wintering; for in writing to Sir H. Calvert from England at this time, his royal highness treats the apprehensions of Count Walmoden and General Harcourt very lightly, expressing his opinion that by proper care it would be impossible for the enemy to pass the Waal.

But all hopes of winter quarters were soon at an end, it became evident that the enemy intended to give the British force no rest ; the very elements also lent their aid to drive our troops from their position, for the ice became sufficiently strong to bear artillery. Thus, the very stream which had been looked upon as affording a barrier to the advance of the enemy, became a bridge to facilitate his approach, and greater vigilance became necessary, whilst from the extreme hardships the troops were exposed to, their effective numbers were daily diminishing.

On the 27th the French crossed the ice and surprised the Dutch in the Bommeler Waard, a point of vital importance. They succeeded in gaining possession of the island and town of Bommel, and pursued the Dutch over the Waal, which had also become practicable, and established themselves at Tuil.

FRENCH DRIVEN ACROSS THE WAAL. 199

Matters remained in this way for two days, when a corps of British and Hessians, under Major-General Dundas, attacked the enemy at Tuil, drove them out of that place, and obliged them to recross the Waal.

The allies were not in sufficient strength to attempt the recovery of the Bommeler Waard, but they took four pieces of cannon.*

In this bright little episode, in the dreary retreat of the army, Major Graham acted as major to the light

* HEAD QUARTERS, Arnheim,
January 1, 1794.

Sir—I have the honour to lay before your Royal Highness the report of the success of the attack made on the enemy on the 30th ult. by Major-General David Dundas.

The corps destined for this expedition consisted of ten battalions of British infantry under Major-General Lord Cathcart, Major-General Gordon, and Lieutenant-Colonel M'Kenzie; six squadrons of light cavalry, and 160 hussars, under Major-General Sir Robert Lawrie, of the loyal " emigrés," and of four battalions and four squadrons of Hessians under Major-General de Wurmb

It was divided into three columns The left column to attack by the dyke, the centre to attack in such a manner as to keep the church of Wardenburgh upon its left wing, " appuyè" to the Vliet, to turn Tuyl, and to attack it in the rear

Major-General Lord Cathcart found the road by which his column was to march so impracticable, that being obliged to make a great " detour," he could not come up in time ; and Major-General Dundas finding, at his arrival near Wardenburgh, that the enemy had abandoned it during the night, he thought it advisable to push on with the other two columns and to begin the attack immediately upon Tuyl

This was executed with such gallantry and spirit by the troops

200 MEMOIR OF GENERAL GRAHAM.

infantry battalion, which led the advance of Major-General Dundas's corps.

From this time till the 9th February, the frost continued intense, snow also falling occasionally. During the whole of that time the allies were continually retreating, the enemy close upon their heels, provisions and fuel very scarce; half the army sick, and the other half almost completely worn out with incessant hard duty. Corporal Brown, in his interesting journal, under date January 7, says—" This is now the tenth day since any of us has had a night's rest or had time to undress"

In fact it was a daily alert, the whole army between the Waal and the Leck ought to be considered on picket duty.

At one time a partial thaw afforded a hope that the line of the Waal might still be maintained, but orders

that, notwithstanding the natural strength of this post, the " abbatis" of fruit trees that were made, the batteries of the town of Bommel, which flanked the approach, and the considerable number of men who defended it, it was soon carried, and the enemy driven across the river (everywhere passable on the ice) with considerable loss of men and of four pieces of cannon

General Dundas speaks in the highest terms of commendation of the spirited conduct both of the officers and men during the execution of the several duties which fell to their lot, as likewise the patience and perseverance they shewed by undergoing immense fatigues and hardships, increased by the cold and the severity of the season

(Signed)   WALMODEN, General

AFFAIR AT ELDERMALSEN.

were no sooner issued with that object in view, than the returning frost rendered counter orders necessary. On the morning of the 8th, General Dundas moved in the direction of Beuren, in pursuance of the orders first issued, and then found all the outposts at Lurgen driven in, and the enemy in force in the neighbourhood. Lord Cathcart was therefore detached to reconnoitre with some Hulans, and the light companies, and part of the 27th Regiment. Finding the enemy not so strong as he expected, he determined to dislodge them, and brought up the remainder of the 27th, the 14th Regiment, and some artillery for that purpose. The 14th formed on the ice, the 27th across the inclosure on the right, and the artillery on the dyke, and marched in that order, driving the enemy before them. The enemy passed the river and formed at Eldermalsen, and from there kept up a heavy fire of musketry and grape. The British line advanced without a halt, and the 27th, changing direction as it approached the mill, charged the village across the ice beyond the burnt bridge, and took the cannon, while the 14th entered the town on the right. The enemy retreated with precipitation, but returned and renewed the attack, and the position was only finally maintained at a heavy sacrifice. From this time the retreat was continued until the army reached Bremen and embarked for England.

The sufferings endured by all ranks were hardly sur-

202 MEMOIR OF GENERAL GRAHAM.

passed by those which the Grand Army of Napoleon subsequently underwent on the retreat from Moscow.

Corporal Brown, in his journal already referred to, thus depicts his feelings on the 16th January—"After a very tedious journey, about three o'clock in the afternoon we reached the verge of an immense desert, called the Welaw ; when, instead of having gained a resting place for the night as we expected, we were informed that we had fifteen miles further to go. Upon this information many began to be much dejected, and not without reason, for several of us, besides suffering the severity of the weather and fatigue of the march, had neither eat nor drank anything except water that day.

" For the first three or four miles such a dismal prospect appeared as none of us was ever witness to before , a bare sandy desert, with a tuft of withered grass or solitary shrub here and there ; the wind was excessive high, and drifted snow and sand, together so strong, that we could hardly wrestle against it ; to which was added a severity of cold almost insupportable. The frost was so intense that the water which came from our eyes, freezing as it fell, hung in icicles to our eyelashes ; and our breath freezing as soon as emitted, lodged in heaps of ice about our faces, and on the blankets or coats that were wrapped about our heads

" Night fast approaching, a great number, both men and women began to linger behind, their spirits being

SUFFERINGS OF THE ARMY. 203

quite exhausted, and without hopes of reaching their destination ; and if they once lost sight of the column of march, though but a few minutes, it being dark, and no track to follow, there was no chance of finding it again. In this state numbers were induced to sit down, or creep under the shelter of bushes, where, weary, spirit-less, and without hope, a few minutes consigned them to sleep—but, alas ! whoever slept awaked no more : their blood almost instantly congealed in their veins, the spring of life soon dried up; and if ever they opened their eyes, it was only to be sensible of the last agonies of their miserable existence

"Others, sensible of the danger of sitting down, but having lost the column, wandered up and down the pathless waste, surrounded with darkness and despair, no sound to comfort their ears, but the bleak whistling wind ; no sight to bless their eyes but the wide track-less desert and '*shapeless drift*,' far from human help, far from pity, down they sank to rise no more !

"About half-past ten o'clock at night we reached Bickborge, when, to add to our misfortunes, we could hardly find room to shelter ourselves from the weather, every house being already filled with Hessian infantry, who are in no respect friendly to the English. In seve-ral houses they positively refused us entrance, and in every one refused us admittance to the fire ; at the same time they posted sentries by the cellar doors to prevent

204   MEMOIR OF GENERAL GRAHAM.

the inhabitants from selling us any liquors ; even their
commanding officer pushed with his own hands a number of our men neck and heels out of his quarters. Thus
we were situated, till partly by force, partly by stealth,
we crept in where we could, glad to obtain the shelter of
a house at any rate."

And on the 19th—" Perhaps never did a British
army experience such distress as ours does at this time.
Not a village or house but what bears witness to our
misery, in containing some dead, others dying. Some
are daily found who have crawled into houses singly ;
other houses contain five, six, or seven together, some
dead and others dying, or unable to walk , and as for
those who are able, it is no easy matter for them to find
their way, for the country is one continued desert, without roads, and every track filled up with the drifting and
falling snow. Add to all this, the inhabitants are our
most inveterate enemies, and where opportunity offers,
will rather murder a poor lost distressed Englishman
than direct him the right way, several instances of which
we have already known. It is reported that in the
several columns of the army about 700 are missing since
we left the river Leck "

The antipathy of the Dutch was very much increased
by the conduct of the stragglers from the army. In consequence of the depredations of worthless men of this
description, the Dutch shut up their shops at the approach

EFFECT OF POPULAR EXCITEMENT. 205

of the English, and denied them everything, whilst they received the French troops with open arms, because with them their persons were safe; and if their property was taken for the public service, they received in return for it, at all events, payment in paper money.

On reaching Bremen, the inhabitants claimed the privilege of a neutral town, and objected to having any troops quartered on them; but they afterwards consented to receive some of the Hanoverian troops and the Foot Guards, until the transports were ready for their reception; the rest of the troops marched through, and the whole embarked at the Lake of Bremen about the middle of April.

Whenever reverses are sustained by our arms, the public indignation which is excited resembles the whirlwind in its course, sweeping all before it, and the fame of many a valiant deed of arms is lost on such occasions amid the clamour which is raised against the failure or miscarriage of the general objects of the expedition.

It was sufficient that a British army had landed on the Continent and been compelled to retreat and re-embark. The extraordinary severity of the winter enabling the enemy to cross rivers which in ordinary seasons would have proved strong barriers, the defection of the allies which left the British a mere handful before a powerful enemy, and the sickness which was

206   MEMOIR OF GENERAL GRAHAM.

the natural result of the extreme fatigue, privations, and
cold to which the men were exposed, have never been
sufficiently taken into consideration, and because some
stragglers from the ranks brought discredit on themselves, little account has ever been taken of the fortitude
and discipline exhibited by those who made good their
retreat to Bremen, and embarked for England with their
honour untarnished.

HECTOR M'NEIL'S "WAES O' WAR."

Battle fast on battle raging,
 Wed our stalwart youths awa',
Day by day, fresh faes engaging,
 Forced the weary back to fa'.

Driven at last frae post to pillar,
 Left by friends wha ne'er proved true ;
Trick'd by knaves wha *pouch'd our siller*,*
 What could worn out valour do ?

Myriads dark, like gathering thunder
 Bursting, spread owre land and sea,
Left alane, alas ! nae wonder
 Britain's sons ware forced to flee !

Cross the Waal and Yssel frozen,
 Deep thro' bogs and drifted snaw—
Wounded, weak, and spent !—our chosen
 Gallant men now faint and fa' !

  * Prussian fidelity.

WAES O' WAR.

207

On a cart wi' comrades bluiding,
   Stiff wi' gore, and cauld as clay,
Without cover, bed, or bedding,
   Five lang nights Will Gairlace lay !

In a sick-house, damp and narrow
   (Left behint wi' hundreds mair),
See Will neist, wi' pain and sorrow
   Wasting on a bed o' care.

208   MEMOIR OF GENERAL GRAHAM.

CHAPTER THE FOURTEENTH

Appointed Lieutenant-Colonel—Account of Caribs of St.
Vincents.

FROM the dreary swamps of Holland the current of
events now carries us to one of the most romantic spots
perhaps on the face of the earth.

Were it not for the dread created by the epidemics
which occasionally prevail in the islands of the West
Indies, the enchanting scenery which is there presented
would be more visited, and its charms more generally
known. Amongst all these beautiful works of creation
there is perhaps not one more like fairyland than the
island of St Vincents, the scene of those events which
follow next in our narrative.

In the deed of agreement by which this island was
ceded to the British Crown by the French settlers in
1763, those who prepared the deed unfortunately omitted
to insert a clause protecting the rights of the Carib
settlers, a singular native tribe, of whom the following
description was published by John Davis in the seventeenth century.

CARIBS OF ST. VINCENTS. 209

" They are a peculiar race, having but little communication with foreigners, and therefore preserving most of their ancient manners. They have hair, not wool, on their heads. They are quite naked, and laugh at the idea of covering anything, saying, ' You are to look at us *between the eyes only.*' They have a prejudice against the English, because a story is current amongst them of some of the tribe having been inveigled on board an English vessel under the flag of some other nation, and that when they got on board they were charmed with kindness, particularly aqua vitæ, and thus carried off as slaves.

In their wars they highly esteem stratagems and surprises ; they have a superstition that a war they should begin openly would not prosper, so that having landed in an enemy's country, if they are discovered before they have given the first shock, or that a dog should bark at them, thinking it ominous, they return to their own country.

" They are at the same time one of the most warlike of savage tribes. From being brought into collision with Europeans, they have learnt to keep their ranks, and to encamp in advantageous positions, and make some kind of fortifications. When the French landed at Grenada, they thought it would be an easy conquest, but found the Caribeans in a defensive position to oppose their landing—besides this, they laid ambushes,

K 2

210 MEMOIR OF GENERAL GRAHAM.

and having taken up a position on an eminence which could only be approached on one side, they had felled logs on that side ready to be rolled down on the advancing foe"

The commissioners appointed for the sale of lands on the cession of the island to the British crown in 1763, acted with great indiscretion by disposing of lands actually belonging to and in the occupation of the Caribs. These natives very naturally refused to give up property derived from their forefathers , and the resistance which the purchasers met with in attempting to get possession, brought on the war of 1772.

The commissioners having acted in direct contravention of their instructions, by which they were strictly enjoined to respect the property of the Caribs, their conduct was made the subject of parliamentary inquiry, the result of which was a condemnation of the war as unjust and dishonourable. A treaty was then concluded which was highly favourable to the natives

It might have been expected that the measures thus adopted to redress the wrongs inflicted on the Caribs would have secured their fidelity and attachment for the future, but very different was the return which they actually made

While England was engaged in the war with her North American colonies, French emissaries were employed to seduce the Caribs from their allegiance, in

FRENCH REVOLUTIONARY AGENTS. 211

hich they easily succeeded, and through their instru-
entality, assisted partly, it is alleged, by the inca-
city of the governor, the island once more fell into the
nds of the French, with whom it remained until four
ars afterwards, when on the conclusion of peace be-
een Great Britain and the United States, the island
ain reverted to the English on 1st January 1783.

During the time St Vincents was under the French,
very hostile feeling to the English had been exhibited
the Caribs. This feeling was, in a great measure,
nothered after the restoration of the island until the
riod of the French revolution. That great political
nvulsion made itself felt even in these remote islands,
parated from Europe by the breadth of the Atlantic.

The celebrated Victor Hugues was the leading agent
dissemmating revolutionary doctrines in the Antilles,
d his plans were so skilfully devised, that he suc-
eded in gaining adherents in most of the islands where
rench settlers were located. In St. Vincents he was
articularly successful; and after gaining his country-
en, the next step was through their agency to open
mmunication with the Caribs, to rouse their passions,
d incite them to insurrection, by descanting on the
harms of liberty, and distributing inflammatory pro-
lamations, of which this is a specimen :—

"Behold your chains forged, and imposed by the
ands of tyrannical English. Blush and break these en-

212 MEMOIR OF GENERAL GRAHAM.

signs of disgrace, spurn them with becoming indignation ; rise in a moment, and while we assist you from motives of the purest philanthropy and zeal for the happiness of all nations, fall on those despots, extirpate them from this country, and restore yourselves, your wives and children, to the inheritance of your fathers, whose spirits from the graves will lead on your ranks, inspire you with fury, and help you to be avenged."

Such addresses were grateful to the prejudices and passions of the Caribs. They replied, they were flattered and obliged by these professions of friendship extended to them by the French republic ; they were sensible of their oppressions, and felt uneasy beneath them, and delayed hostilities on no other account but because they wanted a sufficient supply of military stores to support the first avowal of their intentions ; that on being furnished with what was requisite in this respect, they would most cheerfully co-operate with their friends and allies, the delegates of the republic, in promoting their influence and the establishment of their own rights.

The French inhabitants who had taken the oath of allegiance to his Britannic Majesty were the active agents in this treasonable movement, nor did they stop at the crime of treason, for their plans, when matured, included a scheme for a general massacre of their enemies of all ages and sexes throughout the island.

Fortunately an able man presided over the affairs of

FORMATION OF 2D WEST INDIA REGIMENT. 213

e island at that time as governor, and being apprised
time by the president of Grenada of an outbreak in
at island, he was enabled to take such precautions as
:feated the diabolical scheme of the French emis-
ries, in concert with the Caribs, for a general massacre ;
it war had now been entered upon which was not to
: quenched without much bloodshed.

This outbreak had just commenced, and urgent en-
eaties from the colonists for protection and assistance,
id just been received when Major Graham returned
ith his regiment from the continent. The reputation
e had acquired there as an active officer of light in-
intry, was such that on his return to England he was
:quested to attend at the Horse Guards, and was in-
irmed of the intention of the government to raise some
lack corps, to be employed in the war then raging with
ie Caribs in the West Indies, and the question was
ut to him, whether he would remain in the position
e then held, or go out to the West Indies as lieutenant-
olonel of one of the new regiments to be raised for
olonial service. His answer was, that he was ready to
o anywhere for the rank of a lieutenant-colonel

Having received his commission as lieutenant-colonel
f the 2d West India Regiment, he sailed for the island
f St Vincents in June 1795, and landed there in Sep-
ember of the same year, with the officers and non-com-
nissioned officers requisite for the formation of the regi-

214 MEMOIR OF GENERAL GRAHAM.

ment. According to his own memorandums to form the regiment, he received a number of slaves the property of planters, some French blacks from Guadaloupe, some Carolina blacks, in all amounting to 400 rank and file.

ST VINCENTS, WEST INDIES. 215

CHAPTER THE FIFTEENTH.

Lands at St. Vincents—Carib war—Severely wounded

T the same date at which Colonel Graham reached St.
incents, a considerable reinforcement of troops from
ngland also landed at Kingston. These regiments had,
ke himself, only returned from the continent a few
eeks before their embarkation Major-General Irving
so arrived to take command.

The principal Carib camp on the Vigie was one of
ie first points to which General Irving directed his at-
ntion The general features of St. Vincents are lofty
iountains in the central parts of the island, thickly
othed with trees , these mountains diverge in ridges of
lower elevation towards the sea, and are, in their turn,
itersected again by deep ravines, which gradually widen
n approaching the shore, and become valleys capable
f cultivation. The hills rise more abruptly from the
ia on the north-western side of the island than on the
orth-eastern, there being on this latter side an extensive
act of level land, the most productive in the colony
ome distance above Calliaqua, a small town three miles

216 MEMOIR OF GENERAL GRAHAM

west of Kingston, the commanding post of the Vigie (or look out) is situated towards the interior of the island. The different ridges before mentioned are here concentrated into one elevation, with three conical hills ; the largest of these conical hills is surrounded with deep ravines, almost impassable The top of this hill, having an area of about 100 yards in length and 20 in breadth, constituted the Carib citadel, being barricaded all round with sugar hogsheads filled with earth, and within 200 yards one of the smaller conical hills was formed into their first redoubt, and promised to be very serviceable, as it covered the approach to the citadel in the direction by which it was easiest of access. About cannon shot, nearly in the same direction, rose the third of these hills, overlooking the road from Kingston in a most commanding manner. This was the most advanced post or picket guard.

General Irving lost about 100 men killed and wounded in an attempt on this strong position, in the early part of October, but although the Vigie range was gained, it was deemed impracticable to storm the citadel itself, and the troops were withdrawn Had the place been vigorously assaulted, the enemy would, in all probability, have been cut off. As it was they took advantage of the darkness to evacuate and make their escape, and the place was taken possession of the following morning For some days after this, great un-

SKIRMISH AT BLACKETT'S BLUFF. 217

certainty prevailed in the military councils ; plans were formed and then abandoned. During this delay the enemy obtained some supplies of which they stood in want, and then commenced entrenching themselves on Mount Young and Mount William. About the 16th the British army sat down opposite those positions on Bellevue Ridge On the 18th General Irving crossed the Colonarie river and took possession of the north ridge of the Colonarie Vale, when a discharge of artillery from Mount William left no doubt as to the enemy having succeeded in manning their works at that point. Frequent skirmishes took place after that date until the 30th October, when Colonel Graham was ordered to gain a ridge called Blackett's Bluff. The enemy were well aware of the advantage of this position, and therefore drew out almost all their forces to oppose the British column General Irving, on seeing this, recalled Colonel Graham before he had time to effect the object for which he was detached. The loss of the British on this occasion was four killed and sixteen wounded Shepherd, in his account of the Carib war, charges General Irving with a want of enterprize on this occasion, as the Bluff, in his opinion, might have been secured, and the retreat of the enemy cut off from Mount William The caution of the British general he conceives attributable to orders he had received not to attempt anything until he was reinforced, orders framed without a know-

218   MEMOIR OF GENERAL GRAHAM.

ledge of the state of the enemy at the time, as they
were suffering extremely, being obliged to subsist on
mules.

General Irving was relieved in the command on the
17th October, but no movement of any importance took
place until the 8th January '96, when two deserters
having given information to the brigands of a weak
point in General Stewart's position, an attack was
made about four o'clock at the exposed point, which was
a small battery of one field-piece and a cohorn somewhat
advanced up the ridge. Mons. Chenon, a Frenchman,
.ucceeded in surprising two sentries posted considerably
in advance of this battery, and having run them through,
he advanced and shot a third in front of the work, and
then leaped in at the embrasure. He was made prisoner
immediately, but the impetuosity of his followers soon
obliged the officer in charge of the work, Lieutenant
Verity of the 54th, to abandon the post and retire upon
his regiment. The enemy lost no time in pursuing their
advantage, and as the gun they had got possession of
was so placed as to command the whole ridge, the English camp was no longer tenable. The enemy pushed
on and obtained possession of the other batteries, and
obliged the troops to abandon their ground and retreat
to Bellevue ridge. They next attempted to cut off the
English in their retreat by occupying the different ridges
commanding the high road, and pressed them so hard

COVERS THE RETREAT. 219

that if Colonel Fuller and Colonel Graham had not come up in time to check the enemy and cover the retreat, it could scarcely have been effected. As it was, the loss was great, particularly in officers, sixteen of whom were wounded, and 135 privates killed and wounded.[*]

[*] Extract of a letter from Brigadier-General Stewart to Major-General Hunter, dated Kingston, January 13, 1796.

About three o'clock on the morning of the 8th instant, the enemy made an attack on our left, where we had a three-pounder, and a cohorn placed upon a tongue of land, which ran out about fifty yards, thought, from the steepness on each side, to be almost inaccessible. On the first shot, I immediately ran out as fast as the darkness would permit me, and was met by Major Harcourt, field officer of the day. I found the men all paraded, and Brigadier-General Strutt, who had just received a wound in his face, exerting himself much with the 45th Regiment.

I still proceeded to the left, but from the darkness could not distinguish the enemy from our own soldiers (about this time a French officer had got over our works and was taken prisoner); and not being yet certain whether the enemy had taken possession of the battery to the left, I directed Major Harcourt to reinforce the post with the picquet of the 40th; but before this could be done, I had too much reason to believe it was taken, and immediately despatched a messenger to Lieutenant-Colonel Graham to bring up the whole or part of the West India Regiment; but before the messenger had got many yards, a firing was heard on the right from the enemy, and all along the front.

In this situation I left Captain Harrison of the light company of the 54th Regiment most actively employed in using every exertion to keep his men to their duty, and was proceeding to the right by the 40th Regiment to know what was doing there, but I had scarcely reached this regiment, when I heard the battery I had left was taken. I instantly turned about, directing

220　MEMOIR OF GENERAL GRAHAM.

On the 12th January, Major-General Hunter arrived from Martinique to take command. Immediately on landing he made himself acquainted with the position and state of the army, and resolved at once to draw the whole of his force into the heights about the town. On the 14th the enemy appeared in great numbers in the Mariaqua Valley, and shewed a design of attacking the Vigie—Major-General Hunter not considering the occupation of that post as very important at that moment, ordered the abandonment of it, and the Caribs instantly marched in. Between this and the end of the month

Major Harcourt, with all the men of the 40th he could collect, to follow me and retake the battery.

I again met Brigadier-General Strutt between some men, who informed me his leg was shattered, and Captain Harrison shot through the shoulder. I still pushed forward, using my best endeavours, with other officers, to animate the men to their duty, many of whom at that moment were killed and wounded. At this time the troops in front and on the right of the line gave way, and the enemy took possession of the remaining battery. In this dilemma nothing but a retreat could be thought of.

We reached Biabou with inconsiderable loss.

The enemy hung on our right and rear, but from the judicious attention of Lieutenant-Colonel Fuller (who, on every occasion afforded me the most ready assistance), and Lieutenant-Colonel Graham, they were kept off.

Biabou being upwards of twelve miles from Kingston, without provision and little ammunition, it appeared by no means prudent to take post there. I, therefore, as soon as the men had some rest, and it became dark (after having ordered fires to be kindled), resumed our march towards Kingston unmolested.

ASSAULT OF THE VIGIE

several sharp skirmishes took place without any important advantage on either side, after which a pause took place in the operations until the arrival of General Abercromby, in the early part of June, with a fleet of transports conveying a large reinforcement of troops. This force having been disembarked, the following dispositions were made for an attack on the Vigie :—

First column, under Brigadier-General Knox, to Mariaqua Valley.

Second column, commanded by Major-General Hunter, to Calder Ridge.

Third column, commanded by Major-General Morshead, to Carapan Ridge.

Fourth, under Lieutenant-Colonel Fuller, to Belmont Ridge.

Fifth, commanded by Lieutenant-Colonel Dickens, up Warawarou Valley

Sixth, reserve, under Lieutenant-Colonel Spencer, to follow the line of march.

The whole force amounted to 3960 men. The columns gained their several positions that night or early next morning. The duty allotted to the column under Colonel Dickens, with which Colonel Graham served on this occasion, was that of seizing an important pass on the flank of the enemy's position, while the main body stormed the citadel or Vigie. The service allotted to the column under Colonel Dickens was fully executed, but

222 MEMOIR OF GENERAL GRAHAM

the loss sustained by that column in killed and wounded was very severe

The following is an extract from general order which was issued on this occasion :—

"The Commander-in-Chief has the greatest satisfaction in publicly acknowledging that the success of his Majesty's arms on the 10th proceeded from the information he had received from Major-General Hunter, and from the local knowledge of the ground communicated to him by the gentlemen of the colony, who not only pointed out the route by which the column marched, but likewise conducted them ; the plan was carried into full execution by the good conduct of the officers and the intrepidity of the men Lieutenant-General Abercromby begs leave to return his best thanks to Major-Generals Hunter and Morshead, Brigadier-General Knox, Lieutenant-Colonels Fuller and Dickens, who conducted the different columns. Lieutenant-Colonel Dickens and the *troops who served under him* are entitled to a great share of praise, and the Commander-in-Chief is much obliged to Brigadier-General Knox for the well-timed reinforcement which he sent them."

After the taking of the Vigie, Lieutenant-Colonel Spencer, with one column, marched out to the windward quarter, and took possession of Mount William and Mount Young on the 14th Lieutenant-Colonel James Stewart, with the 42d, took post at Colonarie, and Lieu-

CARIBS PROPOSE TO TREAT. 223

tenant-Colonel Graham at Rabacca. The enemy had burned the guns they had taken in the unfortunate affair at Colonarie, and it was not until after some threats were made that they discovered where they were concealed.

The Caribs were now much distressed for provisions and ammunition, and shewed a disposition to discontinue hostilities by sending us a flag of truce. In consequence of this advance on their part, three of their chiefs were conducted to the head-quarters, but their demands were inadmissible. They proposed to retain their lands, saying that they had burned the English houses and cane-fields, and in return their canoes and their provisions had been destroyed, that there was now no further occasion to continue the war. When asked which party had been the first to violate the treaty of friendship, they replied that they had first declared war, but of what were they guilty in consequence?—everybody was then at war. They were told that nothing short of unconditional submission would be listened to, that their lives would then be spared, and they would be treated with humanity. Should they refuse these terms, the whole force of the island would be employed against them, and their extirpation must be the consequence. Against this they remonstrated, but requested a few days to consult with their chiefs.

When the time for their answer had expired, they

224 MEMOIR OF GENERAL GRAHAM.

disappeared from Mount Young ; but as no hostile measures were taken against them, they returned in a few days and commenced trafficking in the old manner. A Colonial Assembly was summoned, and it was decided that the small island of Balliceaux should be appropriated for the reception of the Caribs, and that they should be removed there.

On this being communicated to them, the son of Chatoyer (a great chief who was killed at an early period of the war), in the presence of Lieutenant-Colonel Haffey and his officers, addressed himself to the attendant Caribs to the following effect.—"It is no disgrace to us to surrender to a great nation. The subjects of France, and all great nations, even of England, are obliged to submit to each other when there no longer remains the means of resistance. What else is now left for us? Have we power to continue the war? No! to-morrow morning I will set you the example of submission, by bringing my family to Colonel Haffey, that he may send us to the General. You may do as you please ; I can only be accountable for myself and my family."

These observations seemingly had the effect he pretended to desire, and the Caribs promised to accompany him. But Colonel Haffey was too well acquainted with their perfidious character to place dependence on them, and he therefore ordered Captain Lauder, with two

IN COMMAND OF LIGHT CORPS. 225

companies, to line the deep ravine to the northward of them, while Captain Munro was posted on the southern ridge, and Colonel Haffey himself took up a post to the westward. Upon this, 300 of the Caribs retreated into the woods, amongst them the orator Chatoyer himself, as well as many of those who had been loudest in promises of submission. Captain Munro took prisoners 100, who were retreating towards the Colonarie River. On the 20th, 280 in all of these natives who had been made prisoners, were sent off to Balliceaux. The same day Lieutenant Laborde was detached to Mount Sable with a party to receive the proffered submission of the Caribs in that quarter, and conduct them to Mount Young; but he found their houses abandoned, and themselves in arms, and strongly posted on an eminence, from which they called to him to withdraw immediately, declaring at the same time that they never would submit to the English; and that they did not revolt so much from the prospect of death as from the idea of submission. The inferiority of his force rendered his retreat both prudent and necessary.

It was at the period at which we have now arrived that Colonel Graham was selected by Major-General Hunter to command a corps of light troops, and penetrate across the island through the midst of the settlements of the Caribs. This corps proceeded along the line formed by the bed of the Colonarie River, to a con-

226   MEMOIR OF GENERAL GRAHAM.

siderable elevation; and on the third days' march discovered the enemy strongly fortified behind a formidable abattis in the woods or jungle, for at this part of the island it is almost an impenetrable wilderness. According to the account given in "Shepherd's West Indies," "The Caribs invited Colonel Graham to approach, with the utmost seeming sincerity of friendship, which he did at the head of his men, displaying a white handkerchief in his hand, indicative of his pacific disposition This officer had frequently expressed his good opinion of the Caribs, and of their similar dispositions towards him; but when he had got within a few yards of their works, a whole volley of musketry was poured around him, and severely wounded him and an officer of Santeur's corps, and all his party except Mr. Mathews, their guide. The latter officer fell into the possession of the Caribs, who cut him to pieces."

General Graham, in his own notes on this affair, says that he was rallying a corps of Martinique volunteers, who were giving way before the enemy, when he received a desperate wound through the lungs from a musket-ball, and soon afterwards, a second in the hand from another ball.

Colonel Stewart, in the "Sketches of the Highlanders," thus alludes to the severity of the wounds received by Colonel Graham on this occasion, and the singular circumstances attending it :—" The people, be-

WOUNDS DRESSED BY A SOLDIER'S WIFE. 227

lieving he was dead, rather dragged than carried him over the rough channel of the river, till they reached the sea-beach. Observing here that he was still alive, they put him in a blanket, and proceeded in search of a surgeon. After travelling in this manner four miles they carried him to a military post, occupied by a party of the 42d. All the surgeons were out in the woods, and none could be found. Colonel Graham was still insensible; a ball had entered his side three inches from the back-bone, and passing through, had come out under his breast; another, or perhaps the same ball, had shattered two of his fingers. No assistance could be got, but that of a soldier's wife, who had long been in the service, and was in the habit of attending sick and wounded soldiers. She washed his wounds, and bound them up in such a manner, that when a surgeon saw the way in which the operation had been performed, he said he could not have done it better, and would not unbind the dressing. The colonel soon after opened his eyes, and though unable to speak for many hours, seemed sensible of what was passing around him. In this state he lay nearly three weeks, when he was carried to Kingston, and thence conveyed to England. He was still in a most exhausted state, the wound in his side discharging matter from both orifices. He went to Edinburgh, with little hope of recovery; but on the evening of the illumination for the battle of Camperdown, the

228   MEMOIR OF GENERAL GRAHAM.

smoke of so many candles and flambeaux affecting his breathing, he coughed with great violence, and in the exertion threw up a piece of cloth, left, no doubt, by the ball in its passage through his body. From that day he recovered as by a charm.

CHAPTER THE SIXTEENTH.

Appointed Lieutenant-Colonel, 27th Regiment.—Helder Expedition—Severely Wounded

COLONEL GRAHAM was transferred from the 2d West India Regiment to the command of the 27th Enniskillen Regiment, in January 1797, and took command of the corps at Winchester, on its return from the West Indies in 1798. In command of this regiment he felt himself, to use his own words, in a position in which he fondly hoped to gain distinction, and it was not long before the state of affairs on the Continent seemed to hold out a prospect of his brightest hopes being realized. The armies of Republican France in 1799 were so fully occupied in Italy and Germany, that the English government deemed the time favourable for an effort to wrest Holland from their power, and restore the Stadtholder, and an expedition was therefore prepared, the command of which was entrusted to the gallant veteran Sir Ralph Abercromby.* The 27th was one of the regiments

* Various plans were suggested and considered for the employment of the force, the only one of which that the Com

230 MEMOIR OF GENERAL GRAHAM.

ordered to embark on this expedition. The fleet sailed on the 13th August, but owing to the state of the weather, nearly a fortnight elapsed before a landing could be attempted on the coast of Holland. The point selected was the Helder The troops commenced to disembark at daylight on the morning of the 27th. The landing was effected without much opposition, but the moment the first division began to advance they became engaged, and the action continued from five o'clock in the morning until three in the afternoon. The position taken up by Sir Ralph was on a range of sand hills, stretching along the coast from north to south. In this position his right was unavoidably exposed; in other respects the position had its advantages, as the British had neither artillery nor cavalry, whilst the French army included a proportion of those arms. The British had nowhere sufficient ground on their right to form more than one battalion in line ; the contest was arduous, and the loss very severe , but by the courage and perseverance of our troops the enemy were completely worn out and obliged to retire in the afternoon to a position two leagues in his rear. Major-General Coote's brigade, consisting of the Queen's 27th, 29th, and

mander-in-Chief felt disposed to countenance was an attack on the Helder, in order to capture the Dutch fleet. Ministers therefore decided to leave a large discretionary power in the hands of Sir Ralph as to the adoption of ulterior measures after his arrival on the coast of Holland.

ACTION AT THE HELDER. 231

85th, was one of the brigades hotly engaged on this occasion. In the early part of the engagement Sir Eyre Coote despatched Colonel Graham with two light companies and a part of the 27th to flank the summit of the ridges of sand hills, with this force he succeeded in getting upon the flank of a corps commanded by Colonel Gluck, routed it, and cleared the hills of the enemy. From that time the 27th was drawn up on the ridges parallel to the sea beach until about two o'clock, when the enemy, pressing very much upon the right flank, Sir Ralph Abercromby called upon Colonel Graham to advance his regiment by wings of battalion. In the performance of this service, whilst charging at the head of the right wing of the Enniskillens, he received a severe wound in the left temple from a rifle ball, by which he was completely deprived of the sight of his left eye

As the expedition to Holland had been despatched by ministers more in the hope that through the prudence, skill, and daring of the commander, it would effect *something*, than in the execution of any matured plan, the successful landing at the Helder was a subject of great rejoicing in England; to the Government it was an unbounded source of gratification, as it relieved them from an uneasy weight of responsibility. Mr. Dundas, in writing to the son of Sir Ralph, thus expresses himself —" Thanks to Heaven and Sir Ralph, we stand on a pinnacle of glory and fame ;" and in the public letter of

MEMOIR OF GENERAL GRAHAM.

thanks transmitted by the minister to Sir Ralph through the Duke of York, we find these expressions—" It is impossible for me to convey to you in adequate terms the sense his Majesty entertains of the steady and enterprising bravery of the army under your command in the arduous and ever memorable action of the 27th ultimo. High as the character of the British army stood before this event, it is impossible that the landing at the Helder point, preceded and attended by so many untoward difficulties, and the battle by which it was immediately followed, should not attract the admiration of Europe, and raise that character still higher in every part of the world as it has done already in the eyes of the Sovereign and their countrymen at home."

It must often be difficult for a General, in writing a despatch, to decide upon the names of those he shall point out as particularly distinguished; and amidst the multifarious subjects engrossing his attention after an action, he may sometimes overlook services which deserve special notice. It seems as if something of this kind had occurred in the case of Colonel Graham after the action of the Helder. Twice singled out as he was for special service, upon one occasion by the direct order of Sir Ralph himself, it seems strange that no special mention should have been made of the conspicuous share in the glory of the day to which he and his brave Enniskillens are so justly entitled.

CURE OF WOUND. 233

For the cure of the wound received at the Helder, it was necessary for him to return to England, and upon this, as upon all other occasions when on leave of absence or at home suffering from wounds, he resided in Edinburgh with his sister, the wife of Dr. Thomas Hay, son of Lord Huntingdon, one of the Lords of Session, and lineal descendant of Hay of Limplum. Dr. Hay's uncle John, of Restalrig titular Count of Inverness, was private secretary to Prince Charles (the Chevalier St. George), over whom he is said, by Horace Walpole, to have exercised unbounded influence. In consequence of this family connection General Graham often rallied his sister in a jesting manner upon her having no ill will in her heart to the Jacobite cause.*

In June 1800, Colonel Graham was sufficiently recruited to join his regiment, then stationed at Swinly camp. In the following August the regiment embarked with the force under Sir J. Pulteney, on a secret expedition. The fleet made for Ferrol; but Sir J. Pulteney, after landing the troops and making a reconnoissance,

---

* After some days' stay at Leghorn, we continued our journey by Pisa, Florence, and Sienna, to Rome, where, after about six weeks' stay, we took our leave of the king to return to Spain. His Majesty, who knew that we were in want of money, sent his *favourite Mr. Hay* to the Pope to desire him to advance him 1000 Roman crowns on his ordinary pension, which the other refused on pretence of poverty.—*Fragment of a Memoir of Field Marshal Keith, written by himself*, 1714-1734.

L 2

234 MEMOIR OF GENERAL GRAHAM.

caused the men to be re-embarked, considering the place too strong for a *coup de main*. The following is Sir J. Pulteney's despatch detailing his operations:—

On Board H. M. S. Renown, at Sea,
27th August 1800.

Sir—I have the honour to inform you that the fleet, on board of which the troops under my command were embarked, arrived before the harbour of Ferrol on the 25th inst. I determined immediately to make a landing, with a view, if practicable, to attempt the town of Ferrol, being certain, if I found either the strength of the place or the force of the enemy too great to justify an attack, that in the landing there was no considerable risk.

The disembarkation was effected without opposition in a small bay near Cape Prior; the reserve, followed by the other troops as they landed, immediately ascended a ridge of hills adjoining to the bay; just as they had gained the summit the rifle corps fell in with a party of the enemy, which they drove back. I have to regret that Lieutenant-Colonel Stewart, who commanded this corps, was wounded on the occasion. At day-break the following morning, a considerable body of the enemy was driven back by Major-General the Earl of Cavan's brigade, supported by some other troops, so that we remained in complete possession of the

FERROL EXPEDITION. 235

heights which overlook the town and harbour of Ferrol, but from the nature of the ground, which is steep and rocky, unfortunately this service could not be performed without loss. The first battalion of the 52d Regiment had the principal share in this action. The enemy lost about one hundred men, killed and wounded, and thirty or forty prisoners.

I had now an opportunity of observing minutely the situation of the place, and of forming, from the reports of prisoners, an idea of the strength of the enemy When comparing the difficulties which presented themselves and the risk attendant on failure on one hand, with the prospect of success and the advantage to be derived from it on the other, I came to the determination of re-embarking the troops, in order to proceed without delay on my further destination. The embarkation was effected the same evening in perfect order and without loss of any kind

I am under the greatest obligations to the Admiral, Sir Jno. Borlase Warren, and the officers of the navy, for the judicious arrangements made for the landing and re-embarkation of the troops, and the activity with which they were put in   The immediate direction of this service was entrusted to Sir Edward Pellew, who performed it in a manner highly creditable to himself and advantageous to the service.

(Signed)   JAMES PULTENEY.

236 MEMOIR OF GENERAL GRAHAM.

Killed and wounded of the troops landed off Ferrol, 27th August 1800 .—Total, 16 rank and file killed, 1 lieutenant-colonel, 3 captains, 3 subalterns, 3 sergeants, 1 drummer 59 rank and file wounded Officers wounded Captain Torrens, first battalion, 52d Regiment, dead of his wounds ; Hon Lieutenant-Colonel Stewart, 67th Regiment ; Captain Hamilton, 27th Regiment ; Captain Trevers, 79th Regiment ; Lieutenant Edmonston, second battalion, Royals, wounded.

EGYPT. 237

CHAPTER THE SEVENTEENTH.

Expedition to Egypt.

On arriving at Gibralter the first battalion, 27th, under Colonel Graham, joined the army under Sir Ralph Abercromby. Circumstances over which the brave and distinguished commander-in-chief had no control occasioned changes in the destination of the fine force under his command.

After the attempt on Cadiz was abandoned, Italy and Spanish America in turn came under consideration; at length the surrender of Malta appearing calculated to favour a landing in Egypt, that plan was decided on, and on the 30th November a part of the fleet arrived at Malta, the remainder joining on the 14th December.

The long detention of the troops on board ship having proved detrimental to their health and spirits, a partial disembarkation of the force took place at Malta, by which the men were so much refreshed that they were generally in a fit state to proceed as soon as the ships had undergone cleaning, and the necessary supplies had been put on board. Sickness, however, still continuing

238 MEMOIR OF GENERAL GRAHAM.

to prevail in the first battalion, 27th Regiment, a longer residence on shore was deemed necessary for the men, and the regiment did not in consequence arrive in Egypt until the month of April.

The glorious victory under the walls of Alexandria had therefore been gained before the first battalion, 27th, reached the coast of Egypt, but there still remained much arduous work to be done by the troops, and the position of the army was one which might well excite anxiety in the mind of the General, demanding as it did the utmost prudence and skill on his part. When General Hutchinson assumed command, he did so undoubtedly under favourable auspices, inasmuch as the campaign had commenced with a decided and brilliant success, but as yet no material superiority had been gained. An army more numerous than his own was opposed to him, strong places had to be taken, climate to be endured, supplies to be obtained from the interior, and a communication to be established with the Vizir, as well as with the army expected from India under Baird, and, independent of these formidable difficulties, the plague, and other diseases menaced to reduce his force Lord Keith also assured him that after October he could no longer remain on the coast with the shipping, on account of the weather, and the state of the vessels.

General Hutchinson fortunately proved himself equal

SOUTH SIDE OF ALEXANDRIA INUNDATED. 239

to the position in which he was placed, possessing prudence and daring as each in turn became necessary.

The want of provisions for his troops, as well as the want of water for the fleet, demanded his first attention, and he therefore as speedily as possible directed an attempt to be made on Rosetta and Fort St. Julien, with a view to obtaining command of the Nile.

A letter from General Menou, which was found in the pocket of General Roiz, killed in the action of the 21st, had disclosed the advantage to be expected from cutting across the isthmus separating the lake of Aboukir from the dry bed of lake Mariotis, thus inundating the latter, and circumscribing the means of communication between Alexandria and the interior. Great as were the advantages to be expected from this measure, it was not adopted by General Hutchinson without much anxious consideration, for the Arabs could give no idea as to where such an inundation might stop, or what might be its mischievous effects, and although it promised to prove serviceable to the operations of the British army, it was also evident that it would at the same time strengthen the south front of the French position.

The advantages appearing to outweigh the disadvantages, the cut was made on the 13th April, and the torrent of water immediately rushed violently down a declivity of six feet, carrying away large portions of the

240 MEMOIR OF GENERAL GRAHAM.

embankment, and speedily producing an inundation sufficiently deep for a flotilla of gun-boats.

The castle of St. Julien, commanding the mouth of the Nile, surrendered on the 19th April.

The capture of this important place encouraged General Hutchinson to press on his operations against the interior, and leaving General Coote to hold the lines against the east front of Alexandria, he advanced against Rahmanich on the 9th May. Having gained possession of that place, he continued his march to Cairo, and his operations in that direction were crowned with complete success, by the surrender of General Belliard, with his whole army, as prisoners of war, on the 28th June.

During these operations, the 27th had remained in camp with the force in front of Alexandria, and nothing of any great importance had occurred, except an attempt made by the French to form an inundation between the lines of the two armies on the eastern side of the town, by making a cut in the canal in front of Green Hill Had the French succeeded in their design of leading the waters of the canal into the plain before the eastern front of Alexandria, the front for operations against that side of the town would have become too contracted. General Coote therefore very judiciously caused a dam to be constructed so as to check the inundation, in which way their scheme was completely frustrated.

In order to complete the investment of Alexandria,

ATTACK ON THE WESTERN FRONT. 241

it was necessary to organize an attack on the western front of the place.

The execution of this portion of General Hutchinson's plan was intrusted to General Coote, who received instructions to proceed with a force of about 4000 men in boats, by the inundation which had been formed on Lake Mareotis, and effect a landing at the most convenient and eligible spot.

General Hutchinson's opinion of the difficulties before him, is thus expressed in a despatch written about this time :—

"The siege of Alexandria will probably be attended with many difficulties ; the works towards the east side where we are encamped are prodigiously strong, and can hardly be approached on account of the narrowness of the space between the lake and the sea, and the nature of the ground ; towards the west the works are not so strong, but, however, the difficulties in approaching them are also numerous ; the corps there is completely in the desert, the communication with us (by whom they must be supplied with everything) is tedious, and the boats employed have most severe duty to perform : on the whole, I cannot flatter myself that Alexandria will be in our possession in such a short time, unless some event takes place of which we are not at present aware."

On the evening of the 16th August the boats as-

242

MEMOIR OF GENERAL GRAHAM.

sembled in the inundation on the left of the British position, and embarked the troops destined for the expedition to the westward—

Consisting of the brigade of Guards under Lord Cavan.

Two battalions 27th Regiment, and the 44th, under Major-General Lord Ludlow.

26th, and two battalions 54th, under Major-General Finch.

With 100 of the 20th Dragoons,—in all about 4000 men.

The flotilla sailed to the westward as soon as the troops were received on board.

To distract the attention of the enemy, and favour the landing of General Coote's division, an attack on the outworks of the eastern front of Alexandria was organized for the morning of the 17th.

It was General Coote's intention to have landed between Alexandria and Fort Marabout, but seeing a corps of the enemy in occupation of some commanding ground above the shore, he left General Finch's brigade to make a feint at that point, while the remainder of the division stood on and landed without difficulty about three miles further on.

The first measure after landing was to get possession of Fort Marabout, which was accomplished on the 21st. On the following morning General Coote advanced

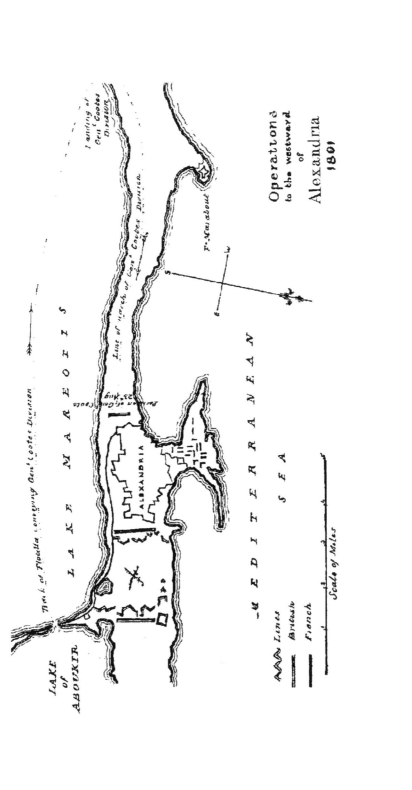

ENNISKILLENS IN ADVANCE. 243

against the French General, Eppler, who, with a corps of 1200 men, had taken up a position on a high ridge of sand hills, his right defended by four pieces of artillery, his left covered by two batteries mounting 18-pounders.

The order of march of the British was in three columns; the right column moved along the flat between the lake and ridge of hills, the centre was directed through the hills, and General Ludlow's brigade marched on the left on the flat near the harbour. The first battalion of the 27th, commanded by Colonel Graham, and a detachment of Lowenstein's chasseurs under Major Pepongay, with 200 of the guards commanded by Colonel Joliffe, formed the advanced guard. Immediately followed the six field-pieces, commanded by Major Cookson, and the dragoons marched in rear of the left Captain Stevenson commanded the gunboats in the lake, Captain Cochrane those in the harbour.

Almost as soon as the movement commenced the advanced guard fell in with the picquets, when a scattered fire of musketry commenced on each side. A Turkish corvette bore down upon the battery on the right, which had begun firing as soon as the ships got under weigh; the corvette never returned a shot until quite close, when luffing up she discharged a broadside which effectually silenced the battery.

The French now opened from all their guns a heavy

244 MEMOIR OF GENERAL GRAHAM

fire, the British pieces unlimbered and played upon them whilst the army continued to advance. The French finding that a serious attack was intended, and afraid of being forced with the bayonet, retired from their position, abandoning the heavy guns ; they, however, formed again on another ridge, and maintained from thence a galling fire of musketry and grape

General Coote had now succeeded in his first object, but anxious to push on to the works of Alexandria he ordered the march to be continued

The French retired reluctantly, and had evidently not contemplated the chance of being forced to retreat, as they were obliged to abandon their tents and baggage.

On arriving within 1400 yards of Alexandria, a halt was made to give time for the heavy artillery to arrive

The French lost in this affair about 200, killed, wounded, and prisoners, with seven pieces of cannon; the loss of the British was three killed and forty wounded The action was maintained entirely by the 27th Regiment, the Lowenstein Rangers, and the detachment of Guards with the Artillery , the rest of the army never fired a shot, although every part was exposed to the enemy's fire, which was very heavy (particularly in grape), and would have been very destructive but for the inequalities of the ground.

The view which now presented itself to the troops (quoting from Sir R. Wilson) was striking from its ani-

BOLD POSITION OF COOTE'S DIVISION. 245

mation and gaiety, as well as replete with historical interest; the town of Alexandria, with its busy harbour and quays, lay at their feet, while, at the same time, the eye rested on the catacombs of Alexandria, the temple of Diana, and the baths of Cleopatra.

No time was lost in communicating intelligence to General Hutchinson of the success which had been gained. The general-in-chief, on learning the boldness of the position taken up by General Coote, at once despatched a reinforcement, and apprehensive that before its arrival the enemy might make a vigorous sortie on General Coote, he therefore planned a feint on the eastern side, to divert their attention to self-defence.

On the morning of the 23d two batteries were ready to open against the redoubt Des Bains, the advanced work on the western side, but the platforms giving way the firing was suspended during the day; fortunately they were repaired in time to take part in the repulse of a determined sortie made by the French in the night, with a view to recover the ground they had lost.

On the morning of the 26th the English batteries on the eastern side, containing ten 24 pounders and six 12 pounders, and two howitzers, commenced playing on the right of the French position.

General Menon had expressed himself very indignant at the capitulation of General Belliard, and declared his determination to bury himself in the ruins of Alex-

246   MEMOIR OF GENERAL GRAHAM.

andria, but, on the morning of the 26th, he found himself reduced to propose an armistice for three days. An
officer was sent instantly to General Coote, who arrived
in time to prevent his making a lodgment on the hill
above Pompey's Pillar. The occupation of that post
would have secured the fall of Alexandria, as it is not
above 150 yards from the walls of the old town, and it
is also nearly equal in height to Forts Cretin and
Caffarelli

On the 31st August General Hope went into Alexandria to sign the capitulation. Sir R. Wilson says,
" General Menon received him with every mark of attention, and invited him to dinner. The repast was only
horse-flesh , but those who are acquainted with the
French general well know that his society would amply
compensate for the want of a more luxurious diet."

CHAPTER THE EIGHTEENTH

Marriage—Serves on Staff in Scotland and Ireland—Letters.

IN November 1801 Lieutenant-Colonel Graham returned with his regiment to Malta, and, shortly after his arrival there, was sent home by the medical staff, in consequence of being threatened with the loss of the sight of his remaining eye.

Previous to his return to England, the Commander-in-Chief, as a mark of the sense he entertained of his services, had appointed him to the Lieutenant-Governorship of Dumbarton* Castle—a command reported vacant

---

* Pennant describes Dumbarton Castle as seated on a two-headed rock of a stupendous height, rising in a strange manner out of the sands, and totally detached from every thing else The sides of the rocks are immense precipices, and often overhang, except on the side where the Governor's house stands, which is defended by walls and a few cannon, and garrisoned by a few invalids From its natural strength it was in former times deemed impregnable ; so that the desperate but successful scalado of it in 1571 may vie with the greatest attempts of that kind—with the capture of the Numidian fortress in the Jugurthan War by Marius ; or the more horrible surprise of Feschamps by the gallant Bois-rosé.

248   MEMOIR OF GENERAL GRAHAM.

in consequence of the death of General Islay Ferrier. The announcement of the death of General Ferrier turned out to be incorrect, and the appointment was therefore cancelled ; and, strange to say, General Ferrier lived to see his niece married to the identical officer thus abruptly appointed to take his place. The Lieutenant-Governor was highly incensed at being so unceremoniously deprived of his life and his situation at one and the same time, and vented his indignation in the following laconic advertisement in the newspapers :—

" I, Islay Ferrier, am not dead "

The Lieutenant-Governorship of Stirling Castle becoming vacant soon after this occurrence, the appointment was immediately conferred on Lieutenant-Colonel Graham.

In 1802 Lieutenant-Colonel Graham was promoted to the rank of full colonel, and in 1804 was placed on the Staff in North Britain as brigadier-general.

This appointment to the Staff in Scotland was followed by his marriage to Jane, eldest daughter of James Ferrier, Esquire, one of the Principal Clerks of the Court of Session ; an alliance productive of all the happiness which can be conferred on man by a sensible and devoted wife.

The personal attractions of Miss Ferrier having excited the muse of the immortal bard of Scotland

BURNS' LINES ON MRS. GRAHAM. 249

[Robert Burns], no memoir of the General would be complete without including such a tribute to the wife of his choice. The lines are as follows :—

Madam,

> Nae heathen name shall I prefix,
> Frae Pindus or Parnassus,
> Auld Reekie dings them a' to sticks
> For rhyme-inspiring lasses
>
> Jove's tunefu' dochters, three times three,
> Made Homer deep their debtor,
> But gi'en the body half an e'e,
> Nine Ferriers wad done better
>
> Last day my mind was in a bog,
> Down George's Street I stoited,
> A creeping, cauld, prosaic fog,
> My vera senses doited.
>
> Do what I dought to set her free,
> My muse lay in the mire ;
> Ye turned a neuk—I saw your e'e—
> She took the wing like fire.
>
> The mournfu' sang I here enclose,
> In gratitude I send you,
> And pray in rhyme sincere as prose,
> A' GUDE THINGS MAY ATTEND YOU.
>
> ROBERT BURNS

St. James' Square,
   Saty. Evening.

The concluding lines have reference to a copy of his elegy on Sir J. H. Blair which the poet enclosed.

250   MEMOIR OF GENERAL GRAHAM.

Owing to Mr. Ferrier's position as Clerk of Session, a friendly intercourse subsisted between his family and that of his illustrious contemporary in the Court of Session, Sir Walter Scott A connection also existed between Mr. Ferrier's family and that of the late Professor Wilson (Christopher North), by the marriage of Mr. Ferrier's eldest son to the Professor's sister ; and Mrs Graham's own sister has since become well known as Miss Ferrier, authoress of " Marriage and Inheritance." Mrs. Graham was thus frequently brought into the society of the most celebrated literary people in Scotland of that day One of the friends of her early life, the beautiful and accomplished Lady Charlotte Campbell, greeted her with the following note on her wedding-day —

> " For Mrs. Brigadier-General Graham
>
>   " This comes to felicitate J. C.
>
>   (Inside the cover) " Miss Ferrier,
>
>   " *per ultima volta.*

" Is it not strange that I should write for the last time to Jane Ferrier without sorrow ? A thousand joys to Jane Graham. You have not time or power to read a long epistle I merely trace these lines expressive of my best and kindest wishes that since I cannot in person be present at the ceremony my heart may wing its way to you. My husband, after *his fashion*, manifests his sincere joy, and would have been very witty if I had

SHERIDAN ASKS A FRIEND TO DINNER   251

allowed him.   God bless you, my dear friend, not less so
as a married than you ever were as a single woman; and
in this pleasing belief, I remain, with pleasure, as well as
affection, Jane Graham's heartily affectionate

" C. M. CAMPBELL."

The following original letter, from the celebrated Sheridan to the Hon. H. Erskine, preserved in Mrs Graham's
portfolio, is very characteristic, and does not appear to
have been hitherto published —

" Saturday.

"Dear Sir—The Mrs. Crowe, who, like the merry
knights, is not only witty herself, but the cause of wit
in others, who has been admired and sought after by
all the men of wit and genius of the age, must not leave
Edinbro' without the homage of your talents being paid
to her, and as there is no time for verse writing or composition (for she goes on Monday), you must come in
person and cut the best figure you can 'extempore.' She
is here to see the lions and 1 am appointed showman.
Now, in this case you know, the word lion implies all
that is agreeable, entertaining, or interesting. Is it
strange, therefore, in seeking for them that you should
start into my mind, and that I shall consider my task
unaccomplished if I have not the pleasure of shewing
you. Mrs. Crowe has commissioned me (venturing upon
her intimacy with your brother, as well as a slight ac-

252 MEMOIR OF GENERAL GRAHAM.

quaintance with yourself) to request your company to dinner to-morrow, Sunday, at Dumbucky, five o'clock , if you can't come to dinner, come in the evening, if not in the evening, come in the middle of the night, but do pray come —Yours most truly,   T. SHERIDAN.

"Honourable H. Erskine."

In the same repository from whence the foregoing letter has been selected, some lines from the pen of Leyden are preserved which may serve as a pendant to Sheridan's lively ebullition.—

"Mr. Leyden is amazed that Miss Ferrier could suppose that any engagement would prevent him from waiting upon her and Lady Charlotte. He does not profess much attention to promises—

> "For promises, as writers mention,
> Serve but to mark the mind's intention ;
> Now, since we never think it strange
> To find one's best intentions change,
> Should promises, like rope or halter,
> Confine intentions ne'er to alter

—" but the promise which promises so much pleasure in the performance has a superior claim to validity. Compliments to Mr. Ferrier.   Sunday"

During the time Brigadier-General Graham was on the staff in North Britain, he had under his command

DISCIPLINE WITHOUT THE LASH. 253

a force of about 7000 volunteers and yeomanry In June 1806 he was struck off the staff and remained unemployed until June 1808, when he was appointed to the staff in Ireland and took command of the garrison at Cork.

The following instance of the General's kindness of heart, and method of managing delinquents, is given upon the authority of an old sergeant of dragoons, for a long time a respectable inhabitant of Surling —"When the sergeant was stationed with his regiment at Cork, a private was tried by a district court-martial for striking a non-commissioned officer, and was sentenced to be flogged The troops in garrison being assembled to witness the infliction of the punishment, Major-General Graham, who then commanded at Cork, rode into the square, and after the sentence had been read, addressing the prisoner, said 'The conduct of the distinguished regiment to which you belong has been so exemplary, that I would much regret seeing a man belonging to it flogged I shall therefore remit your punishment, if any officer of your regiment will speak in your favour.' No one came forward 'Well,' continued the General, 'I make the same offer if any non-commissioned officer will do so' Still no move. The General went on—'Surely some one of your companions will come forward , if so I shall forgive you.' But not a man moved. The General then addressing the prisoner, said, 'You are the most

254 MEMOIR OF GENERAL GRAHAM

unfortunate man it has ever been my lot to encounter. If the predicament in which your conduct has placed you does not work reformation no amount of flogging will Remove the prisoner. It is impossible for any man to be more degraded in the eyes of his regiment.'" For some years afterwards the cats were not seen in that regiment; crime was in a manner banished, thanks to the brave, kind-hearted General ; and the circumstance had also a most beneficial effect on all the corps that were present.

While General Graham commanded at Cork, Major-General Hill, to whom he had been known in his previous service, passed through Cork to enter upon his glorious career in the Peninsula, and proposed to General Graham that he should accompany him to Portugal. At that time some personal matters rendered it inconvenient for him to do so ; and repeated efforts made at subsequent periods to obtain more active employment than the Home-Staff afforded, met with no success. It would appear by a letter from Sir W. H Clinton, dated in 1812, that he had been in correspondence with him on the subject of employment in the Peninsula

" Onil, 25 Miles N.W. of Alicant,

" <i>7th April</i> 1813.

" Dear General—I must not leave unacknowledged your letter of the 24th of January, delivered to me the day before yesterday by Colonel Schroeder of the Brunswick Hussars. I thank you for it, and for all you were kind enough to say in it. It would have given me much pleasure, indeed, to have served with you; but had I seen the hard service you have seen, and to boast of the honourable marks you have, indeed, my dear general, I should think no more of service, and you may rely on it I should have staid quietly where I was, in the enjoyment of one of the pleasantest situations a military man can have.

" I threw myself in the way of service, more especially because it had been intimated to me that whenever I attained to the rank I *now* hold (locally), I must vacate my situation in Ireland. Where should I have then been? I could not, I may say I would not, have accepted service abroad with my then rank had it been then offered to me, so that I looked forward to being very soon on the shelf; I have thus lost a place of great emolument without any adequate return, but I have at least the satisfaction of feeling that I have served, and I hope, in the eye of the world, have done right. It has been judged right not to shew in mine, or in my brother's instance, the same favour which *in two instances* was granted to poor Anstruther, and in a very marked manner to my immediate predecessor Sir John Cradock, as admitting staff situations at home to be held whilst employed on foreign service.

256 MEMOIR OF GENERAL GRAHAM.

" Your letter found me soon after the army moved from the position near Alicant. Sir John Murray having arrived here and found Lord William Bentinck not yet arrived, he assumed his command. We presumed we were waiting for Lord Wellington's instructions; however, here we are ready to act the moment the weather will let us; this and last month are the most unsettled of the year—the spring equinox has been particularly rainy and unpleasant. In ten days we may expect fair weather, then, I presume, we shall go on. The French have hitherto shewn no enterprize; they contented themselves with a skirmish at Alcoy, since then they have hardly shewn themselves; whether this be 'ruse' to draw us out, or really that they wish to shun an action, a short time will prove Our army is numerous, but we have yet to ascertain whether part of it will fight Of the two Spanish divisions of Whittingham and Rich, the former 4000, the latter 2000 men, we have reason to think tolerably. A Sicilian and Italian are rather more questionable; however, the former deceives us much if they do not do well; the army is formed into four divisions: two British and Sicilian, mixed, and two Spanish; M'Kenzie commands one, I the other, British; Lord F. Bentinck has our *diminutive* cavalry; Colonel Adam has the advance, consisting at present of three battalions, viz., 2d, 27th Calabrian (light corps), and the first of the Italian Legion, all light.

EARLY SHOEING AFTER A VOYAGE 257

" If I can shew any attention to your recommendation of Colonel Schroeder, I shall be glad to do so ; I
shall tell Floyd to give you some account of us and our
movements in future ; he recollects with great warmth
your kindness to him, and when I shewed him what
you said of his good father, his young blood seemed to
glow again.

" You probably may have heard the hussars arrived
here in sad plight, and the horses have not been improved by early shoeing. There has been a sad over-
sight somewhere, we were in too great a hurry to have
the services of the cavalry, and we probably shall suffer
for the hurry all the campaign ; I know not exactly
where the blame lies. You must not expect much from
our numbers here ; we have some excellent officers opposed to us, and we have also some good troops. Suchet
commands, and has under him Generals Arispe, de
Lordt, and Habert. We have a beautiful country in
our front, but it has been sadly plundered by the
French ; they will not leave us much to save for the
poor inhabitants—Believe me to be, my dear general,
sincerely yours, W. H. CLINTON.'*

---

* Lieutenant-General Sir W. H. Clinton, K.B, M.P, son of
Sir H Clinton who commanded the army in America, entered
the service in 1784, and served with the Guards in the campaign of 1794 in Holland, and was afterwards employed as aide-
de-camp and military secretary to his Royal Highness In 1812,

M 2

258 MEMOIR OF GENERAL GRAHAM

Some letters from other correspondents shew that he had also made endeavours about this time to get employment in India. On his promotion to the rank of major-general he was transferred from the command of the garrison at Cork to the Perth district in North Britain, where an extensive depot of French prisoners was at that time established.

His residence at Cork brought him into frequent intercouse with Sir John Floyd,* who commanded the southern district, and a friendly intercourse was kept up after they had both left Cork.

In 1812 Sir John writes :—

having attained the rank of major-general, he applied for active employment and was sent to Sicily with the rank of lieutenant-general From there he was dispatched in command of a corps of Italians, Calabrians Sicilians, Majorcans, and some British and Germans, to Alicant, to co-operate with the Spanish He was afterwards opposed to Suchet, and rendered important services both in keeping possession of the principal places in Catalonia against very superior forces, and in preventing the junction of Suchet with Soult at Thoulouse, which might have proved disastrous to our operations in that part His services were specially recognised by the Duke of Wellington

* General Sir John Floyd entered the army in 1760 as cornet in Elliot's Dragoons and was present at the battle of Emsdorf; he was subsequently employed for eighteen years in India in various commands of cavalry; at the siege of Bangalore, 1791, at the battle of Seringapatam, 1792, at the siege of Pondicherry he was second in command, and he was also present at Malavelly, and at the siege of Seringapatam in 1799 His daughter married the Right Hon Sir Robert Peel

SIR JOHN FLOYD.

TUNBRIDGE WELLS, 2d *November* 1812

Major-General Graham.

My dear General—We have long been living after the manner of exiles. Not long after we came to London I bought a house in Cavendish Square, and great part of the furniture, the property of Mr Hope, who has two houses in that square—one great and magnificent—the other, my object, small, clean, new furniture, and very pretty. Next day a gentleman offered £1000 for my bargain, which I declined. After being long in expectation of the title, it appeared at last that the house could not be sold. I had paid £1800 deposit-money, and after great plague recovered my money only about a week ago. Meantime, I bought another house in Mansfield Street, near Cavendish Square. I got possession about a month ago; but as it is undergoing a thorough repair, cleaning, etc, we shall not be able to inhabit it much before the first of next month. Meanwhile, we have made Tunbridge Wells our headquarters, from whence we have made various expeditions into the country. We passed three weeks at Lord Pembroke's, Wilton House, said to be, and I really think it is, the finest house in Europe. It has been long a mine of the finest sculpture, paintings, and books. The present earl has now arranged the whole, with the assistance of Mr. Wyatt, with infinite taste and judgment, and at very

MEMOIR OF GENERAL GRAHAM.

great expense. There still remains a great deal to be done. From Wilton House we were singularly fortunate in an excursion to Fonthill Abbey, in the *absence* of the owner Mr. Beckford—a most singular personage, with whom no one associates. His most positive orders are in existence, to admit no one to see the abbey. We, however, got in and saw all , and a very extraordinary *all* it is. Mr. Beckford built it with the assistance of Mr Wyatt. It stands on very high and very beautiful ground, and overlooks the whole country, and has the outward appearance of an abbey, with a very high octagon tower or dome in the centre. A great folding-door in the middle of the front, 54 feet high, was opened by a dwarf, and might have been opened by an infant, so justly made are the hinges, said to have cost £500, and so well poised the great mass of door. From this a stone staircase, of about 30 feet wide, leads to the apartment which I am not able to describe. A famous yellow room leads into the library, which is a gallery of 334 feet long, 15 or 16 wide, in the centre of which rises the high dome, an octagon, all clear from top to bottom Every circumstance of furniture, painted glass windows, books, is of the most costly kind ; cabinets of every kind the most expensive , every article is a curiosity. The light coming through the painted glass windows sheds a curious mellow lustre on everything. The gallery and most of the apartments are hung with red cloth ;

FONTHILL ABBEY 261

the double curtains red and purple The costly magnificence of all within the building is not to be described, at least by me There is neither sculpture nor painting in the whole abbey, except a few bad pictures of old English kings, and a figure of St Anthony on the altar, at one extremity of the gallery The whole building is of stone

"It is with great pleasure I learn that you have obtained the pension to which your services and your wounds so fully entitle you Long may you, my dear General, enjoy every mark of honour and of comfort that can be bestowed on you

"I have just seen a severe example of the fate of war in Colonel Packenham, who is here at his sister's, Lady Wellington He received seven or eight balls quite close to the enemy's platoon in the breach He considers himself recovering, but is shockingly mangled Lord Wellington has still an arduous task before him. The French have upwards of an 100,000 men in Spain still ; I trust Bonaparte is ill at his ease in Moscow A Russian winter before him, and a Russian army behind him, are no trifles to contend with. None of my people know of my writing, or a quire of paper would not contain all they would have to say Pray, assure Mrs Graham of my sincere regards, and believe me, my dear General, most faithfully yours,   J. FLOYD."

262 MEMOIR OF GENERAL GRAHAM.

In 1814, Sir Frederick Adam, who had served with him in the Enniskillens, thus writes to him in allusion to his old corps, for which he always retained a just partiality :—

"6 Sackville Street,

"London, 11*th February* 1814.

"My dear Sir—If Lieutenant Drysdale's own merits as an officer had not fully entitled him to my aid in procuring the company vacant by the promotion of my old friend Mill, you may be quite sure that your feeling an interest in Mr. Drysdale would have ensured whatever I can do to assist him.

"I am, as you observe, still very partial to my old friends the Enniskilleners; and though the younger brothers are not to be compared in fineness of materials to the elder branch, they have always shewn themselves to be of the same good breed—to drop metaphor, the second battalion fights admirably, which is, after all, the great essential. Your friend Paddy Reeves, with all his originality, is a good officer, and I was lucky in the hour of trial to have him and his gallant battalion.

"I am very sorry to hear your eye is affected, but I hope only temporarily so. My wounds are getting better I shall not only save my fingers, but eventually recover the use of them; in the mean time I suffer considerable pain by the exfoliation of bone from my arm. Poor Reeves, when I last heard from him, was still complain-

APPLIES TO SERVE IN HOLLAND. 263

ing.—With every good wish, believe me, my dear general, very sincerely and truly yours, FREDERICK ADAM."

During the time Sir Thomas Graham commanded in the Netherlands, he addressed the following reply to an application which General Graham made, in the hope of obtaining employment under his command :—

"Calmhout, 26*th March* 1814

"Sir—I had the honour of receiving your letter dated 2d December 1813, only by the last mail. I cannot guess what has occasioned so extraordinary a delay.

"There certainly could be no apology necessary for making the offer of your services, for I know well the estimation you was held in by Sir Ralph Abercrombie. But there has been no opening that could have suited you, nor is there any probability of there being one, for, in the event of any fortress being taken, the Dutch Government would certainly name a governor of their own immediately, as they have done at Breda and other places which the Russians got possession of. I regret, therefore, being under the necessity of saying, that it is not in my power to be of use to you.—I have the honour to remain, with great regard, sir, your most obedient humble servant, "THOMAS GRAHAM.

"Major-General Graham"

264 MEMOIR OF GENERAL GRAHAM

CHAPTER THE NINETEENTH

Stirling Castle—Sieges—Stirling Heads—Rise of the enthusiasm about Scotland—Sir Walter Scott.

THE conclusion of peace in 1814 was followed by a large reduction in the staff of the army. Major-General Graham being amongst the officers struck off the staff at that time, retired to his government at Stirling Castle, where he principally resided for the remainder of his life.

Recent improvements in fortification and artillery have tended to diminish very much the importance of Stirling Castle as a fortress; and anything like disloyal feeling in the country having expired, it seems improbable that the scenes of strife from which it took its name will be repeated under its walls; the office of governor has therefore, in modern times, been abolished; but at the period of General Graham's appointment, a few years, comparatively speaking, had elapsed, since the castle stood a siege, and the name of its gallant defender, Blakeney, was still familiar as household words, the post of governor therefore continued to be an object of ambition to an old officer. It stamped him as a tried

SIEGES OF STIRLING CASTLE

servant of the Crown—a man in whom his Sovereign placed confidence, and gave him a certain degree of military consequence in his declining years, which is gratifying to a man whose life has been spent amongst soldiers.*

Few places in the country are connected with such a number of romantic traditions and stirring events in history as Stirling. Undoubtedly a Roman station, it was afterwards an important pass in the line of demarcation between the Scottish tribes occupying the country north of Stirling, and the Romanized Britons inhabiting the country south of the Forth. In the twelfth century it was one of the four principal fortresses in the kingdom, and as such was given up to the English in 1175, with the other three, Edinburgh, Roxburgh, and Berwick, as part of the ransom stipulated for the release of William the Lion at the treaty of Falaise.

In the wars of Edward First, it was frequently taken and retaken, after protracted sieges, and was evidently at that time a place capable of an obstinate defence.

By the victory of Bannockburn it fell into the hands of Bruce, who had been long endeavouring to get possession of it.

* "In 1447, James, styled Lord Livingstone, being a nobleman of great courage and prudence, was constituted captain of the Castle of Stirling, and had the custody of the young king committed to him by his father when he was the king's governor"
—*Crawford's Peerage*

MEMOIR OF GENERAL GRAHAM.

It was besieged and taken by Monk in 1651 ; and in 1681, the seizure of Stirling was planned by Lord Dundee, and the adherents of James Second, although they failed in the execution of their scheme.

In the reign of Queen Anne the fortifications were improved ; and the successful defence of the Bridge of Stirling by the Duke of Argyle in 1715, with only 1500 men, against the army of Mar, supposed to number 10,000, in a great measure checked that insurrection , while in 1745, Prince Charles, on his march to the south, did not attempt to pass the Forth at Stirling, but selected a ford at Frew, six miles from Stirling. It was in the following year that General Blakeney answered the summons to surrender, by saying that he would defend the place to the last extremity , for as he had lived so he was determined to die—a man of honour The town surrendered on the 8th of January, and the adherents of Prince Charles then proceeded to lay siege to the castle. The siege lasted until the 1st of February, when, in consequence of the advance of the Duke of Cumberland, the besiegers abandoned their works, after blowing up the principal magazine, which was kept in the church of St. Ninian's, a small village about a mile from Stirling.

During the course of this siege, General Blakeney, in order to destroy the idea which was propagated by the Stuart army, of their invulnerability, would not suf-

GARRISON CORPS 267

fer them to bury their men who were killed in the trenches and batteries. As many as sixty of them were thus exposed to view in one day. The siege-work was quite unsuitable to the habits and mode of warfare of the highlanders, and in consequence, the Irish Brigade, and Drummond's Regiment from France, were as much as possible employed upon that duty.

Until the year 1802, which was subsequent to the appointment of General Graham as deputy-governor, the castle was garrisoned by a corps of about a hundred men, who were commanded by a lieutenant and ensign, and wore a dress decidedly different from all other British uniforms. The men had a small French-looking cocked hat, a long red coat with green facings and long black leggings. The officers wore clothes of superior materials, but of the same hue and fashion, the drummer alone having a short coat of a different colour, namely of green. At a former period the breeches were blue and the belts black ; latterly, the breeches were as stated, and the belts white. The arms were latterly a musket and bayonet with a sword, but at a remoter period, they are said to have carried Lochaber axes, like the Town Guard of Edinburgh.

This uniform is said to have been first established by Mary of Guise, wife of James the Fifth of Scotland, and is supposed to have been the Lorraine uniform, but this tradition, although a popular one, does not seem to

268 MEMOIR OF GENERAL GRAHAM.

rest on certain grounds. In the other fortresses appointed by the Act of Union to be kept up in Scotland there were similar corps ; the whole were broken up in 1802.

The dress of the governor, previous to that period, was also faced with green instead of blue, the present colour.

General Graham had always a great predilection for gardening and the study of botany, a peaceful pursuit, often found to be the delight of those who have had to encounter perils and tempest on the ocean of life ; it seems as if in the evening of their days they found a peculiar charm in contemplating the contrast between the rude passions of men and the smiling face of nature in a garden decked as she there is in her most winning garb. We read in Plutarch, that Sertorius the Roman general, at one period of his life, tired of war, resolved on settling in the Canaries (or, as the poets called them, the Fortunate Islands), where some have placed the Hesperian gardens ; and that his intention was only frustrated through the treachery of a part of his crew. A long list might be furnished of poets, philosophers, statesmen, and warriors, who have shewn their love for gardens and shrubberies ; but among them all, few can have had to encounter the difficulties which the elements oppose to the formation of a garden on the top of the castle rock at Stirling. The bitter east wind

STIRLING HEADS 269

which so often sweeps over that high and exposed situation, sparing nothing in its course, would have deterred one of a less enterprising disposition from making even the attempt, but in this very difficulty, perhaps, there was a charm for the old soldier.

It was very evident from the commencement, that, unless some shelter could be obtained, nothing would grow, the plan he therefore proposed to himself was to obtain this shelter, in the first instance, by a circular belt of evergreens ; but the very raising hardy evergreens was a work of time and difficulty, and he was obliged to protect his belt of shrubs during their infancy, by a circular stockade something like a New Zealand pah. By dint of perseverance, in the course of a few years his plans were rewarded with a fair share of success.

In the antiquarian treasures of Stirling, Mrs. Graham, as well as the General, found an inexhaustible resource ; and in the " Stirling Heads,"* a work published in 1816, Mrs Graham has bequeathed to the lovers of antiquarian lore a volume of great interest and value.

The original heads represented in the work are superb oak carvings which once decorated the roof of the presence chamber in the palace of the kings of Scotland, forming, in all probability, a complete series of portraits of the most eminent personages of the times, in the exact costume of the age in which they lived. These

* " Lacunar Strevelineuse."

270 MEMOIR OF GENERAL GRAHAM.

heads are about the size of life, and with each a portion of the figure is represented, the whole being enclosed in a circular frame also of carved oak; the diameter of each, frame included, is probably about two and a half feet, and as they are entirely made of solid oak, the weight of each is, of course, very considerable. The damage which was apprehended by their falling is the reason assigned for the demolition of the roof, but any such necessity cannot be accepted as an excuse for the vandalism perpetrated in the rough treatment and careless dispersion of these precious relics—the boys in the streets having, it is said, been seen trundling some of them as hoops, while others, it is supposed, were actually cut up to heat the bakers' ovens. Mrs. Graham had not been long in Stirling Castle before her attention was attracted to the value of these works of art, and she spared no pains to trace out as many as possible, and to preserve the remembrance of them by careful drawings, the result of which was the production of the elegant work just mentioned.

The royal palaces of Scotland attest the cultivated taste of the royal race of Stuart, and their encouragement of the liberal arts ; the carvings now alluded to are also monuments of the perfection to which the Scotch had attained in wood-carving at an early age. In an excellent article in Blackwood's Magazine (Nov. 1817) on the Stirling heads, the writer, believed to be Fraser Tytler, says,

SCOTIA'S CHARMS, HOW AND WHEN UNFOLDED. 271

" They illustrate the history and manners of the age. By addressing themselves to ' the eye,' they embody, corroborate, and elucidate, those contemporary historical and poetical descriptions which till now have only met ' our ear,' and presented, through this sense, but a vague and indefinite idea." He supposes, that as the art of working in stucco advanced, it superseded or supplanted the art of carving in wood, which had previously been brought to great perfection ; and that as the art of adorning in stucco had attained considerable perfection in the very early part of the seventeenth century, these carvings, in all probability, belong to a date anterior to that period.

An ardent love of country and kindred are strongly marked features in the Scottish character. Thousands of Burns' countrymen can sympathize in the wish he expressed, to have it in his power, unplagued by business, to make leisurely pilgrimages through his native country ; to sit on the fields of her battles ; to wander on the romantic banks of her rivers, and to muse by the stately towers and venerable ruins, once the honoured abodes of her heroes. We may also quote instances of enlightened Englishmen travelling through the country a century ago, and expressing their delight and gratification.

" On returning to Edinburgh," says Pennant, " it was impossible not to recall the idea of what I had seen , to

272　MEMOIR OF GENERAL GRAHAM.

imagine the former condition of this part of the kingdom, and to compare it with the present state ; and by a sort of second sight, make a probable conjecture of the happy appearance it will assume in a few years. Nor could I forbear repeating the prophetic lines* of Aaron Hill, who seemed seized with a like reverie : —

> ' Once more, O North, I view thy winding shores,
> Climb thy bleak hills and cross thy dusky moors ,
> Impartial view thee with a heedful eye,
> Yet still by nature, not by censure tiy.
> England thy sister is a gay coquette,
> Whom art enlivens, and temptations whet ,
> Rich, proud, and wanton, she her beauty knows,
> And in a conscious warmth of beauty glows
> Scotland comes after like an unripe fair,
> Who sighs with anguish at her sister's air,
> Unconscious that she'll quickly have her day,
> And be the toast when Albion's charms decay.' "

But Pennant and Aaron Hill are exceptions ; and we believe the fact to be, that the charming scenery which Scotland presents, and the thrilling incidents interwoven with her national history, were not in themselves sufficient to attract much attention beyond the Tweed until comparatively a very recent period.

The romantic glens and rivers, the battle-fields and venerable ruins, were to be found and seen when Dr. Johnson visited the country, yet he saw nothing he liked so well as Fleet Street.

* Written on a window in North Britain

INFLUENCE OF SCOTT'S WORKS. 273

The magic touch of Walter Scott was required to throw a light over the pages of Scotia's history, illuminating at the same time, in the back ground, her beautiful valleys and heath-covered mountains.

In the effect produced by Scott's novels, we have a striking example of the wonderful power of language, as well as of the fact, that the pleasurable emotion derived from a description of any object is not dependent on the intrinsic beauty of the object itself; for we cannot ascribe the enthusiasm created in favour of Scotland by the Waverley Novels, solely to the natural features of the country in which the scenes are laid. Much is to be attributed to the admirable manner in which emotions are excited, in connection with the glories or the horrors of the scenery described.

No one understood better than Scott, that every scene, to be complete, must be associated with something which affects the imagination—must be distinguished by some event in which the mind can take an interest.

The result of this skilful interweaving of events with the materials of the world of nature, is, that the same land where Johnson found nothing worth looking at, has become the land of pilgrimage of thousands, eager to gratify themselves by viewing in reality the scenery depicted on the glowing canvas of the "Author of Waverley;" thus realizing to themselves, as far as possible, the incidents of his story.

274   MEMOIR OF GENERAL GRAHAM.

The same Stirling, on which, in the rude ages of the past, so many eyes were fixed, by reason of its being an important pass, the possession of which was eagerly coveted, has lost none of its importance as a *pass*, the causes only which gave it importance have changed. It is no longer a military position for which barbarous races are engaged in perpetual contests, but it is the great gateway through which peaceful travellers, in quest of the picturesque and romantic, must pass, standing as it does on the confines of some of the most remarkable and interesting scenery in the country.

"From the top of the Castle," Pennant says, "is by far the finest view in Scotland. To the east is a vast plain rich in corn, adorned with woods, and watered with the river Forth, whose meanders are, before it reaches the sea, so frequent and so large as to form a multitude of most beautiful peninsulas, for, in many parts, the windings approximate so close as to leave only a little isthmus of a few yards. In this place is an old abbey, a view of Alloa, Clackmannan, Falkirk, the Firth of Forth, and the country as far as Edinburgh. On the north, the Ochill hills and the moor where the battle of Dunblane was fought. To the west, the strath of Menteith, as fertile as the eastern plain, and terminated by the Highland mountains, among which the summit of Ben Lomond is very conspicuous."

And a little further—" The whole ride from Stirling

STIRLING CASTLE

LETTER FROM SIR W. SCOTT. 275

to Queensferry (near Hopetoun House) is not to be paralleled for the elegance and variety of its prospects, the whole is a composition of all that is great and beautiful, towns, villages, seats, and ancient towers decorate each bank of that fine expanse of water, the Firth; while the busy scenes of commerce and rural economy are no small addition to the still life. The lofty mountains of the Highlands form a distant but august boundary towards the north-west, and the eastern view is enlivened with ships perpetually appearing or vanishing amidst the numerous isles."

General Graham's circle of acquaintance was very extensive; he was at the same time always delighted to make the acquaintance of those who could understand and sympathize in those feelings which Stirling Castle is calculated to awaken; thus it frequently happened during his residence in the Castle, that visitors became acquainted with him through letters of introduction either to himself or Mrs. Graham; or in consequence of their being more than commonly enthusiastic in examining the locality. Among the letters of this description which have been preserved, the following is from the Great Wizard of the North himself:

Dear Mrs. Graham—May I presume upon your kindness so far, as to say that the bearer is my son, who is taking his first flight from home, and for whom I am

276 MEMOIR OF GENERAL GRAHAM.

anxious to secure General Graham's countenance, and yours, in passing through Stirling. I should particularly wish him to see what is worth noticing in your Castle, connected as it is with so many noble reminiscences; and I hope I do not trespass too much upon your goodness in hoping you will facilitate his progress. His travelling companion is Mr. Allan, son of Mr. Allan of Edinburgh. I need not say that when you have a friend who wishes to see what *lions* we have to shew on Tweedside, no one can be so happy to offer some small requital for the honour he now solicits, than, dear Mrs. Graham, your truly respectful, and obedient servant,

WALTER SCOTT.

Abbotsford, 24*th July*

From the same hand Mrs Graham received upon another occasion, the following graceful acknowledgment for some small service which she had been enabled to render :—

My dear Mrs. Graham—I scarce know a subject (after good morals) on which a father should be more anxious for his son on his entrance into life, than that of securing him good society, and I feel proportionably your kindness in sending me such valuable introductions for Walter to your friends at Cork. He is a bashful lad, as becomes his extreme youth, but I think well

RADICAL COMMOTIONS. 277

disposed to profit by your kindness in a matter of so much consequence. He left us on Wednesday to swim with bladders in the great sea of human life, and greatly shall I be obliged to any that will hold up his chin occasionally. You will think I have scarce got free of the technical language of the bath at Mr Gunn's, but at least I have the pleasure to say, that after a relapse which followed my getting out here, my health has at length mended, and seems now in the way of being quite confirmed. In fact, I am more absolutely free from all sort of stomach complaints than I have been at any former period of my life, only I am still weak, to which the remedy, that is the constant use of calomel, has contributed. Should any wind favourable to us blow you towards this quarter, we should be delighted to see you, the general, and all the family. I will shew you Melrose in great style. Mrs Scott and the girls offer best regards, and I am ever, dear madam, your obliged and grateful servant, WALTER SCOTT.

Abbotsford, 16*th July*

278　　MEMOIR OF GENERAL GRAHAM

CHAPTER THE TWENTIETH.

Radical Movement—Union Societies—Bonnymuir Prisoners in
Stirling Castle—Veteran Battalions

DURING the great revolutionary war with France, the
naval supremacy of England obtained for her a mo-
nopoly of the carrying-trade of the world. The requirements of the war, and foreign exports, afforded ample
employment to the artizans and mechanics in the country, while the high price of farming-produce was con-
ducive to the interests of the agriculturists.

On the return of peace, this state of general prosperity was succeeded by a state of wide-spread distress
and suffering

At that period the great political convulsions of the
preceding century in America and France began first to
exhibit visible effects on the institutions of this country.

The prevailing distress, caused by the termination of
the war, was made use of by political demagogues to
excite a feeling of hostility to all established authority
The sufferings of the people were ascribed to the weight
of the national debt, and the tyranny and oppression of

TREASONABLE PROCLAMATION. 279

the aristocracy ; and a thorough reform in Parliament declared to be the only panacea for the existing misery and distress

These notions and principles were studiously impressed on the people, and promulgated far and wide by means of pamphlets and itinerant orators.

Large bodies of men were assembled to listen to inflammatory harangues, under pretext of petitioning the King and Parliament. The numbers assembled on some occasions exceeded 50,000. One of the most numerous of these meetings was held at Manchester in August 1819, and its dispersion caused a serious sacrifice of life.

Various enactments were immediately after this passed, which had the effect of suppressing these meetings, but the disaffected in Scotland immediately organized " Union Societies," in which a considerable portion of the operative classes enrolled themselves.

These societies held weekly meetings, and soon put themselves in communication with corresponding societies of reformers in England, by means of delegates, who received regular pay , and these men finding their business thus profitable, spared no pains to exaggerate the strength and progress of the cause of radical reform.

" Towards the end of March 1820, a general rising of the unions was talked of in the neighbourhood of Glasgow ; and it was said that the disaffected had not only been provided with arms, but by repeated drilling, had

280 MEMOIR OF GENERAL GRAHAM

thoroughly instructed themselves in the effectual use of them."*

On the 1st of April an address was posted up in Glasgow, Paisley, and other manufacturing towns, calling upon the people to take up arms for the redress of their grievances, and announcing the full determination to proceed to hostility against the constituted authorities ; declaring equality of rights, though not of property, to be the object for which they contended, and bidding the troops remember the glorious conduct of the soldiery of Spain, and follow their example. It concluded by requesting, that during the continuance of so momentous a struggle, all persons should desist from their labour, from and after the 1st April ; and further, recommended to the proprietors of public works to put a stop to them until the restoration of order. The proclamation ended thus :—" And we hereby give notice to all who shall be found carrying arms against those who intend to regenerate their country, and restore its inhabitants to their native dignity, that we shall consider them as traitors to their country, and enemies to their king, and treat them as such.

" By order of the Committee for forming a
" Provisional Government"

The injunction to suspend work was very generally

* *Annual Register*, 1820

observed by the weavers, cotton-spinners, and a great number of artizans and mechanics of other denominations followed their example. In Glasgow and its neighbourhood, 60,000 persons it is supposed struck work. The consequence of this was, that the streets were crowded with idle people menacing the public peace.

Proclamations were issued by the magistracy, cautioning the people against taking part in any tumult, and the necessary measures were adopted for the preservation of, and for restoring order, if necessary, by force of arms. Stirling Castle was denuded of troops, their presence being required to aid in making up such a force as the expected crisis in Glasgow appeared to require; and a superb corps of volunteers, named the Glasgow Sharpshooters, may still be remembered for their military appearance and patriotic spirit; but the number of those who have any recollection of that alarming era is fast diminishing; a generation almost has passed, and the present generation have little conception of the excitement in the country at the period of which we are speaking.

Men's minds were familiarized at the time with the idea of a collision between the military and the people by the conflict which had taken place at Manchester; a repetition of that scene, or an outbreak of a much more formidable character seemed imminent, day after

282 MEMOIR OF GENERAL GRAHAM.

day rumours were afloat that the insurrection was on the point of breaking out.

At length on the 5th April, while this state of excitement was at its height, intelligence was brought to the Castle of Stirling that a battle had actually taken place between the radicals, as they were called, and the military, and that the former had been routed and dispersed, and a number of them taken prisoners. This report was speedily succeeded by the approach of a troop of cavalry (10th Hussars and Stirlingshire Yeomanry) escorting a number of prisoners, together with some carts in which wounded men were lying. The long pikes which had been taken from the prisoners were now carried by the dragoons in rest, like lances ; and the martial procession, winding its way to the old castle over the esplanade, by which the drawbridge and gate are approached, was extremely picturesque.

Until Lieutenant Hodgson of the 10th Hussars, who commanded this detachment, made his report to General Graham, nothing was known with any certainty as to what had actually taken place, or what might be expected next.

From this officer's report, it appeared that intelligence having reached him of a gathering of armed men in the direction of Bonnymuir, he had proceeded there from Kilsyth with a detachment of his own regiment and some of the yeomanry cavalry, then on permanent

SKIRMISH AT BONNYMUIR.

duty, on arriving at the locality indicated, an assemblage
of men, with arms in their hands, became visible on a
rising ground, the base of which was skirted by a stone
wall, through which there was only one opening, affording access to the position taken up by these people
The lieutenant immediately led his men to this gap, but
before he reached it, the insurgents descended the slope
with a cheer, and posted themselves in such a manner
as to oppose the passage of the gap. In forcing his way
through, the lieutenant received a severe wound in the
hand from a pike, and his serjeant, who followed him,
was also very severely wounded in the arm; and some
of the cavalry horses were seriously injured or killed
After the cavalry passed fairly through the gap, all resistance was very soon at an end. Such of the insurgents as could make their escape did so, and the others
threw down their arms and surrendered.

A few of the men who were taken had suffered from
the swords of the cavalry, and it was believed that one of
them had been killed. The prisoners taken amounted
to nineteen No correct estimate of the number present at the commencement of the fray could be given,
but it seemed probable that it did not exceed fifty in all

The prisoners were all tried for high treason, and
being convicted, were sentenced to be hanged and beheaded, but only two of them suffered the extreme
penalty, the sentence on the others being commuted to

284 MEMOIR OF GENERAL GRAHAM.

transportation for life Baird, one of the men executed, and who was the commander of the party, had been a corporal in the Rifle Brigade Hardie, his fellow-sufferer, had been a serjeant in the militia.

Mr. Peter M'Kenzie of Glasgow has published a very circumstantial account of the enterprize led by Baird and Hardie ; and he argues with great force, that these men and their followers were the victims of foul treachery

The zeal shewn by Baird and Hardie to the last, for the cause of reform, leaves no room to doubt their feelings on that subject ; and their superior intelligence and determination of character accounts for their having been selected to take a lead in the revolutionary proceedings in which they engaged ; but it is evident from Mr. M'Kenzie's book, that neither of them planned the expedition to seize the Carron works, which seems to have been the object of the party who assembled at Bonnymuir. The active agents in promoting the enterprize are named in Mr M'Kenzies book, and the conclusion to be drawn from what is therein stated is, that the promoters of the scheme were base traitors, and enticed Baird and Hardie and their followers to take a part in it, solely with a view to betraying them into the hands of Government.

In consequence of the state of the country at this period, a call was made upon all discharged soldiers in

VETERAN BATTALIONS.

the receipt of pension, and capable of serving, and veteran battalions were formed of the men who came forward to enrol themselves

Stirling Castle was selected as the rendezvous for one of these battalions, and a number of men were speedily obtained ; but there was a want of officers to command them In this emergency General Graham accepted the temporary services of some retired half-pay officers who had made Stirling their residence, and came forward in the most patriotic way and expressed their readiness to do duty if required

By means of the assistance thus obtained, an officer's guard was mounted for some time while the popular excitement was at its height *

* General Graham always expressed himself greatly indebted to Major Peddie, acting fort-major, for his zeal and activity at this critical period.

No proper places of confinement existed in the Castle at the time these prisoners arrived, yet during the time they remained no accident of any kind occurred, nor was any complaint of any description ever brought to the notice of the governor—(*See Appendix*). Major Peddie had previously greatly distinguished himself at the siege of Bergen-op-Zoom, where he would certainly have gained the Victoria Cross, had that institution been in existence, having rescued his commanding officer, Colonel Henry, as well as another wounded officer, under a very heavy fire.

CHAPTER THE TWENTY-FIRST.

Artists at Stirling—Letters from Sir D. Wilkie, Dr. Gregory, Mr. Williams, and Mr. Herman Ryland—Visits to Sir Robert Abercromby—Death of General Graham.

STIRLING has long been a favourite place of resort for artists, and any gentlemen of that profession who visited the castle while General Graham resided there, were always welcome to the governor's house. Amongst those who thus became more than transient acquaintances may be numbered the celebrated Wilkie.

During one of Wilkie's visits to Stirling he greatly admired a piece of oriental carpet of the texture of tapestry, which he found in one of the churches—an edifice which had been for some time shut up. The General, on hearing of the circumstance, undertook to procure the carpet for him, and succeeded in doing so through his butcher, a very worthy member of the Town-Council. For this little service Wilkie always expressed himself much indebted, as he found it serviceable in some of his pictures, from the rarity of the

SIR D. WILKIE. 287

pattern, and also owing to some peculiar arrangement of the colour. The following is a letter from the great painter himself on the subject :—

> " Phillimore Place, Kensington,
> " London, *Nov.* 2, 1817.

"Dear Sir—I have but now returned to this place, and was much gratified at finding a letter from you waiting for me. It gives me great pleasure to hear of you and Mrs Graham again, and to find myself remembered in so friendly a way, as I find I have been, by your kindness in obtaining for me the grant from the corporation of the carpet I wished so much to have. I have now to request that you will be so kind as send it by the coach to Edinburgh, to *Mr. Brown, bookseller, North Bridge Street,* who has got directions from me to pack it properly, to be sent by sea to London. You will also oblige me much by mentioning whether you were put to any incidental expenses in the way of obtaining the carpet, such as fees or so to people connected with the corporation, that I may have the pleasure of defraying them

" Your supposition of its having belonged to the royal palace, is the most probable way of accounting for its coming there. Perhaps some authentic knowledge about this might be got from a book that has been published by a Mr Thomson, giving an inventory of the jewels and wardrobe of the Kings of Scotland.

288   MEMOIR OF GENERAL GRAHAM.

"It might be curious to know whether carpets are mentioned, and what sort of them. I am still persuaded that it can only be of Persian manufacture. That of there being wild beasts and dragons upon it, which I think there is, I am told is an objection to this, as Mahometans are not allowed to represent natural objects; but I suppose this would apply more to the Turkish than to the Persian manufactures. It would be curious, indeed, if it had really belonged to that interesting apartment now a part of your drawing-room. It is evidently an ancient relic, and as such I shall consider it a great curiosity.

"I beg, sir, to thank you for the friendly interest you have taken in this affair. I beg to be most kindly remembered to Mrs Graham; and with sincere esteem and regard, I have the honour to be, dear sir, your very faithful servant,   DAVID WILKIE."

The celebrated Dr. Gregory of Edinburgh, proposing to pay a visit to Stirling, thus announced his intention to the General :—

"Edinburgh, 19th April 1818.

"The first time that the wheel of fortune shall whirl me to Stirling I shall not fail to storm your castle and put your whole garrison to the *pill*—a much surer weapon than either *sword* or *gun*. Yourself I shall carry in

MR. WILLIAMS. 289

triumph to the *Borestone*,* where, *nolens volens*, you shall read me a military lecture on the battle of Bannockburn   J. G."

The following is from Mr Williams the eminent landscape painter in Edinburgh —

> " 65 North Castle Street,
> " 14th *July* 1826.

" Dear Sir—Our friend Mr Geddes, when I was in London a few days ago, entrusted to my care a print of the Duke of York, to be presented to you for your acceptance. I have now the pleasure of sending it, along with a small parcel from myself, to your excellent lady.

" This fine weather must bring innumerable strangers to your magnificent abode, which will give a regal expression to it, but I fear your time and hospitality must be sadly intruded on. This beautiful evening exhibits a charming amber sky towards the west, and I almost fancy I perceive your castle rising among the purple clouds. How I should rejoice to be able to devote a whole month to the scenery of Stirling alone.

" Please tell Mrs. Graham that the ' Exhibition' this

* On an eminence, overlooking the celebrated field of Bannockburn, near Stirling, a stone is pointed out, to which the name of the " Borestone" has been given, from a round hole in its centre, in which it is said Bruce's standard was fixed on the day of the battle.

O

290 MEMOIR OF GENERAL GRAHAM

year (in London) was but so so. Turner, of course, is always paramount ; and Lawrence stands at the head of portrait painters His pictures of Peel and Canning were excellent, full of truth and character I am glad to say, too, that Geddes is getting on very well His portraits are much admired ; he was painting the Bishop of Limerick when I saw him, and succeeded extremely well Poor Wilkie, from all accounts, is not much better. He will spend the winter at Rome; but he does nothing with his pencil. I saw a letter from him lately, giving an account of all that he had seen, and a more interesting letter I never read. He, of course, is much made of abroad, and enjoys himself as much as an invalid can do.—Believe me to be, dear sir, yours, with esteem and respect, J H WILLIAMS."

During the remaining years of General Graham's life he seldom quitted Stirling, except to pay an occasional visit to his sister Mrs. Hay in Edinburgh. His favourite walk was to Airthrie Castle, the residence of Sir Robert Abercromby, of whom mention has already been made in the course of this narrative, as bravely sallying from the crumbling ramparts of York Town, at the head of a chosen band, and carrying havoc and consternation into the enemy's works Sir Robert being many years older than General Graham, the latter looked up to him with a degree of filial respect Those

SIR ROBERT ABERCROMBY. 291

now living who knew Sir Robert must recollect him as a vision of a bygone age.

At the time here alluded to, although verging on ninety years of age, he was erect in figure, and with the exception of his sight, which was very weak, he retained all his faculties unimpaired. When walking about the beautiful grounds and park adjoining his mansion, his figure, if not picturesque, was certainly unique. His coat, usually of a snuff-brown, exhibited in its shape a struggle between a predilection for the broad flaps of the last century, and a desire to countenance the prevailing fashion of the day; this antagonism of motives ending in a compromise, and the garment itself ending in belonging to no particular species of the genus coat; a white neckcloth, a double-breasted red waistcoat of an antiquated build, drab knee-breeches, and top boots, completed the costume. Owing to his very delicate eyesight he always wore coloured spectacles, and a green shade over his eyes; and out of doors he generally walked with a green umbrella over his head, forming an agreeable contrast to his waistcoat. In the evening, if he had any guests, he always appeared with the star of the bath on his coat, knee breeches and silk stockings. Punctuality was with him a cardinal virtue; and those who knew his peculiarities always made a point of appearing in the drawing-room before the dinner hour. At five o'clock

292 MEMOIR OF GENERAL GRAHAM.

punctually, an old French butler (Derry was his name), announced to his master, with a French accent, "*dinare* ready, Sir Robert" Everything on the table was faultless, and the whole of the arrangements like clock-work ; Sir Robert's defect of sight was in some degree remedied by the acuteness of his hearing. Being a bachelor, he was in the habit of asking his factor, Mr F——, occasionally to officiate as croupier when he had a dinner party Upon one such occasion, Mr F——, having helped some one to roast beef, and the servant having inadvertently taken away the plate without any gravy, Mr F——, addressing the guest he had just helped, asked whether he would not have some *sauce* with his beef. Sir Robert, hearing what his factor said, corrected him in this way—"Sauce to roast beef, sir' who the devil ever heard of such a thing ? Gravy you mean."

Sir Robert's services had been principally in India, and he had been little with his brother Sir Ralph, under whom General Graham had so frequently served. But as he had been in America with General Graham in the earlier part of his career in the war of independence, they had many mutual acquaintances, and many an anecdote in connection with the history of olden times was recounted when these two old warriors met, of which it is to be regretted that no note was made at the time Sir Robert, although a disciplinarian, was greatly beloved by his household The old French butler who has been

AN OLD FRIEND DISCOVERED 293

alluded to was secured the enjoyment of a delightful cottage on the estate for his life, and Sir Robert's valet, soon after his master's death, fell into a desponding state, and at last, it is supposed, put an end to his life.

In the early part of the year 1830, Mrs. Graham's cousin, Mr. Lewis Ferrier, was appointed chief commissioner of the customs at Quebec, and, the General having accidentally heard that an acquaintance of his early life, Mr. Herman Ryland, was a resident there, took the opportunity of sending a letter to him by Mr. L. Ferrier, to which he received the following interesting reply —

> " Beaufort, near Quebec,
> " *Sunday, 9th June* 1830.

"Never, never, my dear General, have I been more agreeably surprised than I was yesterday, by the receipt of your letter of the 11th April, which was delivered to me by Mr. Ferrier. How often have I thought of you ! How often, during the period of six and forty years have I inquired after you, without ever happening to meet with a person who could give me any information respecting you ! and here now, we are suddenly brought, as it were, face to face, and talking together on matters lang syne gone by, and looking as young as we did fifty years ago ; for you can have no idea of me, at upwards of seventy years of age, nor can I have a recollection of you as being more than seven or eight and twenty. How

294 MEMOIR OF GENERAL GRAHAM.

pleasant it is to hear you!—1 was going to say, revert to scenes of early life—and find such as you advert to, still fresh in your memory. This is the first time since we parted that I have heard a word of the lady you mention. I think I see her now listening at my door, while you were abusing her. What strange turns does human nature sometimes take, and how we all were astonished at hers! Do you remember the scene at poor Gordon's, when I drew on the brother, and got a pink in the arm after the ruffians had knocked me down? Another fair one, whom you must recollect, is still living, she married in London about five years after she went to England, and had three sons by her husband, who died upwards of thirty years ago. They are all doing very well, and were my neighbours when I was last in London. We still keep up an irregular intercourse by letter—a more intimate one never took place after the separation at New York. You astonish me by what you mention about Sir William Campbell.* We have met at different

---

* This has reference to a visit paid by Sir William Campbell to General Graham at Stirling Castle sometime previously.

Upon the occasion referred to, the servant announced to the General a visitor—Sir William Campbell. The General received his visitor in that friendly, cordial manner which was habitual to him; but it was evident to the visitor that the General neither remembered him as an old acquaintance nor knew the nature of his business. In order to dispel the mystery which evidently attended his visit, he lost no time in saying—"I daresay, General, you do not recollect me as Sir William Campbell; but you will,

ELEVATION OF A SERJEANT TO THE BENCH. 295

times when he came down to Quebec ; but I had no recollection of ever having seen him before How he could attain or possibly discharge the duties of a chief justice is to me incomprehensible ! He always appeared to me as an unassuming, good sort of man, who might be qualified to act as a Justice of the Peace in a back settlement on this continent. I think the Judge's grateful attention to you does him credit. To me he was under no obligation, and I had entirely forgotten him.

"I missed of seeing Sir Thomas Saumarez when I was last in England, and had the mortification of learning after I returned here, that we had taken up our quarters in the same hotel at Portsmouth, without either of us knowing that we were so near each other. I had a kind message from him a year or two ago, through a lady of our mutual acquaintance. the wife of a Major Elliot.

"I must now, my dear General, give you a more particular account of my life and adventures since we last parted. You may know that on the evacuation of New York, I returned to England with my friend Mr. Poyntz and the commander-in-chief, Sir Guy Carleton, in the Ceres frigate On our arrival we found all the Spenser

perhaps recollect Serjeant Campbell in your company in the 76th Regiment in the American war ; you see before you that individual, and I am now Sir William Campbell, Chief-Justice of Upper Canada " The General perfectly recollected him as having been in the regiment with him

296   MEMOIR OF GENERAL GRAHAM

connection (my first and kindest protectors) were out of the ministry, and so they continued for many years. About a twelvemonth afterwards I went over to France, and took up my abode in the village of Clichy, near Paris, where I had been at school some seven or eight years before

"Whilst there I had, through the interest of Lord Spenser, nearly got into employment under the royal family of France, but fortunately circumstances suddenly induced me to return to England, or my head might never have had so bald and venerable an appearance as it now has

"At the time of the first contemplated Regency, Lord S., who was nominated by the Prince of Wales to the Vice - Royalty of Ireland, made choice of me for his private secretary, but the sudden restoration of His Majesty's health put an end to this arrangement, and I remained *sur le pavé* till 1793, when Lord Dorchester, then Governor-in-Chief of British America, brought me out with him to Quebec as his confidential secretary, in which capacity I served under the several persons administering the government of this province during a period of twenty years till the summer of 1813, when I gladly resigned the situation under that renowned general Sir George Prevost.

"In 1810 I was sent home by Sir James Craig on the public business of the province, and remained there till the spring of 1812, in official intercourse with the late Lord Liverpool and Mr Peel, then secretary and under-secretary of State for the Colonies Before I left England the Prince Regent was pleased, on the recommendation of his Lordship, to issue a mandamus, calling me to a seat in the legislative council of this Province, as a mark of His Royal Highness' approbation of my public services

"Within a short time after my arrival in England I attended the funeral of General Peter Craig (with whom I had had only one interview), and about a year afterwards that of his brother Sir James, a man of the most amiable character and first-rate talents, to whom I was most devotedly attached. I was in constant intercourse with him from the time he returned home to the time of his decease, and as constantly with my friend Sir James Kempt, our present governor, who had been quarter-master-general under Sir James Craig at the time I was his civil secretary.

"At poor Sir James' funeral I met, for the first time since the evacuation of New York, the late Sir Harry Calvert, but we did not recognise each other—that is to say, we did not speak to each other Some days after the funeral, Thornton, who was then assistant-military-secretary to the Duke of York, and had been military-secretary to Sir James, told me that he had spoken kindly of me to him ; and I can truly say that from the first

298 MEMOIR OF GENERAL GRAHAM.

moment when our acquaintance began at Winchester in Virginia, I uniformly entertained for him sentiments of the most sincere esteem and regard.

"Alas! he and all the rest of a certain class of those you mention have passed away, and you and I, my dear general, must, in the common course of nature, soon follow them to that bourne from whence no traveller returns. Let me entreat you then whilst the possibility of intercourse between us still remains, let me entreat you to continue to favour me with your correspondence. No language can express the high gratification it will afford me, and if either of your sons happen to be destined to serve in this country, let me hope you will desire them to consider me as a parent, and be assured they shall receive from me all the kindness that a parent can shew them.

"But you must allow me to chat a little longer with you about myself and my family, and consider that this is the first opportunity I have had of saying a word to you during a period of six and forty years. At the close of 1794 I married a townswoman of my own, to whom I had long been attached As it was impossible for me to go to her, she yielded at last to my earnest persuasion and came to me by the way of New York. We met in an open boat on Lake Champlain on the evening of the 10th December, after she had been frozen up for some days at Isle aux Noix, and were married the next day

CANADIAN MARRIAGE. 299

at Montreal. By the kindness of providence she is still preserved to be the comfort and happiness of my old age—out of nine children we have four only remaining, two sons and two daughters, all of them of age but neither of them married, nor am I in a hurry to see them so, especially the girls, who are amiable in the highest degree, and the loss of whose society I should not have strength of mind to bear.

"My eldest son, William Deane, resigned his situation of assistant-clerk of the executive council of this province, in favour of his brother George about eight years ago, and with my consent went to England, where he entered himself at St John's College, Cambridge, and after four years study took a bachelor's degree, and has since entered into holy orders. Though the interest of Lord Spenser he obtained the curacy of Sandridge, near St. Albans, where he still remains, praying day and night for better promotion; the curacy being worth only £120 a year, I am obliged to make such an addition to his income as may enable him to hold up his head.

"He bears a high character and has very good talents, which I trust will sooner or later secure him preferment, especially should Lord Spenser's valuable life be continued. In the year 1823 he made a tour with his tutor (a Mr. Spenser, who, I understand, has since been tutor to the Duke of Buccleuch) into Scotland, and on turning to the journal he sent me, I find he was at

300   MEMOIR OF GENERAL GRAHAM.

Stirling on the 26th August of that year. In noticing
the castle he expresses himself as follows.—

"'The castle of Stirling is situated at the summit of a
lofty precipice, the upper part of which is as steep as a
wall, the rest more sloping, and clothed at the base with
trees It is along side of this hill that a walk has been
made for the convenience of the inhabitants of Stirling,
and surely never was beheld a more magnificent prospect
than that which presents itself from this terrace! The
whole country beneath stretches out to an immense extent, in general as smooth as a bowling green, but broken
up in many places into huge hills and rocks, which
resemble islands rising from a sea. Some are steep and
craggy, others covered with wood, and in the distance is
the long range of the Highland mountains, among which
are pointed out Ben Lomond, Ben Nevis, and Ben
Vorlich. The sun was setting with the utmost splendour when I first beheld this scene, and gilding every
object in the prospect with his parting beams—prospect
sufficiently attractive from its natural beauties, but rendered doubly interesting by the storied associations of
the place. At a short distance lay the fields of Falkirk
and of Bannockburn, and on turning my eyes towards
the site of the battle of Kilsyth, I called to mind the
heroic achievements of the gallant Marquis of Montrose'

"But not a word more does he say about the castle,

STIRLING CASTLE. 301

from which I conclude that he had not the good fortune to enter its Gates Oh! had he but known that the governor of that fortress was a man with whom his father had been intimately acquainted at his first entrance into public life, and in whose society the most joyous period of his existence had been passed, how happy would he have been to pay his respects to such a man! Really when I think that he might have had this happiness, that it was positively within his reach, and that through my ignorance of your situation he missed of it, I feel as if I myself had suddenly been deprived of the greatest pleasure I could enjoy. I fear, poor fellow, that there is little chance of his ever making another trip to Stirling Castle, yet I would gladly provide him with the means of going there, did his present situation in the church allow of it.

"What you say of poor dear Colonel Gordon makes me very anxious to see the papers you refer to, and which you have been advised to publish You will be surprised to hear that Asgill refused to pledge himself for the repayment of the monies I advanced him (in case government disallowed the charge), and that a very unpleasant correspondence passed between us on the subject, which is still in my possession.* However

---

* It was natural that Mr Ryland should wish to get his accounts settled, but Sir Charles Asgill may have been quite justified in his refusal to become personally responsible

302   MEMOIR OF GENERAL GRAHAM

both that and the robbery were afterwards passed in my accounts upon a representation from Lord Dorchester

" I am pleased with your having heard of me from Captain Maule of the 79th,* for whom I have a real regard, and will thank you to tell him so if you happen to see him again.

" I have, I believe, noticed every particular in your letter and bored you with a long tale respecting myself and my family, yet I flatter myself you will not think I have trespassed too far on your time after a silence of seven and forty years. On the contrary I will indulge a hope that hereafter you will favour me with frequent intercourse with you by letter.

" Be assured I shall to the utmost of my power cultivate an acquaintance and friendship with Mr Ferrier, both on your account and my own, for he appears to be a most amiable and respectable man.

" And now, my dear general, farewell, no words can express how anxious I shall be to hear from you again. May God preserve you many years, and grant to you and your family every happiness that human nature is capable of enjoying. I am ever, with sentiments of the truest esteem and regard—Most sincerely and affectionately yours,   HERMAN W. RYLAND."

* Now Earl of Dalhousie, late Lord Panmure, secretary of State for War Department

DEATH 303

At this period General Graham was easily affected, as he had been for years, by atmospheric changes, owing to the wound in his lungs, and frequently also suffered from rheumatism, probably the effect of great exposure and hardships in his campaigns , he was more feeble than formerly and unable to walk far without feeling fatigue, but he took the same pleasure as ever in his garden, and no indication of any disease tending to shorten life had displayed itself. The sand of life was, however, rapidly, though imperceptibly, ebbing, and on the 25th January 1831, after having retired to rest as usual, he rose in the middle of the night and complained of feeling very cold. He remained in this state for a few hours, then, on the morning of the 26th, in trying to walk across the room, his strength entirely failed, and sinking down, he calmly said "I am dying," and in a few moments ceased to breathe

His remains rest in the vault of Mr. Graham Moir of Leckie in the church of Stirling.

APPENDIX.

A, Page 30.

THE country in which the armies were engaged at this time was quite uncultivated, and the privations endured by the enemy were quite on a par with those of our own troops Having upon one occasion met with General Isaac Hayes who commanded the American continentals, he told me that a Captain Millar of Tarleton's legion, made prisoner by Lee's dragoons, was brought to his (the General's) quarters at the dinner hour, and was served like himself, and his aide-de-camp and brigade-major, with a cake of Indian meal, a small piece of salt pork, and a ration of rum to mix with some bad water Captain Millar, mortified and uncomfortable at the feeling of being a prisoner, took only the pork and the grog, and left the cake upon his plate. The brigade-major cast an eager glance at the cake and asked the general if he should *take away* the captain's plate, as he seemed to have finished dinner. The general upon this said to Captain Millar, " Sir, he wishes to get your CAKE, but as we shall get no further refreshment till to-morrow, I would recommend to you to put it in your pocket."

B, Page 37.

After our arrival at Petersburg, General Arnold, on whom the command of the force had devolved in consequence of

306   APPENDIX.

the illness of General Philips, ordered a party of the 76th
and 80th to march down to the bridge which had been
destroyed by the enemy a short time before, and make a feint
of repairing it It fell to my lot to command, and while
employed we were saluted by a discharge of grape shot from
the height on the opposite bank I received orders to bring
off my party cautiously, and having collected them in rear of
a house close to the bridge, I told them that the best mode
was to move off singly and rapidly, having a space of three or
four hundred yards to pass under the muzzles of the enemy's
guns ; luckily the place was studded with trees, which partly
intercepted the view from the bank on which the artillery
was placed, and favoured the escape of the whole party.

A sentinel of the 80th regiment, who was one of the last
to effect his retreat, being observed by some of the enemy's
riflemen, who had come down on the bank of the stream,
they called out to him to come from behind the tree which
sheltered him ; the man's name was Pearson, an Edinburgh
baker, and his answer was, " Na, na, I came na sae far from
hame to show sa muckle folly," and while a party was
mustering to take him, he seized a favourable opportunity,
fired his piece and joined his party in safety

CAPTAIN SAMUEL GRAHAM'S LETTER TO GENERAL MORGAN,
AA, Page 68

Sir,—Having been informed that Colonel Holmes's indulgence in allowing 500 of the British prisoners of war to be
quartered in the church in the town of Wynchester has not
met with your approbation, and that you intend to order
these troops immediately to return to the log huts and join
the other prisoners, it is my duty to state to you that on our
first arrival in this place, an equal division of the huts was
made amongst the prisoners, and finding that there was not

APPENDIX. 307

a sufficient number to cover above one half, I made frequent representations to Colonel Holmes, commissary of prisoners, requesting that some immediate steps might be taken for the protection of the other half who are exposed to the inclemency of the weather, as the winter was fast approaching, or to furnish us with tools to build more huts, as we had no money to make such a purchase, he, I have reason to believe, has stated our situation to the commissary-general, but not having it in his power to grant our immediate relief, humanely allowed the 76th regiment, about 500 men, to march into the church in the town, which has been of great use, as the huts possessed by them at the barracks have been distributed amongst the other prisoners; I hope therefore you will be so obliging as allow these men to remain in the church, as it would be a great hardship to dispossess the other soldiers of the huts which were occupied by the 76th regiment, and a still greater hardship to oblige a Highland regiment to construct log huts for themselves, to which work they have never been accustomed, especially when the snow is already on the ground. Should you still persist in your determination to order these 500 men to return to the log huts, you will oblige me by acknowledging the receipt of this, that I may have it in my power to show to my superior officer, that I have not failed in my duty in representing this matter to you.—I have the honour to be most respectfully your humble servant,

(Signed) " S. GRAHAM."

BB, Page 82.

The order to designate an officer for retaliation did not long remain a secret amongst the British soldiers confined at Lancaster, and they expressed their disapprobation of it, by murmurs inside the stockades by which they were enclosed; in consequence of this, various proposals were made by the

308 APPENDIX.

captains, but at length we were swayed by the opinion given by Major Gordon, which was, that we had *only* come to the knowledge of the intended transaction confidentially, through the politeness of General Hazan ; that we could not in honour act upon information thus obtained ; that the treaty had not yet been infringed, and we were bound by our paroles of honour until an infraction of this treaty was actually made. To the honour of the soldiers, I have little hesitation in affirming, that if the officers had gone amongst them, and encouraged them to attempt to disarm the guards, which were not numerous at either of the posts, and break out of their confinement and force their way into New York that they would have tried to do so, however desperate the attempt might appear to be.

AB, Page 86

The following instance of noble and disinterested feeling, exhibited by Captain David Barclay of the 76th regiment, deserves to be recorded in honour of his memory .—

When the American General Hazan, who was entrusted with the duty of designating the officer for retaliation, had in vain begged the officers to select among themselves, he desired his A D C and the commissary of prisoners to retire into the next room to prepare the lots. At the same time, addressing himself to Captain David Barclay, he said, " Sir, I have received a letter from His Excellency General Washington directing me to give you leave to go into New York, I shall therefore not include your name with those of the other gentlemen ." to this Captain Barclay replied, " Sir, I desire that my name may be included, as I insist upon sharing the fate that awaits with my brother officers."

BA, Page 121.

This quotation from Allison appears to be a literal transla-

APPENDIX.

309

tion of the following passage in General Jomini's history of the wars of the French Revolution.

"C'etait pour la cinquieme fois que Clairfayt combattait isolement tendis que 30 milles Autrichiens restaient dans l'inaction a Tournay, et que 6 et 8 mille Anglais sous les ordres de Lord Moira se reposaient à Ostende des fatigues de la traversée."

Jomini in this passage alludes to the defeat of Clairfayt by Macdonald at Hoogléde on the 13th June, thirteen days before the arrival of Lord Moira at Ostend.

C, Page 183.

General Custine, for having failed to relieve Mayence in May 1793, was denounced as a traitor and incompetent, and condemned to death August 1793

A number of the Mayence Club said at the trial, if the proceeding can be deemed worthy of the name of a judicial process, that Custine had allowed himself to be beaten by placing his men at the foot of a mountain "Tout le monde sait que c'est au sommet des montagnes qu'une armée doit etre placée, eh bien lui est resté en bas"

This accusation had great weight with men who had never been out of Paris in their lives, and were here now acting severally and collectively as judges and jurymen

---

D, Page 191

Hochard (or Houchard) like Custine terminated his life on the scaffold In allusion to this circumstance Jomini says, "The Romans beheaded Manlius for having fought and

310 APPENDIX

gained a battle against the orders of the senate, the English punished Byng for not having gained a victory at Minorca, but Houchard is the first instance of a General brought to condign punishment for having gained an important victory, but without annihilating his enemy."

The trial of Houchard, like that of Custine, led to an exposition of the theory of war on the part of the prosecution, but the military principles enunciated in the two cases differ materially in value. When Houchard was arraigned, the orator Barrere, prompted it is supposed by Carnot, who was beginning to infuse life into the war department, thus addressed the unfortunate general — " Depuis longtemps le premier principe pour tirer parti du courage du soldat, le principe etabli par Frederick, et celui de tout les grands generaux, est d'avoir de grandes armées en masses, plutot que de partager ses forces. Au contraire vous n'avez eu que des armées desseminées morcelées meme lorsqu'on les rassemblait en masse des generaux ignorans ou perfides les divisaient et les faisaient battre en détail, en les opposant toujours à un ennemi supérieur. Le Comité a aperçu le mal et a écrit aux généraux de se battre en masse. Ils ne l'ont pas fait, vous avez eu des revers."

BONNYMUIR PRISONERS

In the year 1859 a correspondence appeared in the Stirling Journal, imputing to the authorities in Stirling Castle the exercise of undue severity towards the state prisoners confined in the castle in 1820.

The charge thus brought forward for the first time after a lapse of nearly 40 years, rests upon the authority of a person named M'Millan, himself a prisoner in the castle in 1820, and now a thriving colonist in Australia.

The same publicity which was given to the accusation has, through the courtesy of the editor of the paper, been

APPENDIX. 311

given to a reply from Major Peddie, which seems to exhaust the subject, little more is therefore necessary, than to take advantage of the opportunity which this little work affords, to insert, in a connected series, those articles which have already appeared

The following is the article from the pen of M'Millan It was first published in this country in the Stirling Journal, February 4, 1859

" THE GOOD OLD TIMES —In our obituary to-day will be found announced the death of Mr. Anderson, late of the parish of St Ninians, Stirling. With regard to this gentleman and his compatriots, a correspondent in Glasgow sends us the following particulars —Mr. Anderson was out with Baird and Hardie in 1820, and on the 4th of August in that year John M'Millan, a native of Camelon, and several others, were sentenced to death in Stirling. How or why the sentence was not carried into execution our correspondent does not say, but M'Millan and Anderson, and seventeen others, arrived in due time at Sydney. Mr. Anderson, as we have seen, has just died, but Mr. M'Millan is still alive, and has a residence in Sydney, besides two farms in the country. Mr. M'Millan about fifteen years ago purchased these two farms One of them he named Thrushgrove, in honour of Mr Turner's estate near Glasgow, where the first great Reform meeting was held in 1816, and where Baird and Hardie's monument was erected in 1832. This monument, it will be remembered, was taken down a number of years ago, and it is only those who have seen it who remember where it stood, seeing that there are a great many buildings now erected on Thrushgrove estate Mr M'Millan's other farm is named Clayknowes, after a piece of ground well out the Gallowgate, on which stands Clayknowes pottery, where a great Reform meeting was held during that disturbed time. On one of

312   APPENDIX.

these farms Mr. M'Millan occasionally lives He has still a
vivid recollection of the 'Lion's Den' in Stirling Castle, and
bears a great hatred to it   About twelve months ago he sent
home an account of how he and the other prisoners had been
treated there It appears that after they had been condemned
they were put into the 'Lion's Den,' where they were kept
forty days without bedding, shaving materials, or water   On
the fortieth day Colonel Elphinstone arrived in Stirling with
the famous 33d Regiment, and when going round making an
inspection with General Graham, governor of the Castle,
came to the 'Lion's Den' As soon as he saw the state the
prisoners were in, and learned how long they had been in
that condition, the veteran soldier, addressing the Governor,
said, that he had been all through the Peninsula, that he had
been in French, Spanish, and Portuguese prisons, and had
never seen men used as the unfortunate prisoners in the
'Lion's Den' were He then ordered them to have soldiers'
beds, and sent barbers to have them shaved. He also commanded that the men be brought out to the fresh air,
although when this was done some fell down as if they had
been dead Afterwards, however, they were better treated,
and had leave to walk in the open air daily A few months
ago, continues our correspondent, an article appeared in the
Sydney *Morning Herald*, giving an account of how Orsini
had been treated in the Austrian dungeons, but Mr
M'Millan in writing home assures us that Orsini's treatment
fell far short of what the Bonnymuir men experienced at the
hands of General Graham and Sheriff M'Donald in Stirling
Castle. One of these men, who lives a few miles from Stirling, assured our correspondent, about a month ago, that the
place in which he was put took him to the ankles in water,
and that for a bed he had a bag of straw thrown in to him,
as if he had been a dog Happily scenes of that description
have passed away from amongst us, and we now live under a

APPENDIX. 313

milder reign. Mr. M'Millan is now in independent circumstances, which would not, as our correspondent naively remarks, have been the case had he remained all this time in Camelon."

Those who understand military discipline and etiquette will perceive at once that the drama in the prison is a representation for which we are indebted entirely to the imaginative powers of Mr M'Millan.

Colonel Elphinstone was an old soldier, acquainted with the rules of the service, and being only a subordinate officer in the presence of General Graham, the scene described by Mr. M'Millan never could have taken place. If any representation appeared to be called for, either regarding the requirements of the prisoners, or their security, Colonel Elphinstone knew perfectly how such representation should be made by an officer in his position, and no doubt he would have made any necessary report in the prescribed form. Had any such report been made, the Fort-Major in the castle, from his official position, could not fail to be cognisant of its purport and substance. That no such report ever was made Major Peddie can bear testimony, and he is also in possession of a copy of a letter written to the War Office by General Graham, in which the General distinctly states the gratifying circumstance, that the painful duties required by the state of the country had been discharged without a single instance of a complaint.

The following letter was addressed to the *Stirling Journal*, by Major Peddie, on seeing the quotation from Mr M'Millan's letter :—

"THE BONNYMUIR PRISONERS AND GENERAL GRAHAM,

"*Stirling Castle, 8th Feb. 1859.*
"DEAR SIR—I have never been so utterly astounded as by

P

314   APPENDIX

the perusal of the article in the *Stirling Journal* of Friday
last, headed 'The good old times,' stating, on the authority
of John M'Millan, that the prisoners captured at Bonnymuir,
when they attacked a party of the 10th Light Dragoons and
Kilsyth Yeomanry, were treated, while prisoners in Stirling
Castle, with cruelty beyond that practised in the Austrian
dungeons Why, sir, I have been deluding myself for the
last thirty-eight years with the very satisfactory conscious-
ness that I had, under General Graham, carried out his
orders for the most kind and indulgent treatment of those
prisoners consistent with their safe keeping That such was
the case we have the testimony of Baird and Hardie Their
last act before stepping on the scaffold was to drink the
General's health, and offer their most grateful thanks for the
kindness they had experienced while prisoners in the Castle
At the gate they had taken a most affectionate farewell of
him, shaking his hand most cordially This was witnessed
by the crowd assembled on the esplanade, and is recorded in
the *Stirling Journal* of the day On all occasions of the
General's visiting the prisoners, they expressed their thanks
for his kindness; and when they finally left the Castle they
greeted him with hearty cheers, and for many years afterwards kind messages were sent home by those men, some of
them stating that they had named their children after him.
I assure you that from the first day of their confinement,
their food, washing, and bedding, was the same as that of the
soldier An orderly-officer attended at six in the morning
and saw that their cells had been cleaned out, also at the
breakfast, dinner, and supper, when they were locked up for
the night After their sentence was passed they had six-
pence a day extra to purchase anything they pleased except
spirits; their friends were allowed to see them on Mondays
and Thursdays from ten to three o'clock; they were taken
out daily to walk, books, paper, pens, and ink, were given

APPENDIX. 315

,them, they were visited by the Rev. Doctors Wright, Small, and Smart, and other clergymen; they were under the medical charge of Dr. Vallange, surgeon of the 33d Regiment, now residing at Portobello; the law-agents and advocates had free access to them at all times, among others Lord Jeffrey. With all those facilities for making their grievances known, and not a whisper ever having been heard of this nature, I am justified in asserting that none existed John M'Millan—by the bye, I think his wife was one of the women General Graham was instrumental in getting sent out to their husbands—I perfectly forgive for not admiring the Lion's Den. It is not a very lively place under the most favourable circumstances, but there was no choice, from the great number of prisoners, until barrack-rooms were at a great expense converted into cells, but until recently the cells in the Lion's Den were the only place in the garrison for military prisoners. M'Millan says he was out with the radicals, if so, he must have taken leave of them before the fight, as he was not brought to the Castle for some days afterwards. His attack on Sheriff M'Donald is most atrocious. The prisoners were always pleased to see him, and appeared taken with his polished manner and the kind way in which he offered his advices. The charge against General Graham will astonish every one who knew him. A more kind, benevolent man never existed than the gallant old General.

"I have had a note from Dr Vallange. He says, 'It is a long time ago, yet I have a pretty clear recollection of the circumstances with them; when the 33d Regiment arrived at Stirling Castle the most of the prisoners were confined in the Lion's Den, which was made as comfortable as the place admitted of They were furnished with soldiers' beds, I think, on the floor I had the sole medical charge of them. I do not recollect of any complaint having been made of their treatment. General Graham was considered

316   APPENDIX.

a kind and benevolent man' So much for the Elphinston fiction.

" Loving and esteeming the General as a son should do a father, you must believe that this attempt to asperse his character has caused much pain to—Yours truly,

"W. PEDDIE."

Mr Peter Mackenzie, whose work has been already referred to, on seeing Major Peddie's letter, addressed him as follows.—

"THE BONNYMUIR PRISONERS.

"*Gazette Office, Glasgow, Feb. 14, 1859.*

"SIR—I have not the pleasure of knowing you personally, but I have just read your interesting letter in the *Stirling Journal* of Friday last about the Bonnymuir prisoners of 1820, and I can confidently confirm every word you have stated. I do this the more readily because many of the original letters of Baird and Hardie, before and after their sentence of execution, passed through my hands, and I remember they all bore testimony to the great attention and kindness they had uniformly received from the authorities, and in particular from General Graham. I was the humble means, many years ago, through my old and excellent friend, the late Mr Wallace of Kelly, who was then M.P. for Greenock, and who made a statement in the House of Commons on the subject, of procuring the gracious pardon of his Majesty King William the Fourth, for the whole of the surviving prisoners in New South Wales—John M'Millan included, and I have a duplicate of the pardon of the king in my possession, sent me by Lord John Russell, who was then Secretary of State for the Home Department. Mr J. A. Murray, now Lord Murray, who was then Lord Advocate, gave a willing ear to the application I made to the king for mercy to all those un-

APPENDIX. **317**

fortunate surviving victims; and after the pardon was obtained I corresponded with John M'Millan and others at Sydney on the subject, but I do not remember they ever made the slightest complaint of the kind as has been now imputed as coming from the mouth of John M'Millan. He sent to me and to Mr Wallace, in token of his gratitude, a fine carved ivory walking stick from Sydney, and not having heard of him or from him for many years, I took for granted that he was dead. If you think this spontaneous statement can be of the slightest use to you as bearing out your own most truthful statement, you are perfectly welcome to send it to the *Stirling Journal*, with my respectful compliments to its talented editor, with whom, though a Tory, and I an old Radical of the old Whig *Constitutional* School, I nevertheless can reciprocate compliments, I hope, for the sake of *truth* and *justice* —I am, &c., PETER MACKENZIE

" To Mr. W. Peddie, Stirling Castle."

A further refutation of the calumnies propagated by M'Millan is furnished by Mr. P. Mackenzie's work.

At page 205 of that work, Hardie, in a letter to Mr. Ewing of Glasgow, under date, Stirling, 12th August 1820, thus expresses himself:—

" DEAR SIR—I had a visit this day of my mother and brother, and my friend Helen ——. They let me understand that you and another gentleman had been in this town wishing to give me a visit. I am truly sorry that you were not admitted. If you had sent in a card to me giving me notice, I would have applied to the General to get permission for you to come in, and I have not the least doubt but he would have granted it, as he gives us every indulgence that is in his power."

P 2

318 APPENDIX.

And again, on the 10th August, in a postscript to a letter to Mr. Goodwin of Glasgow, Hardie says:—

" I have still all the indulgence that I formerly enjoyed, that is before I received my sentence, for which I am bound in gr titude to the General and Fort-Major for their kind atten' to me."

It is also related by Mr Mackenzie, that a few moments before Hardie ascended the scaffold, he took leave of the sheriff, and requested him, on behalf of Baird and himself, to please to express to General Graham and Major Peddie their sense of gratitude for the humanity and attention which they had always shewn them.

It is but reasonable to assume that if any difference was made in the treatment of the State prisoners in Stirling Castle, Baird and Hardie, as being the leaders, would have been subjected to the most rigorous form of imprisonment; their testimony, therefore, as to the humanity they experienced, may be taken as conclusive evidence against the truth of M'Millan's statement.

THE END.

CPSIA information can be obtained
at www.ICGtesting.com
Printed in the USA
LVHW080105031121
702312LV00001B/1